ISSUES IN POLICING:

A Canadian Perspective

For my father,

Thank you for your inspiring example.

ISSUES IN POLICING: A CANADIAN PERSPECTIVE

Ronald T. Stansfield Ph.D.

Humber College of Applied Arts and Technology

Thompson Educational Publishing, Inc.
Toronto

Thompson Educational Publishing, Inc.
14 Ripley Avenue, Suite 105
Toroto, Ontario, Canada M6S 3N9
Tel. (416) 766-2763
Fax (416) 766-0398
e-mail: thompson@canadabooks.ingenia.com

Canadian Cataloguing in Publication Data

Stansfield, Ronald T.
    Issues in policing: a Canadian perspective

Includes bibliographical references.
ISBN 1-55077-073-X

1. Police — Canada.
I. Title.

HV8157.S73 1996   376.2'0971   C95-9320420-7

Book/text design: *Danielle Baum*
Cover design: *Mike McAuliffe*

Printed and bound in Canada.
1234 99 98 97 96

Table of Contents

Acknowledgments

This book is the result of the combined efforts of many people. While it is not possible to name all of them, nevertheless, I am profoundly grateful to each and every one.

As always, my partner, Angela, and our four young children, Josh, Zach, Jess and Kyle, supported this project by providing me with the time to complete it. I hope to be able to do the same for each of them one day.

At Thompson Educational Publishing, Keith Thompson and Paul Challen demonstrated extraordinary patience and support throughout this project. Their comments and criticisms were invaluable in improving the overall quality of the book. Similarly, Dr. Livy Visano at York University, Dr. James Hodgson at Longwood College and my colleagues, Scott Nicholls and Art Lockhart at the Centre for Justice Studies at Humber College, all contributed by reviewing the manuscript and offering criticism.

Also, the students in the Law and Security Administration Program at Humber College made an important contribution to this book by questioning my ideas and by answering my questions. Many of these people now are police officers. I consider myself fortunate to have had the opportunity to learn with them. Evelyn Hansen, Liz Crim, and Linda Morris at the Learning Resource Centre of the Lakeshore Campus of Humber College contributed by researching many of the ideas that appear in this book.

Finally, it is important to note that Canadians enjoy some of the most professional police services anywhere in the world. Despite this, police have an ongoing responsibility to improve the services they provide. As a former police officer who has had the opportunity to continue his education and now teach others, I gladly accept this obligation. This book, then, represents my awkward attempt to use my privileged position to influence the police reform agenda.

Despite the assistance of all these people, I alone am responsible for any errors, omissions or inaccuracies that appear in the pages of this book.

Ron Stansfield
Hamilton, Ontario
December 12, 1995

1 Introduction

Purpose

The purpose of this book is to provide the reader with a *general* introduction to and an overview of Canadian public policing. The principal objectives are: (1) to describe key issues in Canadian policing and (2) to use a *multi-disciplinary* approach to analyse these issues critically. For this purpose, charts, graphs, and case studies are used to illustrate the discussion.

It is anticipated that this book will be useful for post-secondary students studying policing. Also, police officers in training, as well as experienced police practitioners may find the theoretical analyse of policing in this book helpful. Finally, "lay" members of the public will find this book useful to help them understand the function of police in Canadian society.

Structure and Rationale

This book is divided into fifteen chapters. This chapter introduces the major topics that are discussed in the remainder of the book. Each of the remaining chapters is devoted to the discussion and analysis of a single issue in policing. These issues were selected for inclusion from the hundreds of possible topics because they are *critical* issues. The importance of these issues can be demonstrated in two ways. First, they are regularly reported in the electronic and print media. In this respect, these issues have *face validity*; that is, they are meaningful to the people in our communities. Second, and as important for the student studying policing, these topics are issues because of the way modern societies are structured and reproduce order. As we will see in our discussion of the history of policing in Chapter 2, once a community commits itself to a particular form of social organization it adopts a compatible form of policing. Similarly, once a community adopts a particular form of policing, inevitably, certain topics surface in the community as *issues in policing*.

The importance of public policing has been temporarily increased by the disorder and chaos being wreaked by the Information Revolution. As this process proceeds, and Canada is transformed from an industrial society into an informational society, the structure used to reproduce order — policing — is also being transformed. The effect of this transformation is to induce a crisis in the old police structure — public policing — and force the development of a new police structure — private policing. Chapter 15 (Future Trends) argues that private policing may eventually displace public policing as the dominant police form, if it has not already. However, during this transition from an industrial order to an informational order and from public policing to private policing, and no doubt because of its historical importance, public policing continues to dominate the public imagination. For this reason, if no other, it behooves us to try to understand this important social institution.

The crisis in public policing is most evident in Canada's large informational centres such as Montreal, Toronto and Vancouver where a steady stream of allegations of racism, sexism, corruption and brutality have plagued public police agencies. More subtle evidence of the crisis is the explosive growth of private policing and the resurgence of vigilantism, which, as we will see in Chapter 15, is being driven by the inability of public police to satisfy the "security needs" of both individuals and organizations in our communities.

The issues discussed in this book define the parameters of the current crisis in public policing. As well, collectively, these issues constitute a predictable and identifiable policing cycle (Figure 1.1). Once a community commits itself to an industrialized form of social organization, with all this entails for the social structure, it sets in motion a chain of events that result in the community developing some form of "public" policing. Similarly, once a community commits itself to using the public police form, certain problems surface in the community as *issues in policing.* [1]

---

1   This is not intended to be an exhaustive list. However, it is the case, that most occurrences involving the public police can be explained by recourse to one or more of these issues.

Figure 1.1
The Policing Cycle

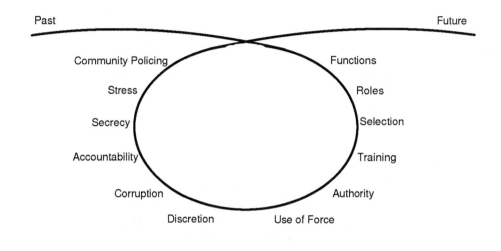

The use of the public police form determines the *function* of police in society. Similarly, the function police perform determines the *roles* both they and their adversaries play. Of course, not everyone is capable of playing every role. Consequently, a process is needed to *select* appropriate police actors. Once the actors have been selected by a police organization, they need to be *trained* to perform their specialized role and function. As well, a specialized role and function creates the need for extraordinary police *authority*. The most important authority police have is the power to *use force*, including lethal force, to resolve conflict.[2] Police are privileged to have extraordinary authority. This privilege obligates police to use discretion and not to use their extraordinary powers arbitrarily. Despite this, from time to time, some police abuse their extraordinary powers and, in doing so, *corrupt* their authority. When police corruption occurs, it creates a need for an extraordinary process to hold police *accountable* for the consequences

---

2   Obviously, police have many special powers such as the power to search for and seize property (see section 487 Canadian Criminal Code) and the power to arrest someone found committing a criminal offence (see section 495.(1) Canadian Criminal Code). However, unlike their other powers, the power to use force pervades *everything* a police officer does (Shearing and Leon, 1976) and, therefore, it is the penultimate power a police officer possesses.

---

of their actions. The competing demands of doing whatever it takes to win the "war on crime," while simultaneously shielding confidential battle plans and corrupt acts from public view, forces police to cloak their actions in *secrecy*. The inevitable result of police having extraordinary authority, accountability, and secrecy is that they experience intense *distress*.

The policing cycle is completed when the community reacts to the way police reproduce order by attempting to *reform* the police: at present, police reform is pre-occupied with community policing. Finally, and rarely, society is fundamentally transformed with the result that there is a dislocation between the old social order and the new social order. The present is one of those extraordinary times and, as a result, it behooves us to speculate about *future trends* in policing.

Content

Chapter 1 provides an *introduction* and overview of public policing in Canada. In particular, trends in the number of police and police expenditures are considered. Based on this information it is suggested that the dominance of public policing in Canada peaked in the 1970s and has been on the wane since.

Chapter 2 discusses the *history of policing*. A "socio-developmental" model is used to analyse police structure and identify the forms of policing that have been used to reproduce order in agricultural, industrial, and informational communities, respectively. Three distinct forms of policing — vigilante, public and private — are identified. These police forms and their corresponding social forms are used to construct a model of police forms and structure.

Chapter 3 discusses the *function* of police in modern industrial societies. Both "functional" and "conflict" perspectives are used to analyse the police function. In particular, the impact of social stratification is used to demonstrate that the police function in society is to reproduce social order.

Chapter 4 discusses the symbolic *roles* played by police. Concepts from Archetypal Psychology are used to analyse the stereotypical roles police, criminals and police spouses play. In particular, the role of police as "crime-fighters" and "lawmen," criminals as "outlaws," and police spouses as "martyrs," are used to construct an archetypal model of police inter-personal relationships. Also, the introduction of new roles to policing are considered.

Chapter 5 discusses the police *selection* process. Concepts from Spectrum Psychology are used to analyse the selection process used by a large municipal police service to screen applicants. The criteria used to screen applicants are classified as selecting physical, mental or spiritual skills. This classification is used to critique the "skill-set" being selected by police organizations.

Chapter 6 discusses the police *training* process. Concepts from Spectrum Psychology are used to analyse basic constable training at a large police training academy. The curriculum used to train police recruits is classified as training physical, mental or spiritual skills. This classification is used to critique the "skill-set" being taught to police recruits. As well, the minimum entry-to-practice requirements for police are compared to several other occupational groups.

Chapter 7 discusses police *authority*. Two types of police authority — "moral" and "legal" — are identified. This distinction is used to facilitate a discussion about the tenuous relationship between police moral authority and their extraordinary legal authority. The discussion is illustrated by an incident that involved a police officer who refused a lawful order by a superior officer because it conflicted with his personal morals.

Chapter 8 discusses the *use of force* by and against police. The role of factors such as socio-economic status, age, race, sex, time, place, and other circumstances of the participants are considered in analysing how force is used in policing. The discussion is illustrated by an incident in which a police officer shot and killed an aboriginal man when the latter refused the officer's request to identify himself.

Chapter 9 discusses police *discretion*. Two types of police discretionary decisions — "legal" and "extra-legal" — are identified. This distinction is used to facilitate a discussion about the relationship between discretion, discrimination and stereotyping. Also, the role of factors such as socio-economic status, age, race, sex, time, place, and other circumstances of the participants are considered when analysing how police make their discretionary decisions. The discussion is illustrated by an incident that involved a rape victim who was arrested by police and imprisoned for a total of twelve days and transported across Canada so she could be a witness against her attacker.

Chapter 10 discusses police *corruption*. Several hypothetical scenarios are used to clarify the meaning of police corruption and demonstrate that low level police corruption is rampant. As well, the roles of factors such as the availability of graft, the strength of the Code of Silence in a police organization and the risk of being caught committing a corrupt act are considered when analysing how police corruption occurs. The discussion is illustrated by an incident that involved a police officer who was forced to resign when it was discovered that he operated a "sex-for-pay" escort service.

Chapter 11 discusses police *accountability*. An ad hoc system of police accountability that includes constitutional, administrative, criminal, and civil processes is described. This description is used to facilitate a discussion about the complexity of police accountability systems and the need for police to be extraordinarily accountable because they exercise extraordinary powers. The discussion is illustrated by an incident that involved a police officer who was found guilty of misconduct by a civilian board of inquiry and forced to resign despite the vehement protests of his colleagues.

Chapter 12 discusses police *secrecy*. Two types of secrecy — formal oaths of secrecy and informal codes of silence — are identified. This distinction is used to facilitate a discussion about the role of secrecy in police work. The discussion is illustrated by an incident in which several police officers were dismissed from their jobs and imprisoned when a colleague revealed that one of them had assaulted a man they had arrested.

Chapter 13 discusses police *stress*. Four stress-styles — excitement, anxiety, depression and relaxation — are identified. These distinctions are used to facilitate a discussion about the causes and cures of police stress. The discussion is illustrated by an incident in which a police officer committed suicide hours before he was to testify before a government inquiry about his role in the investigation of a fatal police shooting.

Chapter 14 discusses the current reform movement in policing — *community policing*. Contemporary community policing programmes are compared to the vigilantism that was used to police farming communities prior to the Industrial Revolution. This comparison is used to demonstrate that true community policing can only be achieved by the combined efforts of several different police forms that include but are not limited to public policing.

Chapter 15 discusses *future trends* in policing. A socio-developmental model is used to analyse recent developments of the police form. In particular, it is suggested that private policing is displacing public policing as the dominant police form.

Public Policing in Canada

Municipalities, provinces and the federal government share responsibility for providing public police services in Canada. Pursuant to subsection 91(27) of the *British North America Act,* the federal government is responsible for legislating criminal law and criminal procedure. For this purpose the Canadian government maintains a federal police service now known as the Royal Canadian Mounted Police (RCMP) to provide police services in the Yukon and Northwest Territories and to enforce all federal statutes, other than the Criminal Code, such as the Narcotic Control Act and the Food and Drug Act. Also, the RCMP provides municipal and provincial police services under contract to the provinces when requested to do so. At these times and in these places, the RCMP also assumes responsibility for enforcing the Criminal Code.

Pursuant to subsection 92(14) of the *British North America Act* the provinces are responsible for the "administration of justice." For this purpose three Canadian provinces[3] — Ontario, Quebec and Newfoundland — maintain provincial police services to enforce the Criminal Code and all provincial statutes such as traffic and liquor laws. Also, the provincial police services in these provinces — the Ontario Provincial Police (OPP), Sûreté du Québec (SQ) and Royal Newfoundland Constabulary (RNC) respectively — provide municipal police services under contract to municipalities when requested to do so. At these times and in these places, provincial police assume responsibility for enforcing the Criminal Code, provincial statutes and municipal bylaws.

Pursuant to the provincial legislation that authorizes their creation, some municipalities (i.e., cities and towns) may be required to provide police services. For this purpose most large Canadian municipalities and cities maintain independent police services to enforce the Criminal Code, provincial statutes and municipal bylaws such as noise and parking bylaws. In Ontario and Quebec, many municipalities contract with the provincial governments to have the OPP and SQ, respectively, provide police services. In the Maritimes and in Western Canada where there are no independent provincial police, many municipalities contract with the federal government to have the RCMP provide municipal police services. An interesting situation exists in Newfoundland where the Royal Newfoundland Constabulary (RNC) — which is technically a provincial police service — provides municipal police services in the capital, St. John's, and two other cities, and the RCMP — a federal police service — provides municipal and provincial police services in the rest of the province. Newfoundland aside, most of Canada's largest municipalities maintain an independent police service (Table 1.1).

---

3   The other provinces fulfill their responsibility for providing police services by contracting with the federal government to have the RCMP provide provincial police services. Also, the Canadian military, Canadian National Railways and Ports Canada are responsibile for providing police services within their respective jurisdictions.

Table 1.1
Population per Officer, Cities over 100,000, Canada, 1993

Police Service	Population	Number of officers	Population per officer
Toronto, Ont.	2,241,100	5,507	407
Montreal, Que.	1,753,200	4,020	397
Peel Region, Ont.	747,500	1,104	677
Calgary, Alta.	732,300	1,177	622
Edmonton, Alta.	629,100	1,126	559
Winnipeg, Man.	616,600	1,074	574
York Region, Ont.	551,100	682	808
Vancouver, B.C.	495,900	1,108	448
Hamilton, Ont.	453,300	648	700
Durham Region, Ont.	419,200	585	717
Niagara Region, Ont.	401,800	582	690
Waterloo Region, Ont.	390,000	548	712
Ottawa, Ont.	344,800	594	580
Halton Region, Ont.	326,800	385	849
Laval, Que.	326,700	440	743
London, Ont.	326,100	428	762
Surrey, B.C.	270,700	303	893
Windsor, Ont.	195,100	379	515
Saskatoon, Sask.	186,600	320	583
Quebec, Que.	184,000	439	419
Regina, Sask.	179,700	325	553
Burnaby, B.C.	168,600	216	781
Sudbury, Ont.	165,800	223	743
St. John's, Nfld.	165,500	273	606
Richmond, B.C.	134,700	151	892
Longueille, Que.	133,700	197	679
Halifax, N.S.	115,200	283	407
Thunder Bay, Ont.	115,100	194	593
Gatineau, Que.	114,500	152	753
Neapean, Ont.	111,800	134	834
Glouster, Ont.	105,600	134	788
Saanich, B.C.	102,000	129	791
Sherbrooke, Que.	100,400	144	697

Source: Statistics Canada, Cat. No. 85-002, Vol. 15 No. 8.

The majority (63%) of Canadian police are employed in the provision of municipal police services. Much smaller numbers of police provide provincial (25%), federal (8%) and other (4%) forms of police services (Figure 1.2). Similarly, only five police services — the RCMP, Metropolitan Toronto Police, Montreal Urban Police, Sûreté du Québec, and Ontario Provincial Police — employed 61% of all Canadian police officers in 1993 (Figure 1.3). No doubt, this concentration of police at the municipal level and among just a few police services reflects the very high level of urbanization in Canada where one in three Canadians lives in either Montreal, Toronto or Vancouver.

The number of police in Canada increased dramatically between 1962 (the first year data were collected) and 1980 and then remained relatively stable in the years following. By 1994 there were 55,946 police in Canada, a decrease of 1.7% from the previous year (Figure 1.4). Similarly, the number of police per 100,000 population increased dramatically between 1962 and 1980 and then remained relatively stable in the years following. By 1994 there were 191.3 police per 100,000 population in Canada, a decrease of 5.4% from the previous year (Figure 1.5).

Figure 1.2
Police Officers in Canada by Level of Policing, 1990

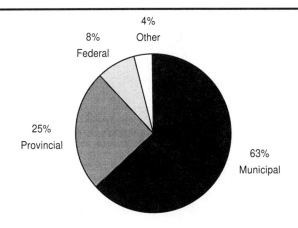

Source: Statistics Canada, Cat. No. 85-002, Vol. 15 No. 8.

Figure 1.3
Police Officers by Major Force, Canada, 1993

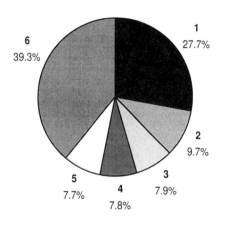

1   RCMP
2   Metro Toronto
3   Surété du Québec
4   Montreal Urban Community
5   Ontario Provincial Police
6   All other

Source: Statistics Canada, Cat. No. 85-002, Vol. 15 No. 8.

Figure 1.4
Number of Police Officers in Canada, 1962-1994

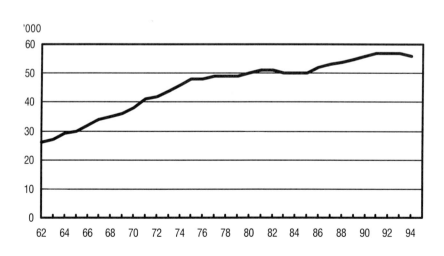

Source: Statistics Canada, Cat. No. 85-002, Vol. 15 No. 8.

Figure 1.5
Number of Police Officers in Canada, by 100,00 Population, 1962-1994

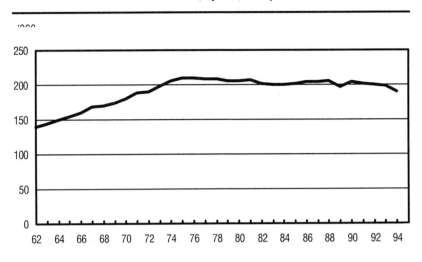

Source: Statistics Canada, Cat. No. 85-002, Vol. 15 No. 8.

Predictably, as the total number of police in Canada has increased, the cost of providing police services has also increased, so that by 1993/94 Canadian policing cost $5.786 billion — a real increase of 20% since 1985/86 (Figure 1.6).[4] The rate of increase was greatest between 1985 and 1990 and then slowed. With the establishment of deficit reduction as a top priority of many Canadian governments, it appears that police expenditures, and therefore the number of police per hundred thousand population, will be stagnant or decrease for the foreseeable future. As we will see in Chapter 15 (Policing Post-Modern Society), the relative decline of public policing is one of the factors driving the growth of private policing.

---

4   1985 was the first year data were collected.

Figure 1.6
Total Police Expenditures in Canada, 1985-1994

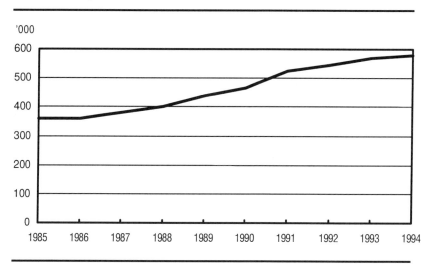

Summary

This chapter provides an introduction and overview of the other chapters in this book. As well, it argues that police structure varies as a function of social structure and that once a community commits itself to a particular form of social organization, such as industrialization, it must develop a compatible form of policing such as public policing. Furthermore, it is argued that Canada is presently on the cusp of a transition from an industrial society to an informational society and that this process is inducing a crisis in public policing. The outline of this crisis and therefore public policing is defined by a series of inter-connected topics or issues in policing that when taken together constitute a policing cycle. Finally, a brief overview of public policing in Canada is also provided.

2 History of Policing

Introduction

Canadian society is being fundamentally transformed by new "information" technologies. Despite the rapid rate of change, there appears to be a pervasive, tacit assumption that public policing always has been and always will be the *only* form of policing. This view implies that policing is a *static* structure that does not change as social structure changes; however, even a cursory examination of the "modern" history of policing reveals that police structure has acquired several different forms during the modern era. A more detailed analysis suggests that the form of policing a community uses to *reproduce* order is determined by the form of social organization that *is* the order. In contrast to the conventional stereotype of policing, this view explicitly maintains that policing is a *dynamic* structure that evolves in response to changes in social structure.

This chapter describes three forms of social organization — agricultural, industrial and informational — and their correlated forms of police organization — vigilante, public and private — respectively. This socio-developmental analysis clearly demonstrates that police organization, like social organization, is a dynamic structure that co-evolves along with the social structure.

Policing in Perspective

To the casual observer it may appear that public police are *the* police. However, a thorough analysis of police forms and structure reveals that policing is a differentiated social structure, and that public policing is only one form of this structure. If conventional stereotypes of what constitutes the police are not valid, then legitimately one may ask: *What is* policing and *who are* the police?

At the psychological level, policing is concerned with the safety and security of the individual. For example, in his now famous statement about the hierarchy of human needs (Figure 2.1), Maslow (1968; 1971) argued that "safety needs" are, after "physiological needs," the most basic needs an individual must satisfy before he or she can progress to higher levels of development. Insofar as "safety" encompasses the *security* of the individual, and a function of policing is to ensure the security of the individual, then policing is intended to satisfy this basic human need. Of course, as we will see in Chapter 3, whether policing ever fulfills this function is determined by a wide range of factors that includes, but is not limited to, the distribution of wealth, power and privilege in a community. Very simply then, at one level (i.e., the psychological), policing *is the activities a community utilizes to ensure the safety and security of the individual.*

Figure 2.1
The Hierarchy of Needs

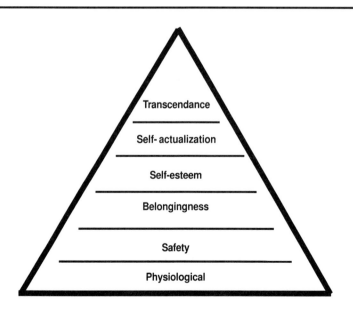

Source: Maslow (1968, 1971).

At a related but different level — the sociological level — policing is concerned with the reproduction of order. For example, Shearing and Stenning (1987: 10) noted that:

> An appreciation of the character and meaning of policing in the latter half of the twentieth century can no longer afford to assume that it is most typically (or even most importantly) about crime, law enforcement, or punishment ... policing must nowadays be understood more broadly as quintessentially about *order*, and the myriad ways in which it can be established and maintained.

Similarly, Ericson (1982: 7), noted that "their (the police) everyday actions are directed at reproducing the existing order ... (t)hey are one tool of policing in the wider sense of all governmental efforts aimed at disciplining, refining, and improving the population." At the sociological level then, policing *is the process of enforcing laws that reproduce order.*[1] Using these definitions as our guide, let us explore the history of policing.

Policing in the Agricultural Era

Contemporary Canadian police practices find their roots in England, which prior to the Industrial Revolution was an agricultural society. The vast majority of people then worked as farmers and lived in the country in or near small villages (Lenski et al., 1991). The basic unit of social and economic organization in these communities was the extended family or kinship group. In essence, these communities *were* extended families (Toffler, 1980: 28).

Critchley (1972: 2) notes that villages were organized into groups of about ten families known as "tythings." As well, groups of tythings were organized into a "hundred," which was headed by a "hundredman" or royal reeve (ibid.). Above the "royal reeve" was the "shire reeve," better known to us today as the "sheriff." The sheriff was responsible for the "conservancy of peace in the shire" or county (ibid.). As you might expect, policing these small farming communities was a very different proposition than policing modern communities.

---

1   These definitions are in sharp contrast to more conventional definitions of policing. For example, Bayley (1985: 7-11) defines police as the "people authorized by a group to regulate interpersonal relations within the group through the application of physical force." Like other conventional definitions of policing, Bayley's is derived from the so-called "liberal frame of reference" and cannot explain the fundamental changes that are occurring in contemporary policing; whereas, the definitions utilized here attempt to "reframe" policing as urged by Shearing and Stenning (1987), to facilitate a "paradigm shift" in our understanding of policing.

The problem agricultural communities faced was: How to maintain order (i.e., police themselves) with limited natural resources?[2] The solution was to utilize the kinship ties (i.e., human resources) that existed naturally within the community and, consequently, did not have to be contrived. Critchley (1972: 2) notes:

> From very early times, certainly from the reign of King Alfred, the primary responsibility for maintaining the King's peace fell upon each locality under a well-understood principle of social obligation, or collective security.[3]

As we saw above, each "locality" was in fact a group of families (i.e., a tything). Similarly, "collective security" is just another way of saying that "all members of a community accepted an obligation for the good behaviour of each other" (ibid.). Policing in the Agricultural Era then was first and foremost a "family affair."

By the time the Normans invaded England in 1066, the system of "collective security" used to police English communities had become known as "frankpledge" (ibid.). Frankpledge was "a system of compulsory collective bail fixed for individuals, not after their arrest for crime, but as a safeguard in anticipation of it" (ibid., 3). In addition to frankpledge, these communities used several other police strategies to reproduce order. For example, "hue and cry" was an alarm system that alerted other members of the community to the presence of a felon. Also, once a hue and cry had been raised, the shire reeve would muster a "posse" and give chase to the "fleeing felon." As well, farming communities used an informal system of informers which required villagers to make "presentments." A presentment was a requirement "to report to the sheriff's tourn any suspicions they might harbour about one another ... " (ibid., 4).

In short, policing in the country during the Agricultural Era was an informal, part-time, volunteer activity that was organized by communities and proceeded according to the principle of *shared responsibility*. Maintaining order in the towns, however, was not as simple a matter. When people moved from the country into towns kinship ties were weakened. As a result, towns had to do more than villages to maintain order. The solution they arrived at was to create a bureaucracy (Marx and Engels, 1989 [1846]: 69) and *assign* rerponsibility for guarding the town at night to certain individuals (Critchley, 1972).[4]

---

2   Agricultural communities are, on average, much poorer than industrial communities (Lenski et al., 1991). As a result, agricultural communities have relatively few options for maintaining order. For example, unlike most industrial communities, they cannot afford a full-time, paid police service.

3   "Alfred the Great" was King of England in the second half of the 9th century.

4   For obvious reasons, night-time was the most likely time for criminals to attack.

Critchley (1972: 6) notes that the Statute of Winchester in 1285 described a system of policing in the towns known as "watch and ward."[5] Very simply, watch and ward was a surveillance system in which all able bodied men acting under the supervision of a "constable" (formerly the Saxon tythingman) were required to take turns guarding the gates to the town during the nightly curfew (Critchley, 1972: 6; Bowsky, 1972: 34). Anyone found violating the curfew could be arrested and imprisoned (Bowsky, 1972: 34). If a violator resisted arrest, the night watchman was authorized to give rise to a "hue and cry" compelling other members of the community to join him in capturing the fugitive. In practice, the wealthier men in the community hired someone to perform their tour of duty in exchange for a fee (Critchley, 1972: 10). As we will see in our discussion of policing during the Industrial Era, the delegation of authority by the wealthy was a key step in the transition from "vigilante" policing to "public" policing.

Another important provision of the Statute of Winchester required able-bodied males between the ages of sixteen and sixty to maintain an "assize of arms" (literally a cache of weapons), under the supervision of the constable, to assist in keeping the peace (ibid.). Of course, farmers had many tools, some of which were easily converted into weapons. As a result, this requirement did not impose an undue burden on people.

Briefly then, policing in towns during the Agricultural Era was a semi-formal, part-time, volunteer activity that was organized into a bureaucracy[6] and proceeded according to the principles of shared responsibility and delegated authority. The system of policing in the country (i.e., frankpledge), and the system of policing in the towns (i.e., watch and ward) in England and elsewhere during the Agricultural Era were community policing in the truest sense of the term. Truly, this was a time when *the police were the public, and the public were the police*. As we will see below, contemporary community policing initiatives bear more than a passing resemblance to these police practices, practices that we shall call "vigilante" policing.

---

5   "Watch and ward" is a term Critchley (1972) coined to describe the system of policing that prevailed in English towns during the Middle Ages. Bowsky (1976: 34) describes a system of "night guards" that was in use in the Italian city of Siena in the 13th and 14th centuries, that is identical in many respects to "watch and ward". It appears that "watch and ward" in one form or another was a common response of farming towns to satisfy their policing needs.

6   As we will see, the development of a bureaucracy to organize volunteer police was an important step towards the creation of public police.

Policing in the Industrial Era

Vigilante policing, as we have referred to it, remained the "average mode of policing"[7] in England until the Industrial Revolution. Industrialization transformed English society from a rural farming society regulated by kinship ties into an urban industrial society regulated by the State. For example, the introduction of mechanized farming tools dramatically reduced the number of people needed in the country to work on farms. As a result, cities generally, and London particularly, swelled as dislocated farmers relocated in search of employment. While many farmers succeeded in securing employment in urban factories, many more did not. As well, the kinship groups that formed the bases of communities during the Agricultural Era were destroyed as individuals and nuclear families relocated to cities. Lenski et al. (1991: 243-44) note that the destruction of kinship groups had important consequences for the way industrial communities were organized:

> ... Serious problems resulted from the disruption of social relationships. Long standing ties of kinship and friendship were severed and could not easily be replaced, while local customs and institutions that had provided rural villagers with some measure of pro-tection and support were lost for good. Thus, it was an uprooted, vulnerable mass of people who streamed into towns and cities and were thrown into situations utterly foreign to them, and into a way of life that often culminated in injury, illness, or unemployment. A multitude of social ills — poverty, alcoholism, crime, vice, mental and physical illness, personal demoralization — were endemic.

The old "vigilante" system of policing was strained to the breaking point as communities re-organized to accommodate the new industrial mode of production (Critchley, 1972: 21; South, 1987: 75). Matters were made worse by the fact that the old vigilante system of policing had been seriously corrupted in London by this time (Critchley, 1972: 21). The deplorable conditions that resulted were immortalized by Charles Dickens in *A Tale of Two Cities*, his fictional account of life in London during the 1770s:

> ... There was scarcely an amount of order and protection to justify na-tional boasting. Daring burglaries by armed men, and highway robberies, took place in the capital itself every night; families were publicly cautioned not to go out of town without removing their furniture to upholsterers' warehouses of security; the highwayman in the dark was a City tradesman in the light, and, being re-cognized and challenged by his fellow-tradesman whom he stopped in his character of the Captain, gallantly shot him through the head and rode away ...

---

7   The "average mode of policing" is the form of policing that predominates during a particular technological era. For example, communal, public, and private policing were the average modes of policing during the agricultural, industrial and informational eras, respectively (Figure 2.1).

Faced with these chaotic conditions, and large numbers of frustrated and desperate people, English authorities were compelled to invent a new system of policing. A turning point appears to have occurred in 1780 when there were several incidents of civil disobedience in the City of London that eventually culminated in the Gordon Riots. These riots signaled the end of vigilante policing in the City of London (Critchley, 1972: 18).

By the turn of the 19th century, the needs of London's industrial society made the development of a new form of policing inevitable (ibid., 35). Clearly, the transition from an agrarian society to an industrial society was a key factor in the development of the formal police institution, now widely known as "public" policing (Trojanowicz and Bucqueroux, 1990: 42; Uchida, 1989: 17). [8]

English authorities responded to the crisis in public order in and around London in the late 18th and early 19th century by creating a publicly funded and State controlled para-military police service (Critchley, 1972). It is illuminating to read Sir Robert Peel's address to the English Parliament when, as Home Secretary, he introduced the legislation authorizing the creation of the new police:

> ... The time is come, when, from the increase in its population, the enlargement of its resources, and the multiplying development of its energies, we may fairly pronounce that the country has outgrown her police institutions and that the cheapest and safest course will be found to be the introduction of a new mode of protection. Addressing himself now to "those who live in agricultural districts," he demanded: "Why, I ask, should we entrust a grocer, or any other tradesman, however respectable, with the direction and management of a police for 5,000 or 6,000 inhabitants? Why should such a person unpaid and unrewarded be taken from his usual avocations and called upon to perform the laborious duties of a night constable?"[9]

This passage clearly demonstrates that when Peel introduced the legislation creating the first public police force, he was aware that vigilante policing had been made obsolete by the transformation of England from an agricultural society into an industrial society. His simple yet effective response to this situation was to create a full-time, publicly funded, State-controlled, para-military police force.

---

8   Bayley (1985: 7-11) is the only one to seriously question this point. As the author has noted elsewhere (Stansfield, 1992), Bayley employees an unnecessarily narrow definition of policing that limits his ability to recognize revolutionary developments in the police form.

9   Reported in Critchley (1972: 48).

After several aborted attempts and numerous experiments in "public" policing, Sir Robert Peel was instrumental in creating the first public police system in the City of London in 1829 (ibid., 49).[10] The resulting police "force" was modeled on the English military. It included: a central line of authority reporting to the Home Secretary; a bifurcated rank structure featuring commissioned and non-commissioned officers; uniforms; and personal weapons (ibid., 51-52). "Constables," as they were known, were men selected, according to strict criteria, from the lower ranks of the military. Every "constable" had the powers of a constable at the "common law" and authority to enforce the law within a prescribed jurisdiction — "up to seven miles from Charing Cross" (a London landmark). As well, they were paid a weekly wage in exchange for patrolling a set "beat." Peel's primary objective in creating the force was to produce a "homogeneous and democratic body in tune with the people" (ibid., 52). What he actually created was a police force that operated according to the principle of *parens patriae*.[11]

As we have already seen, Peel's objective in creating the public police was entirely consistent with how policing was practiced during the Agricultural Era, but it bore only a passing resemblance to how policing was to be practiced during the Industrial Era. In a phrase, public policing is *apart from* the community not *a part of* the community. This is particularly ironic in light of Peel's claim that "the police are the public and the public are the police." In fact, as we shall see in our discussion of the police selection process in Chapter 5, public police always have been and still are exclusionary *not* inclusionary organizations. Until public police practices begin to *include* all parts of our community, not just the interests of special elites, they must be seen for what they really are — "special interest" policing.

The Metropolitan Police Act was the model other industrial communities followed when establishing their public police forces. During the next century, industrial communities around the world adopted the public police

---

10   Bayley (1985: 33) correctly notes that public police appeared as early as Classical Roman. However, as the author has noted elsewhere (Stansfield, 1992), Bayley fails to distinguish between the leading edge of policing (i.e., public policing in Classical Rome), the average mode of policing (i.e., public policing during the Industrial Era), and the trailing edge of policing (i.e., public policing during the Informational Era).

11   *Parens patriae* means literally "parent of the country" and refers traditionally to the role of the state as sovereign and guardian of persons under legal disability." In this context it is intended to convey that, as delegates of the state, public police are responsible for the safety of the public, much like a parent is responsible for the safety of their child. Piaget (1977) refers to this type of "parent-child" relationship as "unilateral respect"; the inferior is expected to respect the superior, but not vice versa.

model. Peel's innovation has become so successful that, in the minds of many people today, public police are the *only* police. Not only do most people not consider other forms of policing to be important, they do not even consider other forms of policing. This myth hides the fact that public policing did not become the "average mode of policing" until the Industrial Era and, as we shall see, by the second half of the 20th century, public policing no longer was the dominant police form in Canada.

Policing in the Informational Era

Public policing remained the average mode of policing in Canada and other parts of the industrialized world until the middle decades of this century when, by most accounts (Toffler, 1981; Naisbitt, 1984; Lenski, 1991; Drucker, 1993), the Informational Era began. Informationalization literally is transforming Canadian communities from urban, centralized industrial communities regulated by the State, to rural, decentralized communities regulated by individuals and corporations. For example, the introduction of robotics is dramatically reducing the number of people needed in manufacturing industries such as the automobile industry. At the same time, increasing numbers of information workers are choosing to live alternative lifestyles. This is being made possible by the widespread availability of personal computers and sophisticated telecommunications tools that bring information resources into the home via the Internet.

The precise nature of the informational social order is still unclear. However, the general outline is emerging. It appears that informational communities will produce a larger economic surplus than industrial communities (Naisbitt and Aburdene, 1990). As well, informational communities are organized into "networks" rather than "hierarchies" (Drucker, 1993). Informationalists are highly mobile (i.e., they are "intermittent nomads" rather than sedentarists), changing occupations and residences more frequently than industrialists (Naisbitt and Aburdene, 1990; Drucker, 1993; Toffler, 1980). Finally, large numbers of informationalists are choosing alternative lifestyles, such as living alone (Toffler, 1980: 212), living in the country (Naisbitt and Aburdene, 1990: 305), and raising children outside marriage (Lenski et al., 1991: 342; Toffler, 1981: 212).

The transition from an industrial society to an informational society is, at once, rendering the traditional public police system obsolete and creating a demand for a new police form to reproduce the new informational order (Naisbitt, 1984: 171; Stenning, 1989: 181). The result has been a rapid expansion in the size of private policing in Canada so that, at present, private police outnumber public police by at least a two to one margin (Normandeau and Leighton, 1990: 131; Statistics Canada, 1994). [12] The dramatic growth of the private police system over the past three decades "points to one inescapable conclusion, which is that when Canadians experience policing ... it is more likely to be 'private' policing than 'public' policing" (Stenning, 1987: 172).

During the early stages of the Information Revolution it appeared that private policing would be "cloned" from the public policing form, distinguished only by the fact that it was operated and controlled by private interests. However, as the Information Revolution progresses, recent developments of the private police form suggest that it has far more radical implications for the future of policing than a simple comparison to public policing would suggest (Shearing and Stenning, 1989).

In their analysis of the private policing model in use at Disneyland in Florida, Shearing and Stenning (1987: 317-19) argue that it is "a design for the future." For example, they note:

> Control strategies are embedded in both environmental features and structural relations. In both cases control structures and activities have other functions which are highlighted so that the control function is overshadowed. Nonetheless, control is pervasive. For example, virtually every pool, fountain, and flower garden serves both as an aesthetic object and to direct visitors away from , or towards, particular locations. Similarly, every Disney Productions employee, while visibly and primarily engaged in other functions, is also engaged in the maintenance of order.

The most important consequence of "this process of embedding control in other structures is that control becomes consensual (ibid.)." [13] In effect, many people are willing to surrender their constitutional rights to private police in order to gain access to the goods and services corporations control. Ironically, some people will not "cooperate" with the public police when they are enforcing the law but will cooperate with them when they are enforcing corporate rules. For example, when public police "moonlight" and provide "security" at a private sporting event — technically working as private police — most people will agree to allow police to search their belongings *because they know it is a condition of entering the stadium.*

---

12   Similarly, the number of private police in the United States has increased dramatically (Spitzer and Scull, 1977) to the point where, by 1982, they outnumbered public police by a three to one margin (Naisbitt, 1982: 171).

13   Elsewhere (Stansfield, 1993), the author has argued that just because control is embedded, and therefore instrumental, does not make it consensual. Rather, embedding control transforms the form of coercion from physical to psychological. Despite this transformation, coercion is coercion — albeit, psychological duress is a subtler, more efficient form of coercion than brute physical force.

Table 2.1
The History of Policing: Summary

Era	Hunting and Gathering (Pre-history — 10,000 B.C.E.)	Agricultural (10,000 B.C.E. — 1750 A.D.)	Industrial (1750 — 1950)
Social Form	- scavenging economy based on primitive technologies (i.e., bow and arrow etc.) - population: 30 to 40 - community structure is a large nuclear family - racially, ethnically, and religiously homogeneous community - nomadic lifestyle - little or no economic surplus - little or no private property - little or no stratification - division of labour between the sexes; males hunt; females gather - female role is highly valued - temporary dwellings with little or no privacy - sharing is a core community value	- farming economy based initially on hoe technology and later on plow technology - population: hundreds to ten thousands - community structure is a few, large extended families - less homogeneous than hunter-gatherer communities but more homogeneous than industrial communities - sedentary lifestyle - small economic surplus - limited material private property (i.e., real estate, farms, animals and implements) - highly stratified communities (i.e., 5% of the population control 99% of the wealth) - rural living in permanent dwellings - privacy between but not within nuclear families - husbandry (i.e., saving) is a core community value - social services (i.e., health care, education and law enforcement) are provided from within the resources of the community	- manufacturing economy based on industrial technology - population: thousands to millions - community structure is large numbers of small nuclear families - less homogeneous than farming communities but more homogeneous than informational communities - sedentary lifestyle - large economic surplus - extensive material private property - communities are stratified but not to the same extent as farming communities - urban living in permanent dwellings - privacy both within and between families - the State provides basic social services (i.e., education, health care and law enforcement)
Police Form	- absence of private property and heterogeneity ensures that there are relatively few conflicts - conflicts are mediated by community members - if conflicts cannot be resolved, disputants are expected to live apart - some forms of behaviour (e.g., abortion, infanticide, euthanasia etc.) are tolerated by the community	- the existence of stratification, private property and some diversity produces conflicts that threaten the status quo; farming communities develop a range of strategies for reproducing order in their communities that includes: - **frankpledge**: a form of preventive bail in which members of the community are required to post a bond with the Shire Reeve (i.e., Sheriff) in case someone in the community commits a crime - **watch and ward:** a surveillance system in which adult males are required to stand guard at the gates of the community at night to prevent strangers from entering - **hue and cry:** an alarm system in which members of the community sound a verbal alarm when they detect the presence of a stranger in the community - **presentments:** a system of informants in which community members are expected to spy on one another and inform the Shire Reeve if they detect a crime	- 1829: in response to a series of violent riots in and around London, Sir Robert Peel tables legislation for the creation of the "first" public police force - the public police are organized into a para-military hierarchy complete with ranks, uniforms and weapons - police "constables" are authorized to exercise extraordinary powers such as the power to use force including lethal force - police forces are empowered to function within clearly defined geo-political boundaries - police forces tend to operate on an exclusionary principle that excludes females, racial and ethnic minorities, gays and lesbians and the elderly

However, if the same police officer asked the *same* person for permission to search his or her automobile after the game, most people would object.

Shearing and Stenning (ibid., 322-23) claim that "instrumental discipline" is the future of social control. Furthermore, they suggest that it is more like Huxley's vision of consensually based control than Orwell's vision of totalitarian control. [14] Whatever else the future of policing may be like, it is clear that it will bear about as much resemblance to public policing as public policing does to vigilante policing.

Summary

Despite the conventional stereotype of who the police are, and what the police do, at least three different police forms can be identified in the modern era. In every instance, a specialized form of policing has developed in response to a new form of social organization. Beginning with vigilante policing in the Agricultural Era, there was public policing in the Industrial Era, and there is private policing in the Informational Era. Essentially, vigilante policing was an informal, part-time, volunteer activity controlled by the community, which operated according to the principle of shared responsibility. In contrast, public policing was a formalized, full-time, mercenary activity controlled by the State, which operated according to the principle of *parens patriae*. Finally, the private policing model that is emerging appears to be a formalized, part-time, embedded activity controlled by corporations, which operates according to the principle of instrumental discipline.

---

14   Huxley and Orwell described their visions of the future of social control in *Brave New World* and *1984*, respectively.

3 Functions

Introduction

Traditionally, police have been viewed as necessary for the smooth and orderly functioning of society. This view is reflected in the police motto: "to serve and protect." According to this view, the police function in society is to enforce the law independently and impartially. An implicit assumption of this view is that society is essentially homogeneous and there is a social consensus regarding the distribution of wealth, power and privilege in society.

An alternative view of the police is that they enforce laws that are designed to reproduce the existing social order. This view is reflected in the actions of individuals and groups who accuse police of oppressing the rights of the powerless. According to this view, the police function in society is to enforce laws that are designed to perpetuate the dominance of elite groups in society. An explicit assumption of this view is that society is essentially heterogeneous and that most power, wealth and privilege is controlled by a relatively small group of elites and that this stratification promotes conflict between individuals and groups in society.

This chapter will consider both of these points of view and attempt to combine them into a coherent and comprehensive view of contemporary policing.

Functionalist Perspective

The classic statement of the police role in a democratic society was provided by the Canadian Committee on Corrections (C.C.C.) (1969: 39) who noted:

The primary functions of the police are:

(a) To prevent crime.

(b) To detect crime and apprehend offenders. This latter function involves the gathering of evidence sufficient not only to warrant the laying of a charge against a specific individual, but also to establish the guilt of that individual in a court of law.

(c) To maintain order in the community in accordance with the rule of law.

(d) The control of highway traffic has also become an important police function in modern times.

This description of the police role is known as a "functionalist" perspective because it emphasizes the *functions* police perform in society. Many criminologists (cf. Kirkham, 1974; Peak, 1993) and most government commissions (cf. Royal (U.K.) Commission on the Police, 1962; Canadian Committee on Corrections, 1969; National (U.S.) Advisory Commission on Criminal Justice Standards and Goals: The Police, 1973) have a functionalist perspective of policing.

An important feature of the functionalist perspective is that it *assumes* there is a social consensus about the status quo and how it is perpetuated (Chambliss, 1973: 3). At the heart of this view is the idea that society is ruled by laws. Pearce (1976: 63) notes:

> This (the rule of law) claims that the legal system is an expression of the people's will; that the meaning of the law is interpreted by an independent judiciary; and that the laws are impartially enforced by an apolitical police force whose *modus operandi* is legally circumscribed.

Two examples that nicely illustrate the functionalist perspective are Sir Robert Peel's famous declaration that the "police are the public and the public are the police" and the Metropolitan Toronto Police motto: "To serve and protect." Peel's oft-repeated declaration explicitly claims that police are fundamentally no different than the public and vice versa. Similarly, the police motto implies that police serve and protect *all* members of the society — not just a select few.[1] As we will see below, both assumptions can be disputed.

1　This is the motto of the Metropolitan Toronto Police Service. Similarly, the motto of the Los Angeles Police Department is "to protect and serve".

Serving and Protecting

Typically, an analysis of the essential elements of the police function identifies two basic types of police duties: crime control and social service. Crime control refers to those police duties that are directly related to law enforcement — such as the detection, apprehension and prosecution of criminals. Social service refers to those police duties directly related to providing services to the public such as controlling traffic, public education and mediating disputes. While it is simplistic to classify police functions in this manner, it is useful to clarify certain features of the police function. [2]

Section 42 (1) of the Police Services Act in Ontario states:

42.(1) The duties of a police officer include,

(a) preserving the peace;

(b) preventing crimes and other offences and providing assistance and encouragement to other persons in their prevention;

(c) assisting victims of crime;

(d) apprehending criminals and others who may lawfully be taken into custody;

(e) laying charges, prosecuting and participating in prosecutions;

(f) executing warrants that are to be executed by police officers and performing related duties;

(g) performing the lawful duties that the chief of police assigns;

(h) in the case of a municipal police force and in the case of an agreement under section 10 (agreement for the provision of police services by O.P.P.), enforcing municipal by-laws;

(i) completing prescribed training.

It is easy to see in this list of duties an uneasy mixture of "social service" and "crime control" functions. For example, 80 percent of these *assigned* duties qualify as "crime control" functions whereas only 20 percent qualify as social service functions (Table 3.1). This is in sharp contrast to the distribution of *actual* duties police perform. For example, several studies

---

2   Shearing and Leon (1976) have argued that it is problematic to characterize police functions as either "social service" or "crime control". They note that the defining characteristic of modern police is the power to use force to resolve conflict. As a result, even when police perform "social service" functions, the capacity to use force is latent in the transaction.

have revealed that police spend approximately 80 percent of their time performing social service functions and only 20 percent performing crime control functions (Reiss, 1971: 96; Ericson, 1982: 206; Hodgson, 1993).[3]

In view of the large disparity between what police are assigned to do and what they actually do, it should not come as a surprise to learn that police are confused about their role (Ericson, 1982: 63), and that many police and most members of the public erroneously believe that police spend the majority of their time enforcing laws (Ericson, 1982: 5; Thomas and Hepburn, 1983: 345).

Confusion about the precise nature of the police function in society may explain the often observed and widely documented cynicism of police (Ericson, 1982: 63-64; Vincent, 1990: 145-150; Westley, 1970: 147-148; Sewell, 1985: 180). Examples of this cynicism are Ericson's observation (1982: 61) that *the* rule of patrol police is "cover your ass," and the author's experience that the motto "to serve and protect" actually means "to serve summonses and protect your ass."[4] The fact that Peel's lofty ideals have been debased is, at once, cause for concern and in need of further explanation.

Table 3.1
Classification of Police Duties According to "Service" or "Enforcement"

Service	Enforcement
- assisting others in crime prevention - assisting victims of crime	- preserving the peace - preventing crimes and other offences - apprehending criminals - laying charges - prosecuting and participating in prosecutions - executing warrants and performing related duties - enforcing municipal by-laws - performing duties assigned by the Chief

3   Hodgson (1993: 180-181) classified his calls for service as "social services," "order maintenance" and "criminal investigations." Social service and order maintenance calls combined consititued 81.8% of his calls for service whereas criminal invesiagions constituted only 18.2%.

4   This was a popular police "joke" when the author was a police officer.

Conflict Perspective

Whereas the functionalist perspective assumes that there is a social consensus in regard to the status quo, the conflict perspective assumes that conflict between individuals and groups in society is endemic (Chambliss, 1973: 3; Turk, 1982: 12). While this may appear to be a minor difference in emphasis, it has profound implications for how conflict theorists view social structure generally, and policing more particularly. Where functionalists see order, conflict theorists see disorder; where functionalists see cooperation, conflict theorists see exploitation; where functionalists see consensus, conflict theorists see conflict. In short, conflict theorists and functionalists have opposing points of view on most things relating to the law and justice.

The conflict perspective maintains that the function of law in society is to reproduce the existing social order (i.e., the status quo). It does this by selectively stigmatizing and punishing certain types of behaviour such as theft, robbery and fraud (i.e., behaviours that tend to redistribute property and wealth) and by not stigmatizing and therefore implicitly endorsing other types of behaviour such as usury, competition, and accumulation (i.e., behaviours that tend to accumulate property and wealth).

The effect of selective stigmatization and law enforcement has been to perpetuate the existing social order and minimize movement between social classes. So, for example, the Economic Council of Canada (1992: 25) reported that "... in any given year, between 42 and 45 percent of the poor population was made up of people who were poor in all five years ..."[5] Similarly, Lenski (1966: 411) reported that only one person in three is upwardly or downwardly mobile in most industrial societies. Typically, people die in the class in which they are born. This lack of mobility ensures that, for most people, life proceeds according to the old adage: "the rich get richer and the poor get poorer." Or, as Reiman (1984) cynically noted, "the rich get richer, and the poor get prison."

Social Stratification

Industrial societies everywhere, including Canada, are politically, economically, and socially stratified (Lenski et al., 1991). The effect of this stratification is to concentrate most power in the hands of a small group of elites (ibid.). So, for example, Ross et al. (1994: 43) note that in 1991 "the top 20 percent of Canadian households receive(d) about nine times the

---

5   The Council's figures were based on poverty rates among working-age Canadians between 1982-1986.

income of the bottom 20 percent (Figures 3.1 and 3.2)." In case the reader thinks that this result was atypical or that Canada is not representative of other industrial countries, it should be noted that this result was consistent with the findings from previous years (ibid.) and that the distribution of household income and poverty (Figures 3.3 and 3.4) in Canada resembles other industrial countries.[6] Very simply, Canadian society is stratified so that a relatively small group of *elites* control most of the country's wealth, power and privilege, while a much larger group of *poor* are relatively impoverished, powerless and disadvantaged.

Another striking feature of the social organization of industrial societies, including Canada, is that typically these societies are stratified according to demographic characteristics such as: occupation, educational attainment, race, ethnicity, age, sex, and ability (Lenski et al., 1991). Stereotypically, the poor in Canada are blacks and natives, females, children, and the physically and mentally disabled; whereas, stereotypically, Canadian elites are white, adult males. For example, Ross et al. found that in Canada in 1991 over one-quarter (26.9 percent) of all children, one-quarter (25.4 percent) of all disabled peoples, more than one-half (57.2 percent) of all single mothers with dependent children under 18, more than half (53.1 percent) of unattached elderly women, and a high percentage of aboriginal peoples were living in poverty.[7] Again, in case the reader thinks Canada is atypical of industrial societies, it should be noted that the composition of the poor and elites in Canada resembles other industrialized countries (Lenski et al., 1991).[8]

Inevitably, the large disparities between elites and poor in industrial societies ensure that as individuals and groups compete to improve their life chances, there are conflicts between these groups (Dahrendorf, 1979; Turk, 1982). Left unchecked, these conflicts can, and sometimes do, undermine the existing social order. While it is possible to use the military to maintain order, it is also very costly and in time it may deplete the wealth of the society leaving less for everyone — elites and poor (Turk, 1982). Thus, it is vastly preferable, from the point of view of the elites, to establish a system of rules (i.e., laws) and rule-enforcers (i.e., police) — that is to say, a legal system to reproduce order and maintain the status quo (Chambliss, 1973: 5; Turk, 1982: 15).

---

6   In 1994, Statistics Canada established the low income cut-off (i.e., people below this income level were living in poverty) at $16,609 for one person and $34, 939 for a family of five living in a city with a population of more than 500,000.

7   Ross et al., (1994: 40) note that precise estimates of poverty among the Aboriginal population were not available at press time. They estimate (ibid., 41) that aboriginal poverty is about 20 percentage points higher than in the Canadian population in general.

8   Significantly, Lenski et al. (1991) note that as stratified as industrialized societies are, they are less stratified than agricultural societies.

Once elites commit to maintaining order by using a legal system, it is important for the system to be perceived as fair and equitable, otherwise the poor would have little or no reason to participate or compete. At a minimum, equity and fairness includes *real* opportunities for the poor to improve their social standing and *effective* guarantees they will not be arbitrarily imprisoned when they try to realize these opportunities. If, at any time, the poor conclude that the social-legal system is unfair (i.e., large numbers of poor are imprisoned for legitimate attempts to improve their social standing) or inequitable (i.e., there is little or no opportunity to move between social classes), they may rebel.[9]

Figure 3.1
Distribution of Total Income by Quintile, Canada, 1992

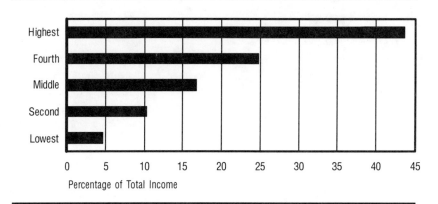

Distribution of Total Income, Canada, 1992

	Lowest %	Second %	Middle %	Fourth %	Highest %	Total %
			Share of Total Income (quintiles)			
Families	6.3	12.2	17.8	24.0	39.7	**100**
Unattached Individuals	5.5	10.5	15.4	24.4	44.2	**100**
All Households	**4.6**	**10.3**	**16.7**	**24.8**	**43.6**	**100**

Source: Ross et al., 1994: 43.

---

9 The possibility of a rebellion by the poor, or by those who sympathize with them, is a formidable threat, since the poor vastly outnumber elites. For example, Ross et al. (1994: 40) reported that 2.76 million Canadian *households* (i.e., 25.4 per cent of all households) lived in poverty in 1992.

Figure 3.2
Distribution of Total Income by Decile, Canada, 1991

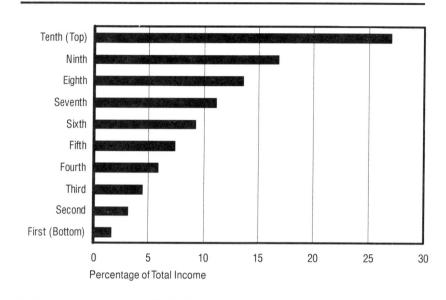

Percentage of Total Income

Decile Shares of Total Income, Canada, 1991

Decile	All Households %
First (Bottom)	1.6
Second	3.1
Third	4.4
Fifth	5.9
Sixth	7.4
Seventh	11.1
Eighth	13.6
Ninth	16.8
Tenth (Top)	27.0
Total	**100**

Source: Ross et al., 1994: 91.

Figure 3.3
Relative Rates of Poverty, Nonelderly Families, Selected Countries, Various Years

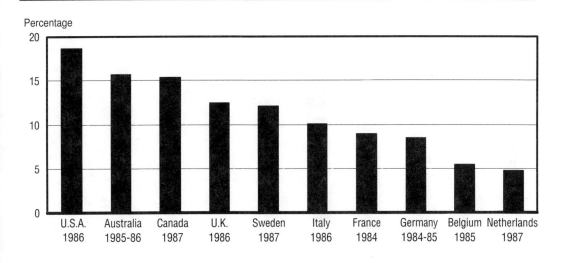

Relative Rates of Poverty for 10 Countries, Nonelderly Families, Various Years

Country	All Families %
Australia (1985-86)	15.7
Belgium (1985)	5.4
Canada (1987)	15.4
France (1984)	8.9
Germany (1984-85)	8.5
Italy (1986)	10.1
Netherlands (1987)	4.7
Sweden (1987)	12.1
U.K. (1986)	12.4
U.S.A. (1986)	18.7

Source: Ross et al., 1994: 111.

Figure 3.4
Poverty Rates Among Nonelderly Families, Before and After Taxes and Transfers, Selected Countries, Circa 1987

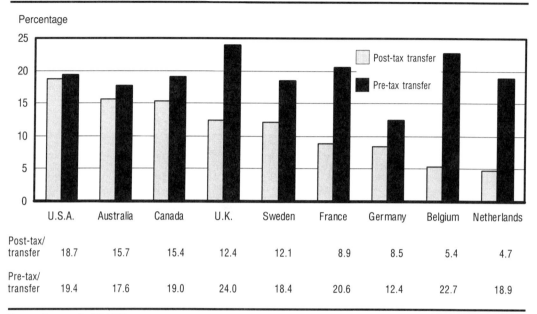

	U.S.A.	Australia	Canada	U.K.	Sweden	France	Germany	Belgium	Netherlands
Post-tax/ transfer	18.7	15.7	15.4	12.4	12.1	8.9	8.5	5.4	4.7
Pre-tax/ transfer	19.4	17.6	19.0	24.0	18.4	20.6	12.4	22.7	18.9

Source: Ross et al., 1994:113.

In Canada, as elsewhere, there is only modest movement between social classes (Economic Council of Canada, 1992: 25). The poor generally, and aboriginals and blacks more particularly, are incarcerated in numbers disproportionate to their representation in the general population (Aboriginal Justice Inquiry of Manitoba, 1991; Royal Commission on the Donald Marshall Jr., Prosecution, Vol. 4, 1989: 60). These historical injustices ensure that rebellion is a clear and present danger to the social order. [10]

---

10   History is replete with examples of rebellions by "oppressed peoples". The American, French, and Bolshevik (i.e., Russian) Revolutions all pitted a poor and oppressed majority against a wealthy and elite minority. Similarly, the Red River Rebellion of 1869-70 led by Louis Riel was a struggle by Canada's aboriginal peoples to achieve equality with European colonialists. Also, more recently, the poor in the United States (i.e., Watts, 1968; South Central L.A., 1993), Britain (i.e., Knightsbridge, 1984) and Canada (i.e., Oka, 1992) have rebelled against the central authority in these countries.

3   **Functions**

Table 3.2
Incidence of Low Income[1] by Selected Characteristics, Canada, 1991

Characteristic	Families (%)	Unattached Individuals (%)
Nationally	13.1	36.5
By Age of Head		
under 25	36.9	33.7
25 — 34	18.6	24.8
35 — 44	12.7	25.5
45 — 54	7.6	29.2
55 — 64	12.0	42.5
65 and over	9.0	43.8
Sex		
Males	9.4	31.0
Females	40.7	41.4
Household type		
couples with children	9.3	NA
couples with no children	9.2	NA
male single parent	16.0	NA
male single parent with dependent children[2]	24.4	NA
female single parent	47.6	NA
female single parent with dependent children[2]	61.9	NA
Other family	17.3	NA

Source: Statistics Canada — Cat. No. 13-207: 170-173.
1   Estimates are based on Statistics Canada low income cut-offs for 1986 bases.
2   Children under 18 years.

When rebellion threatens, elites have only two choices: adjust the status quo so that the poor retain a larger share of society's wealth or use extreme force (i.e., the military) to reinforce the status quo. Since both options involve a major re-distribution of society's wealth, neither is attractive to elites. Rather, faced with the possibility of rebellion, elites attempt to strike a delicate balance: share enough of society's wealth to placate the poor, but share no more than is absolutely necessary. If elites share too much they literally give away their privileged position in society, but if they do not share enough the poor may rise up and take it. In Canada, the elites share more than in some countries (i.e., U.S.A. and Australia) but much less than in others (eg., U.K., Sweden, France, Belgium and Netherlands) (Figure 3.5).

Figure 3.5

Percentage of Total Household Income Received by Top 10 and Bottom 20 Percent of Households in Selected Western Industrial Countries

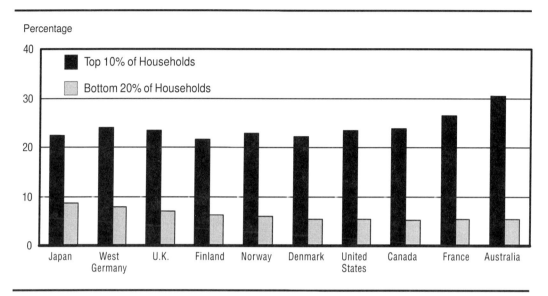

Source: Lenski et al., 1991.

Distribution of Household Income in Western Industrial Societies

Society	Percentage of Total Household Income Received by Top 10 and Bottom 20 Percent of Households		
	Top 10 Percent	Bottom 20 Percent	Ratio of Top to Bottom
Japan	22.4	8.7	2.6
West Germany	24.0	7.9	3.0
United Kingdom	23.4	7.0	3.3
Finland	21.7	6.3	3.4
Norway	22.8	6.0	3.8
Denmark	22.3	5.4	4.1
United States	23.3	5.4	4.1
Canada	23.8	5.3	4.5
France	26.4	5.5	4.8
Australia	30.5	5.4	5.6

Source: Lenski et al., 1991: 323.

Reproducing Order

The function of law in industrial society is twofold: first and foremost, it serves to legitimize the status quo by stigmatizing behaviours that undermine the status quo (eg., theft and various other forms of property redistribution) and secondly, by implication, it legitimizes behaviours that reinforce the status quo (eg., usury and various other forms of property accumulation). Also, it creates a context (i.e., the courts) in which conflicts can be resolved non-violently. However, in order for the law to be effective the State must have a mechanism (i.e., police) for enforcing it.

This then is the function of police in industrial society: to enforce laws that reproduce social order. However, as Ericson (1982: 7) has noted, the police do not reproduce just any order, rather, they reproduce the existing order (i.e., the order of the status quo):

> It is not the mandate of the police to produce a new order. On the contrary, their everyday actions are directed at reproducing the existing order (the "normal and efficient state") and the order (system of rules) by which this is accomplished. They are one tool of "policing" in the wider sense of all governmental efforts aimed at disciplining, refining, and improving the population. As such, most of what they do is part of the social machinery of verifying and reproducing what is routinely assumed to be the case. Their sense of order and the order they seek to reproduce are that of the status quo.

A simplisitic analogy is that police are like "referees" in a "game" between two competing teams whose differing interests (i.e., winning) brings them into conflict. [11] However, this game differs from the games we played as children in two important respects. First, the rules (i.e., the law) are stacked in favour of one team (i.e., the elites), with the result that the referees (i.e., the police) enforce the rules more often against one team than the other. Second, and more ominous, the referees in this game have the power to use force — including lethal force — to enforce the rules. This combination of biased rules and severe sanctions for rule infractions makes this game patently unfair. However, for reasons we will consider below, few of the players on the poor team appreciate the true nature of the game; and because the referees (police) typically are recruited from among the ranks of the middle class, few of them understand their real function in the game. [12]

---

11   Weiner (1976: 14) describes the police function as being like a "buffer" between elites and poor. Similarly, Ericson (1982: 61) notes that the police he studied described their relationship vis à vis the police administration and the public as "a feeling of being caught in a vice ".

12   The poor make particularly good police because they are socialized among the criminal classes and they know "the tricks of the trade" and therefore, they are well qualified to defend against them. Very few police come from the elites because these individuals have other less dangerous opportunities to earn a living available to them.

The poor are also an easy target. Their relative poverty means not only that the poor have a greater incentive to break the law but also that the types of crime that are accessible to them (eg., drug trafficking and street prostitution) are easy to detect because typically they occur in public places. In contrast, the "crimes of the powerful" (eg., fraud, theft, influence peddling) are relatively difficult to detect because typically they occur in the secrecy of private homes and offices.

Not surprisingly, both the poor and the police are frustrated by their respective roles in reproducing the existing social order. Frequently, because they are unaware of the larger picture, the poor blame police for their predicament and police attempt to punish the poor for their deviant lifestyles (i.e., "breaking the rules"). Just as the players on a losing team that has little or no chance of winning occasionally resort to cheating and then blame the referees when they are caught, occasionally referees punish losing teams by imposing penalties (i.e., "unsportsmanlike conduct"). If the poor never win and the elites always win, eventually the poor tire of the game and quit playing (i.e., "drop-out") or, worse still from the vantage of the elites, they may try to "break-up" the game (i.e., rebel). To avoid this, elites have developed sophisticated strategies to keep the poor motivated and, when all else fails, to discourage them from rebelling.

The key to keeping all sides "playing the game" is to convince the poor that they have a reasonable chance of "winning" — that is, that both teams are playing on a level field. This is no small task given the true, exploitative nature of the game — a stratified social order that is reproduced by police differentially enforcing biased laws. The problem for elites is: how to make the social system generally and the legal system more particularly *appear* to be fair and equitable?

One way that is used to foster the impression of fairness and equity is to allow people from one class to move into another class (i.e., "trading players"). So, for example, some elites become poor (i.e., bankrupt) and some poor become elites (i.e., "rags to riches"). Player trades alone, however, are not enough to convince the poor that the game is fair since, as we saw above, relatively few players ever switch teams. As a result, other ways have been found to convince the poor the game is fair.

The solution has been to *mystify* the real purpose of the legal system. Mystification is achieved by cloaking the law in liberal rhetoric that emphasizes the "principles of natural justice." So, for example, the criminal justice system rhetoric emphasizes "fairness" (i.e., a fair trial), "honesty" (i.e., tell the truth, the whole truth and nothing but the truth), "freedom" (i.e., no arbitrary detention), and "humaneness" (i.e., no cruel or unusual treatment or punishment). However the criminal justice system *reality* is distinguished by "racism" (i.e., over-representation of blacks and natives in arrest rates and prisons), "deceit" (i.e., police perjury), "arbitrariness" (i.e., police shooting fleeing felons) and "cruelty" (i.e., indeterminate sentences). It is this "gap" between appearance and reality in the criminal justice system that elites must bridge; mystification is the bridge. This is the context in which the police function is performed.

Clearly, how the police reproduce order — methodically or arbitrarily, humanely or brutally, with integrity or corruptly — is crucial to determining whether "justice is seen to be done." If the police function of differentially enforcing biased laws yet creating the appearance that all is fair and just was not difficult enough, it is complicated by the fact that detecting a criminal offence is actually quite difficult — few people are foolish enough to commit a crime in plain view of the police. As a result, in addition to having extraordinary powers of search, seizure and arrest, police *elaborate* these lawful powers by developing "extra-legal" powers.[13] Examples of extra-legal police powers are: the use of informers, inducing confessions, finessing criminal acts, and differentially targeting the poor for surveillance.

Procuring informers or "snitches" is a common police practice. Typically, offenders are induced to inform by promises of withdrawing or reducing their charges. Similarly, a common police strategy to induce a confession is to promise an accused special treatment. Also, police routinely "finesse" criminal acts by tricking and deceiving suspects. For example, "undercover" police who pose as criminals use trickery and deceit to "finesse" offenders into committing a crime in the presence of police. Of course, police who use these tactics risk entrapping an offender, in which case the courts have the option of dismissing the charges against the accused. In practice, very few cases are dismissed because of police entrappment.

While these extra-legal tactics are adequate to detect and apprehend most offenders, organized criminals develop sophisticated strategies to avoid police detection.[14] As a result, routine police tactics are largely ineffective against sophisticated criminals. This poses a serious problem. Unlike individual criminals acting in isolation who are easily controlled within the authorized parameteres of the law, organized criminals represent a serious threat to the status quo and therefore must be controlled at virtually any "cost." To "level the playing field," police occasionally resort to the use of patently illegal acts in order "to make a pinch." Examples of illegal police

---

13 While not strictly illegal, "extra-legal" police powers are not explicitly authorized by law either. As a result, legally, extra-legal police powers fall into a "grey area."
14 Lavigne (1987) has described the strategies organized criminals such as motorcycle gangs use to evade police detection. Among others these include the use of untraceable mobile cellular phones, spies, and a strictly enforced code of secrecy.

tactics are the use of forged judicial documents, fabricated evidence, coerced confessions and perjured testimony. [15]

The informal system of "extra-legal" and illegal police tactics is known among police as the "Ways and Means Act." Police officers who become accomplished in the techniques of the "Ways and Means Act" are known to their colleagues as "good street coppers"; and those who cannot or will not master the techniques typically are ostracized. The Ways and Means Act makes manageable the difficult police assignment of using the law to control those members of society who represent the most serious threat to social order.

The problem police face is in distinguishing between good people (i.e., law-abiding citizens) and "scrotes," "assholes" and "pukes" (i.e., hard-core criminals). In order to ensure that the credibility of the police and therefore the Criminal Jusrice System is not damaged, police must be careful to limit the tactics authorized by the Ways and Means Act only to criminals. However, the problem is compounded by the fact that many adults, particularly many men, have at some time in their lives engaged in activities that could be classified as criminal (eg., impared driving, possession of marihuana, mishief to property, etc.). This makes the police job of distinguishing between good citizens and "real" criminals much more difficult. Not surprisingly, from time to time, they make mistakes.

Occasionally, police target the wrong (i.e., an innocent) person and the reality of the criminal justice system is exposed. [16] Faced with the choice of acknowledging the repressive reality of the law or compromising the interests of an individual or a small group of police officers, the latter is chosen. In doing so, the impression is fostered among police officers that one of their own is "scape-goated" whenever the "real" face of the law is exposed (Ericson, 1982: 61). Predictably, this results in a siege mentality among police officers that is often expressed in a "cover your ass" syndrome (ibid.). As Ericson (1982: 61) notes, police agencies subscribe to the "rotten apple" theory of organizational deviance because doing so allows them to avoid any wider sense of responsibility or vicarious liability for police wrong-doing.

---

15 Ericson (1981) has documented the use of forged or "left-handed" warrants by Canadian police.
16 Notorious examples of people in Canada and the United States who were wrongly convicted and sentenced to long prison terms on the basis of evidence produced by corrupt police investigations are Donald Marshal Jr. and "Hurricane" Rubin Carter, respectively. Similarly, the graphic Los Angeles police brutality disclosed by the Rodney King videotape undermined police credibility everywhere.

The existence of the "Ways and Means Act," even if only informally, means that the law generally, and the police more particularly, can be unfair and inequitable. Naturally, the brunt of an arbitrary and unjust legal system falls more heavily on some members of society than others — generally on he poor. As a result, like the police themselves, many poor become cynical about their prospects of achieving "justice" in the criminal justice system and of achieving "success" within the social-economic system.

Toward A Synthetic Model of Policing

The preceding discussion underscores the fact that one's perception of the police and their function in society depends on, among other things, one's position in the social hierarchy. Generally, the higher one is in the social order the more likely one is to sympathize with police and to view the police function from a "functionalist" perspective. Conversely, the lower one is in the social order the less likely one is to sympathize with police and the more likely one is to view the police function from a "conflict" perspective. So, for example, typically, the poor view police with ambivalence at best and distrust and hatred at worst. Typically, however, elites view police with benign indifference at worst and ardent support at best. This apparently anomalous situation is easily explained by the two perspectives we discussed above. For the more privileged members of society, the police perform an essential function in society by enforcing laws that ensure the smooth and orderly functioning of society (i.e., functionalist perspective); whereas, for the less privileged, the police are oppressors who differentially enforce biased and therefore unfair laws that obstruct their efforts to achieve equity (i.e., conflict perspective).

Depending on one's position in the social hierarchy, both perspectives can be "right." However, neither explanation alone can produce a comprehensive understanding of policing. A comprehensive understanding requires an appreciation of both perspectives — functionalist and conflict. In the chapters that follow we will borrow concepts and theories from both the functionalist and conflict perspectives to analyse various issues in policing.

Summary

Canada is a stratified society in which the poor and the more privileged are distinguished by demographic characteristics such as race, sex, age and ability. This induces competition between these groups which results in conflict. Left unchecked, this conflict could produce a rebellion by the poor. Recognizing this, a sophisticated system of laws, police and courts exists that is designed to reproduce the existing social order. The police function in this system is to enforce laws that reproduce social order (i.e., the status quo). However, because some members of society represent a more serious threat to social order than others, police improvise extra-legal and illegal ways and means to maintain control. Occasionally they are held accountable for their actions so that the law is seen to be fair.

4 Roles

Introduction

Metaphor is a powerful device for helping us to understand an increasingly complex and complicated world. A typical law enforcement metaphor portrays police as "soldiers" fighting in "a war on crime." Another common law enforcement metaphor portrays criminals as "outlaws" who defy society's rules. Archetypal Psychology maintains that the signs and symbols we use to illustrate our metaphors and myths are products of the subconscious. These "archetypal" images transcend time, place and individuals, reoccuring throughout the world and throughout history. Ultimately, these images influence how communities are organized and, more importantly for our purposes, how communities are policed.

This chapter uses concepts from Archetypal Psychology to analyse law enforcement metaphors and to "tell" the police "story." In particular, the roles of "lawmen," "crime-fighters," "outlaws" and "martyrs" are analysed using archetypal images.

Archetypal Psychology

Actors play roles and, in a sense, we are all actors. As we saw in Chapter 3, police are assigned several different "functions" and, as a result, must play several different "roles." Indeed, a police officer's ability to play several roles convincingly may be the determinant of his or her effectiveness as a police officer. Archetypal Psychology is a powerful tool that can be used to analyse the roles actors play, including the roles played by police.

Archetypal Psychology was founded by the Swiss psychologist Carl Jung (1875-1961) early this century and has been applied in a wide variety of contexts since then, including: mythology (Campbell, 1968), psychoanalysis (Jung, 1968; Shinoda-Bolen, 1985; 1990), ontogenetic (i.e., individual) development (Pearson, 1991; Wilber, 1985) and phylogenetic (i.e., species) development (Wilber, 1986a). Very simply, Archetypal Psychology assumes that every person has a subconscious mind that contains mental patterns called "archetypes" that influence how we experience the world and find expression in our dreams, fantasies and fears (Pearson 1991: 6).

Pearson (1991: 10-11) has identified a total of twelve archetypes: innocent, orphan, lover, seeker, warrior, caregiver, destroyer, creator, ruler, magician, sage, and fool. Each archetype is associated with a "goal," a "fear," a "problem," a "response to task," and a "gift or virtue." For example, the warrior's goal in life is to "win the war." The warrior's fear is "to show weakness in the face of danger." The warrior's problem is how to win the battle without suffering unacceptable loses. The warrior's response to daily tasks is to fight only for what really matters. Finally, the gift or virtue the warrior archetype brings when it is activated is "the courage and discipline" to face and persevere in the face of danger (Table 4.1).

Archetypes are organized in pairs so that, typically, one pair of archetypes is activated in response to certain life issues during each stage of individual development (Pearson, 1991: 6, 237-239). For example, during childhood, typically, either the innocent or the orphan archetype is activated (the other archetype is repressed) in response to the individual's need to establish a safe and secure environment. Similarly, during adolescence, typically, either the lover or the seeker archetype is activated (again, the other archetype is repressed) in response to the individual's need to establish an "identity." This developmental process is repeated throughout the individual's lifetime as new life issues surface (Table 4.2).

Each archetype has three levels of development[1] that determine the precise manner in which an archetype will respond to daily tasks. So, for example, at the lowest level of development, the warrior archetype is committed to the use of violence on behalf of family and friends in a no-holds barred fight to the death. At the second level of development, the warrior is committed to the use of violence on behalf of others (i.e., community or country) but only as a last resort and only if it is in a "fair fight." At the third and highest level of development, the warrior is

---

1   These "levels" correspond roughly to the levels of development in the compound individual (i.e., body, mind, and spirit).

committed to a non-violent struggle on behalf of all things (i.e., all of humanity, the environment, etc.) to achieve greater social justice (Table 4.3).[2] Most people today are "stuck" at the second level of development (Wilber, 1986a).

Table 4.1
The Twelve Archetypes

Archetype	Goal	Fear	Dragon/ Problem	Response to Task	Gift/Virtue
Innocent	Remain in safety	Abandonment	Deny it or seek rescue	Fidelity, discernment	Trust, optimism
Orphan	Regain safety	Exploitation	Is victimized by it	Process and feel pain fully	Interdependence, realism
Warrior	Win	Weakness	Slay/confront it	Fight only for what really matters	Courage, discipline
Caregiver	Help others	Selfishness	Take care of it or those it harms	Give without maiming self or others	Compassion, generosity
Seeker	Search for better life	Conformity	Flee from it	Be true to deeper self	Autonomy, ambition
Lover	Bliss	Loss of love	Love it	Follow your bliss	Passion, commitment
Destroyer	Metamorphosis	Annihilation	Allow dragon to slay it	Let go	Humility
Creator	Identity	Inauthenticity	Claim it as a part of the self	Self-creation, self acceptance	Individuality, vocation
Ruler	Order	Chaos	Find its constructive uses	Take full responsibility for your life	Responsibility, control
Magician	Transformation	Evil sorcery	Transform it	Align self with cosmos	Personal power
Sage	Truth	Deception	Transcend it	Attain enlightenment	Wisdom, nonattachment
Fool	Enjoyment	Nonaliveness	Play tricks on it	Trust in the process	Joy, freedom

Source: Pearson (1991: 10-11).

---

2   An example of the warrior archetype at the first level of development was Malcolm X's famous declaration that he would achieve social justice for black Americans "by any means necessary." An example of the warrior at the second level of development was the Marquis of Queensbury's Rules for "fair fighting." Examples of the warrior at the third and highest level of development were Martin Luther King Jr.'s and Mohandas Gandhi's use of non-violent resistance to the American and British authorities respectively to achieve social justice for all people regardless of their race, colour or caste.

Table 4.2
Archetypes and Individual Development

Archetypal Pairs	Stage of Development	Life Issue
Innocent/Orphan	Childhood	Security
Lover/Seeker	Adolescence	Identity
Warrior/Caregiver	Adulthood	Responsibility
Destroyer/Creator	Mid-life	Authenticity
Ruler/Magician	Maturity	Power
Sage/Fool	Old Age	Freedom

Source: Pearson (1991: 240).

Crime Fighters

Frequently, police are depicted in film and literature as "soldiers" fighting in "a war on crime." Recent examples of this trend in film are the television programmes "N.Y.P.D. Blue" and "Night Heat" and the feature films based on the fictional character "Dirty Harry." Examples from literature are the numerous books authored by the former police officer, Joseph Waumbaugh. While the metaphor of police as crime-fighters is promulgated by the publishing and film industries, it does not end there since our image of police as "crime-fighters" influences both police and community expectations of how law enforcement will be accomplished.

The crime-fighter role comes easily for most police because most are males, and most males are socialized as "warriors" (Pearson, 1991: 260).[3] For example, frequently young boys, but rarely girls, are encouraged to participate in "violent" sports such as football and hockey. As a result, from a very young age boys learn the skills they need to be warriors. When they reach adulthood, these young warriors are expected to use their warrioring skills to compete, and especially to win, at business. This view was illustrated by the late Vince Lombardi's football coaching philosophy which proclaimed: "Winning is not the most important thing, it's the only thing!"

---

3 Interestingly, in art and literature warriors usually are depicted as males although there are a few examples of female warriors such as the Amazons (Pearson, 1991: 96).

Table 4.3
Archetypal Levels

ARCHETYPE	PHYSICAL	MENTAL	SPIRITUAL
Innocent	Unquestioning acceptance of environ-ment, authorities, belief that the world as it is being experienced is all there is; dependence	Experience of the "fall" disillusionment, disappointment — but retention of faith and goodness in adversity	Return to paradise, this time as a Wise Innocent; trust and optimism without denial, naïveté, or dependence
Orphan	Learning to acknowledge the truth of one's plight and feel pain, abandonment, victimization, powerlessness, and loss of faith in people and in institutions in authority	Accepting the need for help; being willing to be rescued and aided by others	Replacing dependence on authorities with interdependence with others who help each other and band together against authority; developing realistic expectations
Warrior	Fight for self or others to win or prevail (anything goes)	Principled fight for self or others abiding by rules of a fair fight or competition; altruistic intent	Forthright assertiveness; fighting or competition for what really matters (not simply personal gain); little or no need for violence; preference for win/win solutions; conflict honestly aired; increased communication, honesty
Caregiver	Conflict between your own needs and those of others; tendency to sacrifice your own needs to what others need or want from you; rescuing	Learning to care for yourself so that caring for others is enriching not maiming; learning "tough love" empowering, not doing, for others	Generativity; willingness to care and be responsible for people (and perhaps also for animals and the earth) beyond your own immediate family
Seeker	Exploring, wandering, experimenting, studying, trying new things	Ambition, climbing the ladder of success, becoming the best you can be	Spiritual searching transformation
Destroyer	Confusion, grappling with the meaning of death, loss, pain	Acceptance of mortality, loss, relative powerlessness	Ability to choose to let go of anything that no longer supports your values, life, and growth, or that of others
Lover	Following your bliss, what you love	Bonding with and making commitments to whom and what you love	Radical self-acceptance giving birth to the Self and connecting the personal with the transpersonal, the individual with the collective
Creator	Opening to receiving visions, images, hunches, inspiration	Allowing yourself to know what you really want to have, do, or create	Experiments with creating what you imagine — allowing yourself to let your dreams come true
Ruler	Taking responsibility for the state of your life; seeking healing of wounds or areas of powerlessness that are reflected in scarcity in your outer life; concerned primarily with your own life or your own family	Developing skills and creating structures for manifesting your own dreams in the real world as it is; concerned with the good of whatever group or community you belong to	Fully utilizing all resources — internal as well as external; concerned with the good of society or the planet
Magician	Experiencing healing or choosing to notice extrasensory or synchronistic experiences	Grounding inspiration by acting on your visions and making them real; making your dreams come true	Consciously using the knowledge that everything is connected to everything else; developing mastery of the art of changing physical realities by first changing mental, emotional, and spiritual ones
Fool	Life is a game to be played for the fun of it (Fool)	Cleverness used to trick others, to get out of trouble, to find ways around obstacles, to tell the truth without impunity (Trickster)	Life is experienced fully in the moment; life is celebrated for its own sake and lived in the moment, one day at a time (Wise Fool or Jester)
Sage	Search for "the truth" and objectivity	Skepticism, awareness of multiplicity and complexity of truth, all truth seen as relative; acceptance of subjectivity as part of the human condition	Experience of ultimate truth or truths; wisdom

Source: Pearson (1991).

Their socialization ensures that warriors excel at competition and thrive on conflict. As a result, warriors are attracted to some occupations more than others. For example, warriors are attracted to "dangerous" occupations such as fire-fighting, policing and the military because these careers offer an environment where not only can the warrior fight, but the warrior also is *expected* to fight (eg., fighting fires, crime or wars). Warriors disdain more mundane occupations such as accounting, business and law because these roles are limited to "sitting behind a desk and pushing a pencil."

A problem faced by warriors who are crime-fighters is that civil society is essentially *peaceful* and often there is no war for them to fight. As a result, police organizations must "invent" a war (eg., the war on crime/drugs), complete with an enemy (i.e., criminals, pukes, scrotes, and assholes), a battleground (i.e., the streets and courts), and a cause (i.e., to rid the streets of crime). Thus, it is assumed that there *is* a war in society. So, for example, police rhetoric talks about the "war on crime," and the "need" for more powerful weapons. As well when police officers are killed in the line of duty, they are given a "hero's" burial with full police "honours."

When soldiers go into battle they wear a uniform to distinguish themselves from the enemy. [4] Similarly, when crime-fighters go into battle it is important that they are easily distinguishable from civilians (i.e., non-combatants) and criminals (i.e., the enemy) alike. To accomplish this, crime-fighters prepare for battle by donning a special costume (uniform) complete with a special hat (adorned with ribbons), special shoes (infantry boots), weapons and medals. This contrasts with the enemy who, typically, is "camouflaged" and whose identity can only be inferred from his [5] appearance (unconventional), attitude (disrespectful), whereabouts (a high crime area or a poor person in a rich neighbourhood), associates (other enemies), and past behaviour (criminal record).

---

4 This helps to minimize deaths from so-called "friendly fire" situations in which soldiers accidentally or mistakenly shoot their colleagues. Not surprisingly, this is a problem for police also (see Chapter 8).

5 In the highly sexist world of police archetypes, it is taken for granted that both police and criminals are males; females and children are limited to supporting roles as victims and sympathizers.

The most important piece of equipment in a crime-fighter's uniform is his gun.[6] Just as a magician needs a magic wand, and a ruler needs a crown, a warrior needs a weapon: the weapon of choice for modern warriors is a gun. And just like the warriors of old, crime-fighters today nurture and care for their "pieces."[7] However, convinced about the strength of the enemy and the terrible dangers of their mission, crime-fighters are never satisified with their weapons and always feel the need to have more and more powerful weapons. The inevitable result of this situation is that there is an ongoing "arms race" between police and criminals to see who will have the most powerful weapons.

The crime-fighter's sense of vulnerability is an inescapable feature of the warrior archetype. Pearson (1991: 99) notes that warriors have only a limited array of conflict resolution skills:

> To a person with only the Warrior archetype evidenced in consciousness, every situation seems like a dragon, and the only options are to run, fight, or be destroyed.

The options for crime-fighters are even more limited than other warriors because "running away" from a fight usually is viewed as "cowardice" within the police subculture and cowardice is not tolerated (Vincent, 1990: 126). Also, the option of losing a fight is not an acceptable alternative because it may be interpreted as a sign of weakness and encourage the enemy. As a result, crime-fighters must always be willing to use force, including lethal force (see Chapter 8) if necessary, to defeat the enemy (Vincent, 1990: 129-32; Reiss, 1971).

The high priority placed on winning, and the virtual absence of retreat as a strategy, means that crime-fighters must be very careful when choosing their battles. This pragmatic view is expressed in the occupational wisdom that "you never rush to a fight — when you get there, the losers go to hospital and the winners go to jail!" Very simply, crime-fighters are expected *not to fight* unless winning is a high probability either because they possess overwhelming numbers or

---

6   Weapons have been present in policing since the beginning. For example, Critchley (1972: 51) notes that when the "new" police appeared in London in 1829 they were armed with "a short truncheon concealed beneath the long tails of the coat." Today, most but not all police in Canada and the United States carry personal firearms (i.e., pistols or revolvers). Notable exceptions are uniformed members of the Royal Newfoundland Constabulary and police auxiliaries who patrol while armed only with a baton.

7   A few of the ways police alter their firearms are by adjusting the firing mechanism to make it more sensitive to pressure and by substituting hollow-point ammunition for solid-point ammunition.

because they have more powerful weapons.[8] Crime-fighters who know how "to pick their spots" without compromising the safety of themselves or their colleagues are known as "good street coppers" and are awarded a high status within the police subculture.

Another key defence for the warrior is secrecy (Pearson, 1991: 102). During wartime everyone accepts that secrecy is necessary to prevent the enemy from "spying." Similarly, crime-fighters know the value of secrecy (cf. Ericson, 1981: 31; Vincent, 1990: 144-5) and they create formal and informal rules to ensure their secrets are not revealed to their enemies (i.e., criminals) (see Chapter 12). The heavy emphasis on secrecy in police organizations ensures that crime-fighters become skilled at deceiving their enemies and at detecting their enemies' deception. Also, severe sanctions are imposed on those who "betray" their colleagues by revealing police secrets (see Chapter 12). Despite these precautions, and because the enemy is often difficult to identify, crime-fighters are frequently suspicious, sometimes bordering on paranoid, about people who want to know "too much" about "police business."

"Lawmen"

Another common police archetype is the "lawman." At the heart of this image is the notion that police are responsible for keeping the peace and maintaining order by enforcing the law. Just like the crime-fighter archetype, the lawman archetype has been a mainstay in film and literature. Perhaps the most famous example of the lawman archetype was the infamous gun battle at the O.K. corral in which Wyatt Earp and "Doc" Holiday among others shot and killed several members of the Clanton family when the latter refused to leave Tombstone before sunset. Also, just like the crime-fighter archetype, the lawman archetype influences police and community expectations of how the law will be enforced.

Like the warrior, the ruler is a role that most young males are socialized to play (Pearson, 1991: 265). For example, frequently young boys, but rarely girls, are encouraged to develop leadership skills (i.e., be captain of a sports team). When they reach adulthood men are expected to use their leadership skills to rule, if not in business, at least within their own family. This view is illustrated by the old adage "a man's home is his castle."

---

8 On those rare occasions when a crime-fighter loses a battle, usually it is because he over-estimates his own abilities or underestimates the abilities of his enemy.

Their socialization ensures that rulers excel at exercising power and thrive on creating order. As a result, rulers are attracted to some occupations more than others. For example, rulers are attracted to para-military hierarchies such as those found in the army and police departments because these organizations offer access to power and an environment in which it can be exercised (eg., giving and taking orders). Finally, rulers disdain networked organizations such as those found in the arts and among street people because, to the ruler, networks are disordered.

Rulers do not like to lead — they *expect* to lead. Indeed, in the medieval period it was the Ruler's "divine right" to lead (Pearson, 1991: 184). In the grand tradition of ruling, lawmen expect *unconditional* obedience when they give an order. As a result, even something as simple as seeking clarification of a lawman's orders may be perceived as a challenge to his authority. When this occurs a lawman's first reaction is to demonstrably reassert his authority so that everyone can see "who's in charge." If, when doing so, the lawman uses "excessive force" (i.e., the warrior gets out of control), those he polices (i.e., rules) may conclude that he is an "ogre tyrant" who is to be feared but not respected. Ironically, this is just the opposite of what the lawman seeks, which is to be admired and respected by all for his kind and benevolent rule.

Another irony associated with lawmen is that their rule is always constrained by a higher authority (i.e., higher ranking officers). This is because lawmen are members of a para-military hierarchy that structures power relations between the members; consequently, lawmen are at once "superior" to lower ranking colleagues and the public and "inferior" to higher ranking colleagues (see Chapter 7). This arrangement creates the unusal situation in which lawmen can be both the "punished" and the "punisher." This may explain the lawman's often observed penchant for dispensing "street justice" (Reiss, 1976; Ericson, 1982). The situation is aggravated by the fact that police organizations emphasize the use of punishment to hold police accountable for the consequences of their actions (see Chapter 11). As a result, lawmen feel that they are "scape-goated" whenever something goes wrong (Ericson, 1982: 60).

Convinced of their own benevolent intentions (i.e., "I'm just serving and protecting") and frustrated by what they consider to be unnecessary attempts to limit their power (i.e., "administrative red tape"), lawmen develop a deep-seated cynicism about the law, the courts and, most important of all, their role in the criminal justice system (Ericson, 1982: 61). Consequently, the law becomes the "Criminal's Code," the courts become "Kangaroo Kourts," and the lawman's role becomes "to serve summonses and protect your ass." To cope with what they feel is an impossible situation (eg., "I'm expected to protect society by catching criminals but everytime I try to do my job somebody dumps all over me!"), lawmen develop a set of "ways and means" for getting the job done (ibid.). Because the "Ways and Means Act" is extra-legal, from time to time police-rulers are caught going "over the line" and are punished for their indiscretions. When this happens it only serves to reinforce the lawman's cynicism.

"Martyrs"

Traditionally, females have been socialized into caregiving roles (Pearson, 1991: 260). For example, frequently young girls, but rarely boys, are encouraged to "play house" and to "play with dolls." As a result, from a very young age many girls learn the skills they need to be "caregivers." When they reach adulthood, women are often encouraged to use their caregiving skills to "raise a family." This archaic view is illustrated by the old adage: "Women should be kept barefoot and pregnant."

Another role that females in this culture are socialized to play is the "innocent." Everyone is born in a state of innocence and, consequently, the innocent is the first role we learn (Pearson, 1991: 254). However, whereas boys are encouraged to relinquish their innocence at a young age, girls are encouraged to retain it. This archaic view is illustrated by the old adage: "girls should remain virgins until they marry" but "boys will be boys." Historically, and to a considerable extent at present, females who flouted this taboo were ostrasized for being "sluts" and "whores"; whereas promiscuous males were idolized for being "studs" and "real men." This double standard has meant that the innocent role remains a powerful influence on some females long past childhood.

The result of the way females in this culture are socialized is that many women are dominated by the caregiver-innocent archetypal combination. Stereotypically, these women are attracted to "helping" careers such as nursing, teaching, and social work because these occupations provide an opportunity for their caregiver to care for "needy" people (i.e., nursing the sick or teaching young children) and provide an environment (i.e., a patriarchal hierarchy) in which the innocent can feel safe and secure.

Often, a policeman (i.e., warrior-ruler) will be attracted to a nurse or teacher (i.e., innocent-caregiver) and vice versa because they literally "need" each other.[9] For example, when a police officer (warrior-ruler) comes home from work (i.e., fighting crime), he "needs" a kingdom to rule and someone to nurse his "wounds." Similarly, when a social worker (caregiver-innocent) returns from her work (i.e., caring for the needy), she "needs" a place of safety and someone to care for. In short, warrior-ruler males and caregiver-innocent females have complementary archetypes. As a result, a chance encounter between these two may produce a "courtship" and a long-term relationship (Figure 4.1A).

A police officer (warrior-ruler) / social-worker (caregiver-innocent) relationship[10] is a stable archetypal pattern until the dynamic is altered — usually by the birth of a child (Figure 4.1B). When this occurs, typically, the wife-caregiver diverts her attention away from the husband to the child, with the result that the husband-warrior may feel unloved or unappreciated. Similarly, typically, the husband-ruler begins to share his attention with both his wife and the child, with the result that the wife-innocent may feel abandoned (i.e., orphaned). When this happens the husband may respond by finding a surrogate caregiver such as his mother or a mistress who will care for his needs. Similarly, the wife may respond by finding a surrogate ruler such as her father or a male lover who will protect her. Because we are primarily concerned with the role of the police officer here, the following discussion will be limited to consideration of the stereotypical situation in which the husband has an "affair" and the wife does not (Figure 4.1C).

When a husband decides to have an affair, the resulting archetypal pattern is inherently unstable. Typically, the husband keeps the affair a secret to avoid destroying his marriage and family (i.e., his kingdom). However, the demands of ruling over an expanded kingdom and fighting on behalf of so many people may overwhelm the ruler's abilities and produce a crisis. For example, if the mistress feels she is not receiving enough attention, she may demand that the husband divorce his wife; on the other hand, the wife may discover the deception and force the husband to make a choice between her and the mistress. If the husband is forced to make a choice, he may choose to end the relationship with his family and preserve the relationship with his mistress. The choice can be rationalized as "she'll be okay as long as she has the kids." One

---

9   This archetypal analysis could also be applied to homosexual and bisexual relationships; however, homophobia has ensured that these relationships are relatively rare in police organizations.

10 The attraction may result in a brief "one-night stand" or it may produce a life-long union. Whatever form it takes, these relationships follow a predictable pattern.

Figure 4.1
Archetypes and the Police Family

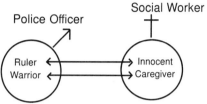

A. The "Courtship"

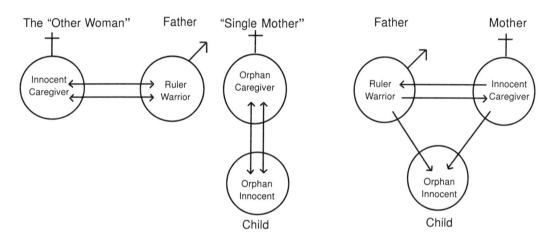

D. The "Divorce"

B. The "Marriage"

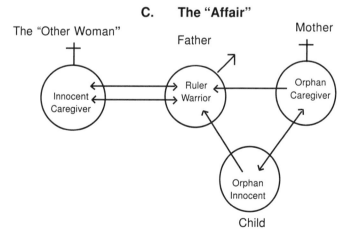

C. The "Affair"

consequence of this choice is the creation of two new families: one is a conventional nuclear family without children and the other is a single parent family headed by a mother (Figure 4.1D). Depending on what the husband learns from this experience, the outcome may be repeated again and again with the result that numerous single parent, female-headed families are created.

"Social Workers"

Historically, women have been either totally excluded from police work or allowed to participate in marginal "caregiving" roles such as working with children and as secretaries. The justification for the exclusion of women from police work has been rooted in the belief that police officers require extraordinary physical strength to be effective law enforcers (warriors). As we will see in Chapter 5 (Selection), while women may be biologically disadvantaged vis à vis males in the area of muscular strength they are not in other areas of physical fitness. As a result, a stereotype developed that women were not "fit" to be police officers.

In part, as a result of the progress made by the women's movement, by the 1970s police organizations had realized that it was no longer acceptable to exclude women and minorities from policing. In an attempt to correct this historic injustice, police organizations began revising their selection practices and hiring more women as police. As a result, the number of female police in Canada has been slowly increasing over the past two decades (Figure 4.2). Despite these efforts, in 1994 women constituted only 9% of all Canadian police officers. The under-representation of women in policing is reflected at all levels of police organizations. For example, 94% of all female officers were constables in 1993 and, by 1995, only two Canadian police services, Calgary and Guelph, had a female Chief of Police (*Mclean's*, August 14, 1995).

The inclusion of increasing numbers of women in police work may yet have a profound effect on both the police role and police organizations. You will recall from our discussion of the police function in Chapter 3 that police typically spend 80% of their time involved in social service functions and only 20% involved in criminal investigations. The skills needed to be an effective social worker — empathy, compassion, tolerance, trust and honesty — are the skills possessed by the archetypes stereotypically associated with females. If police organizations actually hired the sexes in proportion to the skills they actually need (i.e., 80% social service versus 20% crime control), then police organizations would need to employ 80% females and only 20%

males! Of course, this makes about as much sense as the existing arrangement in which more than 90% of police officers are males.

Figure 4.2
Police Personnel by Gender, Canada, 1962-1994

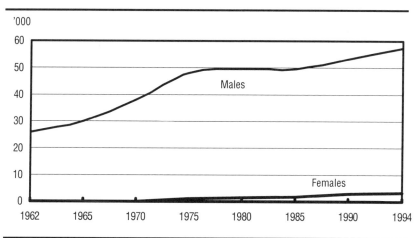

Source: Statistics Canada, Cat. No. 85-002, Vol15 no8.

The qualities stereotypically associated with females provide a much-needed counterbalance to the qualties stereotypically associated with male police officers, such as courage and control. As the feminization of policing continues, it may become possible for police organizations to break free of the war metaphor and to embrace the social service metaphor. Clearly, if community policing is to succeed, police organizations will need the skills not only of women but also of other groups that have been historically excluded from constructive roles in policing such as the elderly, aboriginals, blacks, gays and lesbians, and Asians.

"Outlaws"

In farming communities prior to the Industrial Revolution, an "outlaw" referred to someone who did not belong to an organized community. Because the law only existed within organized communities, to live outside of a community was literally to be outside the protection of the law. Essentially, outlaws had no rights. If an outlaw entered a community it was assumed he or she was there to commit a felony (an offence) and they would be chased away (i.e., a fleeing felon) by a Sherrif's possee. While the term outlaw has largely fallen into disuse outside of Hollywood, the outlaw archetype has been reborn in modern communities in the guise of the "criminal."

As we noted above, traditionally, males in this culture are encouraged to be warriors and rulers (Figure 4.3A). However, depending on a variety of factors, the warrior-ruler combination may not develop. For example, if a young man is prevented from developing his ruler archetype because of personal or institutional barriers, the ruler archetype may be repressed and the destroyer may take its place. When this happens, the individual is unlikely to be attracted to a conventional career in warrioring (such as policing, fire-fighting or soldering) because the para-military structure of these organizations conflicts with the destroyer's need to destroy favoured ways of being and thinking. On the other hand, the warrior-destroyer is very likely to be attracted to unconventional careers in warrioring such as fighting injustice or fighting the status quo by redistributing wealth. Frequently, however, these activities are criminalized because they threaten the existing social order. As a result, the warrior-destroyer may become a social outcast. It is at these times that the "shadow" side [11] of the warrior and destroyer are likely to be expressed (Figure 4.3B).

The criminal who has an active destroyer-warrior combination is cast in the role of "Robin-Hood;" that is, redistributing wealth by stealing from the rich (the elites) and giving to the poor (oneself, friends and family). And, just as Robin-Hood's unlawful ways brought him into conflict with the Sheriff of Nottingham (i.e., the law), so are modern criminals drawn to conflict with the police (Figure 4.3C).

Police and criminals are "natural" enemies: lawmen are sworn to uphold the law and, by doing so, creating order; whereas, outlaws are dedicated to breaking the law and, by doing so, creating disorder. This antagonistic relationship is aggravated by the fact that both police and criminals are dominated by their warrior archetypes. The inevitable result of police who express their warrior-ruler archetypes coming into conflict with criminals who express their warrior-destroyer archetypes is violence, and frequently, because both sides tend to be armed with lethal weapons, the outcome is deadly. As we will see in Chapter 8, usually, but not always, the "victim" is the criminal.

---

11 As well as having a constructive or "positive" side, each archetype has a destructive or "shadow" side that can possess the individual if the archetype is ignored or repressed. For example, Pearson (1991:16) notes that the shadow warrior is "(t)he villain, who uses Warrior skills for personal gain without thought of morality, ethics, or the good of the whole group." The shadow destroyer "includes all self-destructive behaviors ... and all behaviors — such as emotional or physical abuse, murder and rape — that have destructive effects on others (ibid.)."

Figure 4.3
Police and Criminals

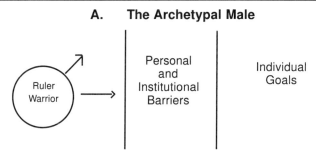

A.   The Archetypal Male

B.   The Archetypal Criminal

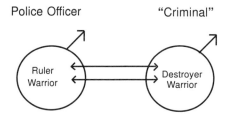

C.   The War on Crime

Police have a natural advantage in the "war on crime" since they are highly trained and well organized and, typically, criminals are neither. Most criminals learn their "skills" by trial and error or from more experienced peers while serving time in a correctional facility. For this reason, most criminals carefully try to avoid open conflict with the police. Instead, they use their usually superior knowledge of the battlefield (i.e., the neighbourhood) and sometimes superior support of non-belligerents (i.e., the public) to fight a "hit and run" "guerrilla war" against police and conventional society. Despite the best efforts of criminals, it is inevitable that they meet the police on the battlefield of justice where a victor and loser will be determined. Depending on the outcome, and your point of view, the result is either a tragedy or a farce.

Summary

In this chapter we used concepts from Archetypal Psychology to analyse aspects of the law-enforcement process. In particular, we looked at the roles of "lawmen," "crime fighter," "outlaws" and "martyrs."

In the course of performing their day-to-day functions, police are required to play several different roles. Key among these are the "warrior" and "ruler." Individuals with active warrior and ruler archetypes are attracted to policing by the opportunity to participate in battles and exercise power. Their fighting and ruling skills often make them excellent soldiers, but poor "peacekeepers."

According to archetypal psychology, to satisfy the warrior's thirst for battle, police must "invent" a war on crime and "find" an enemy to fight. Their search for an enemy leads them to those who break society's rules — criminals. Dominated by the shadow side of their warrior and destroyer archetypes, criminals fight police in a guerrilla war —always waiting for the right opportunity to unleash a surprise attack. When they finally meet in battle, police usually emerge victorious owing to their superior training, organization and weaponry. Notwithstanding these advantages, significant numbers of police also are wounded or die on the field of combat.

In short, police and criminals are actors in a morality play scripted by their archetypes. True to the script, the final scene features a climax in which someone gets hurt or killed. In the end, police and criminals are actors in a real life tragedy in which they kill or are killed by their sworn enemies — each other.

5 Selection

Introduction

This chapter uses concepts from the field of "Spectrum Psychology" to analyse police selection practices. In particular, the selection process of the Metro Toronto Police Services (M.T.P.S.) is analysed by classifying selection criteria as selecting physical, mental or spiritual skills. It is concluded that police selection practices place an undue emphasis on physical skills and practically ignore spiritual skills with the result that the individuals who are hired by police organizations may not have the skills needed to be effective police officers in a multicultural society.

Police Selection Process

Arguably, the human resource is the *most important* resource in every organization, including police organizations. Furthermore, police organizations have only a few options for shaping their human resource. For example, by differentially selecting and retaining (i.e., hiring and firing) those whom they employ, and by training current employees, police organizations can change the attitudes, values and skills of their workforce. It follows, then, that the process a police organization uses to select new members is one of the *most important* functions in the organization.

Essentially, the "criteria" an employer uses to "screen" applicants reflect the skills the employer values. [1] These criteria are like a "snap shot" of the organizational culture: in effect, a picture of how the organization "looks." Just as a picture is revealing, an analysis of the

---

[1]   In this discussion the term "screening" will mean the process of discriminating between acceptable and unacceptable applicants and "criteria" will mean the standards employers use to evaluate applicants.

criteria a police organization uses to select new members can reveal much about the organization's attitudes and values (i.e., its culture). While there is considerable variation between police organizations in how they select new police officers, there are also many similarities.[2] For the purposes of this discussion, we will analyse the selection process of a large municipal police service in Ontario.

It should not come as a surprise to learn that police selection processes are systematically biased, since this is the *raison d'être* of all selection processes: to systematically identify and *include* individuals who possess the desired skills and to *exclude* those who do not. While the selection process is by definition discriminatory, police organizations are bound by law not to discriminate against an applicant on the basis of certain specified characteristics. The "prohibited grounds" of discrimination in employment in Ontario are: age, ancestry, race, religion, creed, colour, criminal record (for which no pardon has been received), place of origin, ethnic origin, marital status, family status, sexual orientation, sex, and handicap.[3] With the exception of this small but important list of "prohibited grounds," police organizations may discriminate against applicants on the basis of any criteria they choose.[4]

The Metro Toronto Police Services (M.T.P.S.) selection process has a total of six stages (see Figure 5.1). The *first stage* consists of a "self screen" and application form. Applicants who attend the police organization's employment office receive an information form that outlines the "basic requirements" needed to become a police constable. The requirements are:

---

2   For example, a review of police selection practices in Ontario in 1992 (Solicitor General of Ontario, 1992: Appendix B)) revealed that despite their differences, these processes were more similar than different.

3   Human Rights Code, R.S.O. 1981, s. 4.

4   A important exception to these prohibitions are "employment equity" guidelines in Ontario. For example, the *Police Services Act* (R.S.O., 1990, Chap. P.15.) requires police organizations "to establish employment equity plans for the elimination of systemic barriers ... and implementation of positive measures" in the recruitment of designated groups: women, racial minorities, Aboriginal people, and people with disabilities. Significantly, homosexuals are not included in the list of "designated groups." This is consistent with the long history of homophobia in society generally, and in policing more particularly (Visano, 1987; Hislop, 1982).

- Canadian citizen or permanent resident of Canada;
- twenty-one years of age or over;[5]
- no criminal record for which a pardon has not been granted and no pending criminal charges;[6]
- a secondary school diploma or its equivalent;[7]
- valid drivers licence and fewer than six demerit points;[8]
- satisfy colour vision, visual field and visual acuity requirements.[9]

An applicant who satisfies these basic requirements is allowed to submit an application for employment. The application for employment solicits information in five areas: personal biographical data; educational history; employment history; personal demographic data; and other miscellaneous data.[10] The information provided in the application for employment is not used at this stage of the selection process. Instead, it is retained on file and used later (i.e., stage 3). Applicants who are successful at this stage of the process are allowed to proceed to the second stage.

The *second stage* of the selection process begins when the applicant is invited to a police training facility for a full day of testing. There, the applicant is tested for physical fitness, general aptitude, and written communications skills in the morning, and spelling skills and

---

5   Even though no upper age limit is specified, the Human Rights Code (R.S.O. 1981) in Ontario permits employers to discriminate on the basis of age against people who are more than 65 years.

6   Criminal record means a conviction for a criminal offence for which a pardon has not been granted (Human Rights Code, R.S.O. 1981).

7   A secondary school diploma is normally awarded after four years of full-time post-secondary study. Equivalencies are approved by the Ontario Ministry of Education.

8   Non-probationary drivers may have accumulated no more than six demerit points and probationary drivers may have accumulated no more than three demerit points (Police Employment Office, June 1994).

9   Applicants are tested for colour blindness, visual field disturbances, and 20/40 uncorrected and 20/30 corrected visual acuity (ibid.).

10 Personal biographical data includes the applicant's name, birthdate, and place of residence, etc. (ibid.). Educational history includes the applicant's educational attainment such as the highest level of education completed, scholarships and awards, etc. (ibid.). Employment history includes information about the applicant's employment, prior employment experiences such as places of employment, and duration of employment etc. (ibid.). Demographic data is used for an employment equity survey and includes information about the applicant's demographic characteristics such as race, sex, etc. This section is voluntary (ibid.). Miscellaneous data includes information about how the applicant learned about the availability of the position. This information is used by the police organization to "track" applicants (ibid.).

Figure 5.1
Stages in the M.T.P.S. Selection Process

1. Self-screen and application form
2. Physical fitness, psychological and aptitude tests
3. Personal interview [1]
4. Background check and "home" interview [2]
5. Clinical interview [3]
6. Medical exam

Source: Police Employment Office, June 1994.

1   This interview is actually a series of two personal interviews that are conducted by police officers from the Police Employment Office.
2   This interview is conducted at the applicant's place of residence by police officers from the Police Employment Office.
3   This interview is conducted by a clinical psychologist.

psychological stability in the afternoon. [11] Physical fitness is assessed by the applicant completing the following tests: a 2.4 kilometre run; body fat measurement at six sites; push-ups; flexibility; grip strength; and curl-ups. General aptitude is assessed by the applicant completing sections two, three, four, and six of the General Aptitude Test Battery (GATB). These sections measure numerical aptitude, intelligence, spatial aptitude and verbal aptitude, respectively. Written communications skills are assessed by the applicant completing two essays on assigned topics. These are assessed for spelling, legibility, grammar, relevance, and maturity of content. Spelling skills are assessed by the applicant completing a written spelling test. Psychological stability is assessed by the applicant completing the 567 item MMPI-2 (the Minnesota Multiphasic Personality Inventory 2). This test measures "a number of the major patterns of personality and emotional disorders." [12] While the

11   Prior to commencing the physical fitness test, an applicant must provide a letter from a physician certifying that the applicant is fit to participate (ibid.).
12   The MMPI-2 has 7 Validity Indicators: Cannot Say, Lie, Infrequency, Correction, Back F, Variable Response Inconsistency, True Response Inconsistency; 10 Clinical Scales: Hypochondriasis, Depression, Conversion Hysteria, Psychopathetic Deviate, Masculinity-Femininity, Paranoia, Psychasthenia, Schizophrenia, Hypomania, Social Introversion; 15 Supplementary Scales: Anxiety, Repression, Ego Strength, MacAndrew Alcoholism Scale-Revised, Over-Controlled Hostility, Dominance, Social Responsibility, College Maladjustment, Gender Role-Masculine, Gender Role-Feminine, 2 Post-Traumatic Stress Disorder Scales; 15 Content Scales: Anxiety, Fears, Obsessiveness, Depression, Health Concerns, Bizarre Mentation, Anger, Cynicism, Antisocial Practices, Type A, Low Self-Esteem, Social Discomfort, Family Problems, Work Interference, Negative Treatment Indicators; 3 Si subscales: Shyness/Self-Consciousness, Social Avoidance, Alienation-Self and Others; 28 Harris-Lingoes Subscales: Subjective Depression, Psychomotor Retardation, Physical Malfunctioning, Mental Dullness, Brooding, Denial of Social Anxiety, Need for Affection, Lassitude-Malaise, Somatic Complaints, Inhibition of Aggression, Familial Discord, Authority Problems, Social Imperturbability, Social Alienation, Self-Alienation, Persecutory Ideas, Poignance, Naiveté, Social Alienation, Emotional Alienation, Lack of Ego Mastery, Cognitive, Cognative, Defective Inhibition, Bizarre Sensory Experience, Amorality, Psychomotor Acceleration, Imperturbability, Ego Inflation.

MMPI-2 is administered at this time, it is not evaluated until much later in the selection process (i.e., stage 6), when it forms part of a clinical interview and assessment conducted by a psychologist. Applicants who are successful at this stage of the selection process are allowed to proceed to the third stage (ibid.).

The *third stage* of the selection process is a personal interview with the applicant. This stage consists of two, one-on-one, semi-structured personal interviews with police officers from the M.T.P.S. employment office. The applicant is required to bring a valid driver's licence, proof of citizenship, and proof of educational achievement to these interviews. The interviews focus on the applicant's employment background, educational history, and social habits. They are intended to assess the applicant's skills in areas such as assertiveness, self-discipline, conformity, productivity, dependability, altruism, and social skills. For example, typically, applicants are asked: Have you ever been suspended from school, fired from a job, or had your driver's licence suspended (i.e., conformity)? How much alcohol do you consume (i.e., judgement)? To what extent are you involved in the community (i.e., altruism)? Why do you want to be a police officer (i.e., altruism)? How are your relationships with peers and colleagues (i.e., social skills)? How often are you late for work/school (i.e., dependability)? Also, the way an applicant responds to the interview process is assessed (i.e., assertiveness). Applicants who are successful at this stage of the selection process are allowed to proceed to the fourth stage (ibid.).

The *fourth stage* of the selection process is a "background check". This stage consists of police officers from the police organization's employment office personally interviewing individuals with knowledge of the applicant's attitudes and values (i.e., former teachers, employers, etc.). These interviews provide an opportunity to verify the results of the personal interviews conducted in stage three. As well, these interviews are intended to assess the applicant's skills in areas such as integrity, leadership, and judgement. Also, as part of this stage, the applicant is interviewed at home. This interview is intended to assess the applicant's risk exposure in two key areas: the risk to disclose confidential information and the risk for the applicant to be corrupted by criminal influences. An applicant who successfully completes this stage of the selection process is allowed to proceed to the fifth stage (ibid.).

As noted above, the *fifth* and next to last stage of the selection process is a clinical interview with a consulting psychologist. At this time the applicant's results on the MMPI-2 are evaluated and form, in part, the bases of a clinical opinion by the consulting psychologist about the applicant's suitability for employment as a police officer. An applicant who successfully completes the fifth stage of the selection process is made an offer of employment that is conditional upon completing the sixth, and final, stage (ibid.).

The *sixth* and final stage of the selection process is a pre-placement medical examination by a physician. Typically, this stage consists of a physical exam and a complete medical history. This stage is intended to ensure that the applicant can perform as a police officer without hazard or risk to himself or herself or others. This is determined by a physician assessing whether the applicant's health is suited to the workplace conditions and the demands of the job. Based on the results of these tests, the physician will issue one of the following recommendations: the applicant is fit to work; the applicant is fit to work subject to restrictions; or the applicant is unfit to work. Once the applicant completes this stage of the selection process, he or she has satisfied all conditions of employment and may become a "sworn" member of the police organization (ibid.).

Police Selection Criteria

The M.T.P.S. is to be lauded for the use of systematic and standardized selection tests to screen applicants for mental aptitude (GATB) and emotional stability (MMPI-2). Both tests have been demonstrated to produce valid and reliable results (Archer, 1992; Keesling, 1985). [13] Unfortunately, the same cannot be said for the selection tests that are used to screen applicants in stages three and four of the selection process. These tests are neither standardized nor systematic and, therefore, they cannot be claimed to produce "valid" or "reliable" results (Kline, 1986). [14] For this reason these "screens" have been omitted from the following analysis.

---

13 Keesling (1985:1645) has suggested that results of the GATB may *not* be good predictors of job performance. Also, concerns have been raised that some of the Specific Aptitude Test Batteries in the GATB are racially and sexually biased (ibid.).

14 Use of non-standardized and unsystematic selection tests to screen applicants appears to be a widespread problem. For example, a report prepared for the Ontario Ministry of the Solicitor General and Correctional Services (1993a: Appendix B: 2) noted "the reliability, predictive value, and fairness of the selection procedures employed (in police organizations in Ontario) are generally unknown," and that "some of the methods employed are, in all likelihood, unreliable and, therefore, biased." This may explain why, after examining police selection practices in Ontario, the Task Force on Race Relations and Policing (1989: 60) concluded, "the current low rate of visible minority and female recruiting and hiring in Ontario police forces reveals systemic barriers within recruitment and hiring practices."

To analyse the critera the M.T.P.S. uses to select applicants we will use concepts from Spectrum Psychology (Wilber, 1986b). Very simply, Spectrum Psychology maintains that every person is compounded of a body, mind, and spirit — in effect, we are "compound individuals" (Wilber, 1986a). The body is exercised in labour, breath, sex and feeling. The mind is exercised in communication, mutual personal recognition and exchange of self-esteem. Finally the spirit is exercised in psychic and subtle transcendence and absolute absorption in Atman (Wilber, 1986a: 261). [15] It follows that each level of the compound individual possesses a "skill set" that can be measured and evaluated. As we noted above, the objective of every selection process is to "screen-in" applicants with desirable skills and to "screen-out" applicants who lack these skills. The concept of the compound individual, then, is ideally suited for classifying the selection criteria police organizations use to select new members.

An analysis of the criteria the Metro Toronto Police Services uses to select applicants reveals that they select physical skills primarily (73.9%), followed by mental skills (26.1%) and spiritual skills (0%) (Table 5.1). The emphasis of physical skills and de-emphasis of mental skills and spiritual skills in the selection process has definite implications for the type of applicant selected. For example, groups that are stereotypically associated with wisdom (i.e., the old and social reformers) would be excluded by this selection process and groups that are stereotypically associated with immaturity (i.e., the young and social conformists) would be included. This means that heroes like Mohandas Ghandi, Martin Luther King Jr., and Mother Teresa would be excluded by this selection process. [16]

The heavy emphasis placed on physical skills in this selection process is a clear indication that the M.T.P.S. values physical fitness in its police constables. This is particularly ironic because, like most police organizations, the police organization under study employs police constables who could no longer pass the physical fitness requirements needed to become a police officer! [17] This contradictory situation suggests

---

15 Readers who are unfamiliar with the concept of "spirit" may think of it as the level of the "self" from which qualities such as honesty, trust, compassion, tolerance, and love emanate.

16 Among other reasons, Dr. King and Mahatma Ghandi would have been excluded because they had criminal records. Similarly, Mother Teresa would have been excluded because she could not have passed the strenuous physical fitness tests.

17 The period of peak physical fitness is between the ages of twenty-five and thirty years (Vitale, 1973: 81). For this reason most police organizations attempt to recruit new members from within this age group. However, typically, police do not retire until they are between the ages of fifty and sixty years. As a result, for most of their careers, most police are not in peak physical condition.

that the physical fitness skills being screened in this selection process *are not* essential qualifications for employment as a police constable. In short, because this selection process utilizes physical fitness tests that are not "age sensitive," it constructively discriminates against most people thirty years of age and older.

Table 5.1

Police Hiring Criteria Classified According to the Level(s) of the Compound Individual They Select

PHYSICAL	MENTAL	SPIRITUAL
2.4 km. run	Ontario grade 12 or equivalent	
body fat composition	general learning ability (GATB)	
flexibility	written communications	
push-ups	spelling skills	
vertical jump	verbal communications	
grip strength	psychological profile (MMPI-2)	
curl ups		
Canadian citizen/ permanent resident		
21 years of age or over		
good physical health		
valid driver's licence		
safe driving record		
colour vision		
visual field		
visual acuity		
no pending criminal charges		
no criminal convictions for which a pardon has not been granted		

Source: Police Employment Office, June 1994.

There is a long, if not distinguished, tradition of age discrimination in policing. Sewell (1985) noted that as recently as the early 1980s Canadian police organizations were using a selection process that explicitly discriminated against "older" applicants — by awarding more points to younger candidates. [18] Lest the reader think this is a uniquely Canadian problem, it should be noted that as recently as 1992, the New York City Police Department discriminated in hiring on the basis of age. [19]

It would be a relatively simple matter for the Metro Toronto Police Services to alter its physical fitness tests to be age sensitive; some police organizations already do so. [20] The fact that most police organizations do not do this suggests that they are ambivalent about recruiting the skills (i.e., wisdom, patience, etc.) commonly associated with older, more mature applicants.

The rigorous nature of these physical fitness tests ensures that they constructively discriminate against most people with physical disabilities. Although handicap is a prohibited ground of discrimination in employment in Ontario and people with disabilities are one of the groups designated for special treatment in that province, the rigorous physical demands of police work have been used to justify the exclusion of the physically disabled from employment as police constables. Thus far, no one has attempted to challenge the status quo in this area, although it is not difficult to imagine this happening.

Historically, as well as the elderly and the physically and mentally disabled, women have been excluded from employment as police officers. Over the years police organizations, including the M.T.P.S., have attempted to address this imbalance by altering their selection criteria. Special attention has been given to altering the physical fitness tests since these were identified as being particularly difficult barriers for female applicants. This raises the question: have these *ad hoc* adjustments had the desired effect?

---

18 Applicants between the ages of 23 and 25 years of age received the maximum of 75 points; five points were subtracted for every year outside this range, with candidates older than 35 years of age scoring zero (Sewell, 1985: 110).
19 The N.Y.P.D. explicitly discriminates against applicants who are more than 35 years of age by refusing to employ them as police constables (N.Y.P.D., 1992).
20 The Ontario Provincial Police physical fitness test utilizes different selection criteria for different age groups (O.P.P. Employment Office, 1994). For physical fitness tests applicants are grouped as follows; 18-29 years, 30-34 years, 35-39 years, over 40 years. However, by setting the same criteria for everyone over 40 years of age, these groupings unfairly discriminate against older applicants.

At first glance, the physical fitness criteria used by the police organization under study appear to (Table 5.2) discriminate against *males* by setting a lower standard for female applicants on most physical fitness tests. [21] However, a more thorough analysis of the physical fitness criteria reveals quite a different picture.

Physical fitness is the result of *balanced* fitness in three major areas: aerobics (i.e., muscular and cardiorespiratory endurance); anaerobics (i.e., muscular strength); and flexibility (i.e., muscle and tendon elasticity) (Getchell and Anderson, 1982: 4-5). Extraordinary development in one fitness modality but not others is inconsistent with good overall physical fitness and may have negative implications for fitness in other areas. As a result, an effective physical fitness conditioning programme attempts to strike a balance in all three areas of fitness (ibid.). An analysis of these physical fitness criteria according to the physical fitness modality they select is revealing.

Table 5.2
Police Physical Fitness Standards for Males and Females

PHYSICAL FITNESS TEST	MALE STANDARD	FEMALE STANDARD
Push-ups (30 sec.)	21-36	12(20)-22(38)
Curl-ups (60 sec.)	30-75	30-75
Grip test (kg.)	90-130	65
Vertical jump (cm.)	30.5-68.5	20.3-58.3
2.4 km. run (min.)	12:20-9:00	13:20-10:00
Body fat (%)	14.1	21.3
Flexibility (cm.)	29-45	32-46

Source: Police Employment Office, June 1994.

Note: The lowest number in the range is the standard to obtain a 50% mark and the highest number in the range is the standard to obtain a 100% mark. Scores of less than 50% in the 2.4 km. run and body fat tests and 22 kg.'s in the grip strength test result in disqualification. Also, an overall score less than 55% results in disqualification. Women are allowed to do either "regular" or "knee" push-ups. The standards for "knee" push-ups are shown in parenthesis.

---

21   A notable exception is the flexibility test for which the standard is more difficult for women than men.

An examination of Table 5.3 reveals that these physcial fitness tests select "anaerobic" skills primarily (57.1%), followed by "aerobic" skills (28.6%), and "flexibility" skills (14.3%). This emphasis on anaerobic fitness suggests that the M.T.P.S. places a high priority on muscular strength. This is important because males, due to larger muscle mass, have a biological advantage over females in anaerobic exercises. Females, because of physiological differences related to childbirth, have a biological advantage over males in flexibility exercises (Vitale, 1973: 83). [22] For example, Kimura (1992: 120-121) found that men tend to perform better than women "in target-directed motor skills, such as guiding or intercepting projectiles" and women tend to perform better

Table 5.3
Police Physical Fitness Standards Classified According to Fitness Modality and Sex

	Anaerobic			Aerobic		Flexibility	
	Females	Males		Females	Males	Females	Males
Push-ups (30 sec.)	12	21	2.4 km. run (min.)	13:20	12:20	32	29
Curl-ups (180 sec.)	30	30	Body fat (%)	21.3	14.1		
Grip test (kg.)	65	90					
Vertical jump (cm.)	20.3	30.5					

Source: Police Employment Office, June 1994.

Note: These are the standards to achieve a score of 50%.

22 Skeptical readers may satisfy themselves that this is true by performing a simple test. Begin by standing with your feet together and your toes touching the wall. Now take three foot-steps (not strides!) back from the wall and place a light chair between yourself and the wall. Bend over and, touching the top, or "crown," of your head to the wall, so that your back and legs form a 45 degree angle, pick up the chair. Now try to stand up straight without bending your knees or using the weight of the chair to "bounce" yourself up. In most cases, males cannot perform this task, but females can. The reason is because, typically, females have a relatively large pelvic region to accommodate child birth and, as a result, a relatively low centre of gravity. In contrast, typically, males have a relatively large upper torso to confer greater physical strength and, as a result, a relatively high centre of gravity.

A police organization that included this "chair-lift" test in their selection process would soon be staffed almost exclusively by women. This is precisely the opposite of what actually occurred in modern police organizations. The situation only started to change when human rights laws were passed which prohibited discrimination on the basis of sex in employment. Most police organizations responded by "lowering" the standards on physical fitness tests for female appli-cants. This is comparable to our imaginary feminist police organization making the chair in the "chair-lift" test lighter in an attempt to select more male applicants. Of course, this "accomodation" would not help most males pass the tests because their problem is their large upper torso, not the weight of the chair. Similarly, allowing female applicants to do fewer or "easier" push-ups than males was not a satisfactory accommodation.

than men in exercises requiring fine-motor coordination. Finally, when differences in muscular strength are eliminated, there appear to be no significant differences between the sexes in muscular endurance (Vitale, 1973: 83).

The emphasis of muscular strength and de-emphasis of flexibility in police physical fitness tests would discriminate against females if the tests did not require males to satisfy a higher standard than females in most tests. However, lowering the standard for women on most tests does not make the tests "fair" since females still are required to pass a physical fitness test that is designed to test the unique physical abilities of males (i.e., muscular strength). A "fair" test would establish different exercises for males and females: exercises that emphasize muscular strength for males and that emphasize felxibility for females. The failure of the M.T.P.S. and other police organizations to utilize physical fitness tests that accomodate female differences suggests that police organizations are ambivalent about recruiting the skills (i.e., compassion, empathy, etc.) commonly associated with females.

Summary

Historically, women, people of colour, gays and lesbians, the aged, and the physically and mentally disabled have been marginalized and excluded from full participation in our society — including the provision of police services. Recent attempts to correct this historic injustice have included efforts by police organizations to hire more people from some of these "designated" groups. Police organizations have correctly reasoned that the key to creating a community police service is to create an equitable selection process.

Despite these efforts, imbalances still exist in the police selection process studied here. This selection process does an effective job of selecting strong, young men who are emotionally stable and who have mental aptitude, but it is much less effective at selecting women, the physically disabled, people more than thirty years of age, and people with spiritual aptitude.

A truly equitable police selection process will not exist until police organizations strike a delicate balance between the various levels of the compound individual (i.e., physical, mental and spiritual) and the various forms of physical fitness (i.e., muscular strength, muscular endurance and flexibility). An equitable process will not automatically exclude gays and lesbians and the physically and mentally disabled or treat women and minorities unfairly.

6 Training

Introduction

As in the previous chapter, this chapter uses concepts from the field of Spectrum Psychology. The process used to train police recruits is analysed by classifying courses several different ways. Also, police basic training is compared to basic training in other occupations. It is concluded that police training is much too short to be effective and does not adequately emphasize the training of spiritual skills with the result that police recruits may not learn the skills they need to be effective police officers in a multicultural society.

Police Training Process

The human resource is arguably the *most important* resource in an organization — including a police organization. Police organizations have only a few options for shaping their human resource — by differentially selecting and retaining those whom they employ (i.e., hiring and firing) and by training current employees new skills and attitudes. Thus, the process used to train police officers is, along with recruiting and selection, one of the *most important* functions in a police organization.

Training is a two-part process. In part one, new students are selected for training; in part two, students are trained with the appropriate skills and attitudes. The skills an organization does not, or cannot, recruit must be taught.[1] As a result, it is important to remember, when examining a training system, that the curriculum that is taught represents the skills and attitudes the organization believes are important but has been either unable, or unwilling, to recruit.

---

1   See the discussion of the police selection process in Chapter 5.

Essentially, there are three types of police training systems: "open," "closed," and "hybrids." Open systems recruit trainers and students from outside the police system, whereas, closed systems recruit trainers and students from within the police system. Hybrid systems, as the name implies, combine students and trainers from both within and outside the police system.[2] For the purpose of this discussion we will analyse the process used to train police recruits at a large Canadian police college.

The police college under study is a centralized facility that provides a closed training environment for all municipal and provincial police in the province. Instructors are either serving police officers who have been seconded from their police organizations, or former police officers who have retired from policing and now are permanent employees of the college. A majority of instructors do not have university level preparation.[3] This may be a consequence of the heavy emphasis placed on practical application in the training process. Also, there are a few full-time instructors, in specialized areas only, such as physical and driver training, who have no prior police experience. Typically, civilians are hired on a temporary contractual basis to teach specific skills that permanent instructors are not available or qualified to teach.

Police training in the province has five levels (Figure 6.1). Level I lasts a minimum of thirty days and consists of a "force orientation with a designated coach officer" (Police College Course Calendar, 1994: 10).[4] This stage is intended to orient the recruit to the rules and regulations of the police service that hired them, and to prepare recruits to attend Level II training at the police college.

---

2   The Royal Canadian Mounted Police Training Depot and the Ontario Police College are examples of closed training environments. The Atlantic Police Academy is an example of a hybrid training environment.

3   The total faculty complement at the police college was thirty-seven instructors, twelve of whom held Baccalaureate degrees and three of whom held Master's degrees (Police College, 1994).

4   The term "coach officer" is used to describe experienced police officers who have been selected, and usually, but not always, trained to train recruits.

Figure 6.1
The Police Training Process

Level I[2]	Level II[1]	Level III[2]
Force Orientation with designated coach Officer (30 days min.)	Basic Training (60 days)	Field Experience (2 years)

Level IV[1]	Level V[2]	Level VI[1]
Intermediate Training (14 days)	Field Experience (3-4 years)	Advaned Training (2-3 weeks)

1 At the Police College.
2 At the police Organization.
Source: Ontario Police College Course Calendar, 1994: 10.

Significantly, Level I and Level III training may vary dramatically from police organization to police organization. This is a consequence of two factors: first, police organizations in Ontario, as elsewhere in Canada, vary considerably in size and funding levels and, therefore, in their ability to deliver employee training; second, local police organizations have sole responsibility for delivering Level I and Level III training. The practical result of this de-centralized and differentially resourced system is that few police officers in this province receive the same basic training.[5]

5   The only exceptions to this situation are police officers who are hired and trained by the same police organization.

Level II training is "an intensive sixty-day diploma course ... (that is intended) ... to provide candidates with a foundation of the laws and procedures police officers require throughout their career (*sic*)" (ibid., 11). During this stage of "basic training" police recruits live in residence at the police college where they are taught by instructors via a traditional, pedagogical process. There is no variability in the training that police recruits receive at this stage of the training process because all police officers in the province must receive this training and the police college is the only facility authorized to deliver it. [6]

Level III training begins when recruits graduate from the police college and return to the police organization that hired them. Similar to the first stage of training, this stage of "field training" takes place under the supervision of a coach officer and, in theory, can last up to two years (ibid., 10). Generally, most recruits complete their basic training within one year of being hired. Here again, there may be considerable variation in the type of training police recruits receive. This is because, like Level I training, individual police organizations are responsible for the design and delivery of Level III training (ibid.).

Completion of Level III of the police training process concludes a police recruit's "basic training." Levels IV, V and VI of the training process, are intended only for "experienced" police officers. For example, Level VI is "advanced training" that is intended for police officers who have not received formal training in a five-year period.

The following discussion is limited to consideration of Level II (i.e., "basic") training because this is the only standardized training that *every* police recruit in Ontario receives. While it is true that police recruits in this province receive other levels of training, the content and consistency of this training may vary so dramatically between police organizations that it makes generalizations impossible.

---

6   The only exceptions to this situation are individuals who have previous police experience from other jurisdictions (eg., R.C.M.P.).

Basic Training

The basic training police recruits receive at the Ontario Police College [7] is an example of what Ferguson (1980) has called the "old education paradigm." [8] For example, this training programme employs a traditional pedagogical approach to education. [9] There is a clear distinction between roles of students and instructors at the police college: instructors are responsible for the design and delivery of curriculum and student evaluations; students are responsible for assimilating content and recognizing or recalling information as required. A total of 12 hours or 3.4% of basic training is set aside for this purpose (Figure 6.2). [10] It is significant that, in most cases, more time is allotted for *evaluating* what is learned than for *learning* new skills.

Once again, as we did in Chapter 5, we will use concepts from Spectrum Psychology (Wilber, 1986b) to analyse the police recruit basic training course. Recall that Spectrum Psychology maintains that every person is a compound of a body, mind, and spirit — in effect, a compound individual (Wilber, 1986a). The body is exercised in labour, breath, sex and feeling; the mind is exercised in communication, mutual personal recognition and exchange of self-esteem; the spirit is exercised in psychic and subtle transcendence and absolute absorption in Atman (Wilber, 1986a: 261). [11] Each level of the compound individual has the potential to develop a set of skills suited to that level. Since the objective of the basic training programme is to teach the individual the skills needed to be an effective police officer, the concept of the compound individual is a useful device for classifying the basic training curriculum according to the level — physical, mental or spiritual — trained.

---

7   A revised police recruit basic training programme was tentatively scheduled to be implemented in January 1996 (Police College, 1994).

8   Ferguson (1980: 289-291) maintains that the "old education paradigm" is a rigid, compartmentalized, hierarchical, authoritarian, and content-oriented structure that emphasizes analytical, left-brain, thinking, external reality, and performance; whereas, the "new education paradigm" is a flexible, integrated, egalitarian, process oriented structure that emphasizes whole brain, intuitive thinking, internal reality, and self image.

9   Knowles (1975) notes that there are two general approaches to education — "pedagogy" and "andragogy." Very simply, pedagogy on the one hand treats the learner as dependent, ignorant and in need of instruction and evaluation from a teacher. Andragogy, on the other hand, treats the learner as self-directed, innately wise and as seeking guidance and feedback from a mentor.

10   The minimum passing standard for all courses in the basic training programme is 75%. A student who fails two or more courses or who fails to achieve an overall average of 75% is deemed to have failed and is required to repeat (Police College Course Calendar, 1994: 7). In practice few students fail, and those who do are not retained by their employers. Significantly, Illich (1970: 114) maintains that "grading" is, ultimately, "degrading" for students because it identifies them as successes or failures. The emphasis on grading in the basic training programme is another example of how it conforms to the "old education paradigm."

11   Readers who are unfamiliar with the concept of "spirit" may think of it as the level of the "self" from which qualities such as honesty, trust, compassion, tolerance, and love emanate.

Figure 6.2
Time Allocation for Subject in Police Training

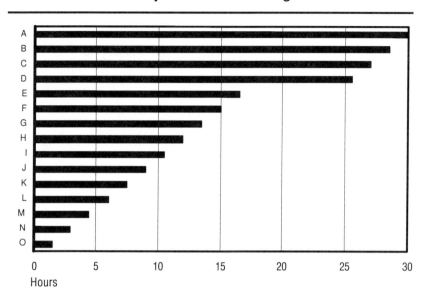

LEGEND

Subject	Title(s)	Hours
A	Traffic Law	30.0
B	Criminal Offences, Physical Training, Provincial Statutes	28.5
C	Firearms	27.0
D	Police Vehicle Operations, Defensive Tactics	25.5
E	Arrest, Evidence	16.5
F	Communications, Accident Investigation	15.0
G	Officer Safety	13.5
H	Examinations	12.0
I	Wife Assault	10.5
J	Anti-Racist Training	9.0
K	Drug Law	7.5
L	Introduction to Law, Induction	6.0
M	Provincial Offences Act, March Past and Review	4.5
N	Victim Sensitivity, Use of Force, Crime Prevention, C.P.I.C.*, Police Ethics	3.0
O	Young Offenders Act, Death Notification, Justice Panel, Notebooks, Crime Scene Preservation, Drill	1.5

Source: Registrar—Police College, 1994.
*   Canadian Police Information Computer

Table 6.1
Police Basic Training Subjects Classified by the Levels of the Compound Individual

Physical	Mental	Spiritual
Firearms	Introduction to Law	Police Ethics
Physical Training	Criminal Offences	Victim Sensitivity
Drill	Arrest	Anti-Racism Training[1]
March Past and Review	Evidence	
Police Vehicle Operations	Young Offenders Act	
Defensive Tactics	Wife Assault	
	Examinations	
	Death Notification	
	Drug Law	
	Crime Scene Preservation	
	Justice Panel	
	Traffic Law	
	Accident Investigation	
	Provincial Offences Act	
	Provincial Statutes	
	Officer Safety	
	Communications	
	Use of Force	
	Crime Prevention	
	Canadian Police Info. Centre	
	Induction	
	Notebooks	

Source: Police College, 1994.

1   In addition to the nine hours of the "manifest curriculum" that has been allotted for anti-racist training, an additional nine hours of the "latent curriculum" (i.e., three hours of practical training in each of Provincial Statutes, Wife Assault, and Use of Force) is *eligible* for training community policing concepts, which include anti-racist training (Police College, 1994). Because this training is "latent" and not "manifest," it occurs randomly and has not been included in the present analysis.

A content-distribution analysis of the basic training programme, according to the levels of the compound individual trained, reveals that mental skills (71.0%) are the top priority and physical skills (19.4%) and spiritual skills (9.7%) are much lower priorities (Table 6.1). Similarly, a time-distribution analysis of the basic training programme, according to the levels of the compound individual trained, reveals that mental skills (64.0%) and physical skills (32.0%) are allotted much more training time than spiritual skills (4.0%) (Figure 6.3). [12]

The emphasis on training mental skills in the basic training programme may be the result of the physical skills bias that exists in the typical police selection process (see Chapter 5). That is, the basic training programme may have been deliberately designed to emphasize mental skills training in order to balance the extraordinary physical skills that are recruited in the typical police selection process. Assuming this is the case, what is not clear is why the basic training programme virtually ignores training spiritual skills, especially since the typical police selection process does not recruit these skills. A *comprehensive* basic training programme would strike a delicate balance between the various levels (i.e., body, mind and spirit) of the compound individual.

Figure 6.3

Time Allotted to Training the Different Levels of the Compound Individual in Police Basic Training

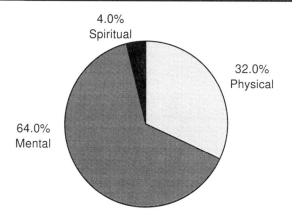

Source: Police College Course Calendar, 1994.

---

12   These values represent the percentage of the total time spent in the basic training programme.

Table 6.2
Police Basic Training Classified by Social Service and Crime Control Roles

Crime Control	Social Service
Firearms	Police Ethics
Physical Training	Victim Sensitivity
Criminal Offences	Anti-Racism
Drug Law	Death Notification
Defensive Tactics	Wife Assault
Provincial Offences Act	Communications
Drill	Crime Prevention
March Past and Review	
Traffic Law	
Police Vehicle Operations	
Justice Panel	
Provincial Statutes	
Accident Investigation	
Use of Force	
C.P.I.C. (Canadian Police Information Computer)	
Notebooks	
Officer Safety	
Crime Scene Preservation	
Young Offenders Act	
Introduction to Law	
Evidence	
Arrest	

Source: Police College Course Calendar, 1994.

An "inter-subject" time-distribution analysis of the basic training programme yields some interesting results. For example, much more time is allotted to learning how to operate firearms (27.0 hrs) and police vehicles (25.5 hrs) than learning anti-racism (9.0 hrs) and victim sensitivity (3.0 hrs). As well, much more time is allotted to learning how to investigate accidents (15.0 hrs) than learning police ethics (3.0 hrs). Perhaps most telling is that "marching" in its various forms (i.e., drill and march past and review; total = 6.0 hrs) is allotted as much time as victim sensitivity and police ethics combined (6.0 hrs).

The time allotted for studying individual subjects in the basic training programme implicitly reflects the priorities assigned by the Ontario Police College to these topics. From this we can see that *inclusiveness* (i.e., anti-racist training and wife assault) is a much lower priority than *exclusiveness* (i.e., criminal, traffic, and drug law). Similarly, *non-violent conflict resolution* (i.e., communications) is a much lower priority than *violent conflict resolution* (i.e., firearms and defensive tactics). Also, *empathy* (i.e., victim sensitivity) is the same or a much lower priority than *technics* (i.e., police vehicle operations and C.P.I.C., respectively). As well, *accountability* (i.e., police ethics) is a much lower priority than exercising *power* (i.e., arrest and evidence).

A content-distribution analysis of the roles taught in the basic training programme reveals that crime control (75.9%) is the top priority and social service (24.1%) is a much lower priority (Table 6.2). Similarly, much more time is allotted to learning crime control skills (84.0%) than social service skills (16.0%) (Figure 6.4). This arrangement reinforces the inaccurate and misleading stereotype that portrays police officers as "crime fighters" and "lawmen" (see Chapter 4) but not "social workers." This situation moved Southgate (1988: 240) to suggest:

> [Police] training should change its character and reflect a different set of priorities. Because the policing task does involve so much dealing with people it is the skills of doing this that should receive priority over the learning of factual information about law and procedure ...

Figure 6.4
Time Allotted to Training Social Service and Crime Control Roles in Police Basic Training

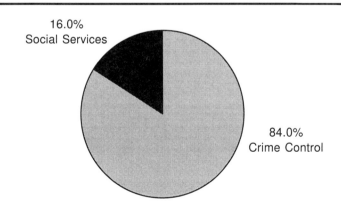

16.0%
Social Services

84.0%
Crime Control

The preceding discussion implicitly assumes that the way content is distributed and the time that is allotted for courses in the basic training programme reflects underlying police priorities; however, it is also true that police training does not occur in a vacuum. Rather, it is subject to a variety of constraints that include fiscal, political and social factors. One speculates that, given the option, police authorities would significantly increase the total length of time allotted for police training, especially for new recruits. [13] This raises the question: how do the "entry to practice requirements" for police compare to other occupations?

Table 6.3
Comparison of Minimum Entry to Practice Requirements of Police and Other Occupations

Education	Police	Nurse	Lawyer	Physician	Professor
Secondary	Grade 12	Grade 12	Grade 13	Grade 13	Grade 13
Post-Secondary					
Diploma	3 months	3 years[1]	NA	NA	NA
BA	NA	NA	2 years	3 years	4 years
MA/LL.B./MD	NA	NA	3 years	3 years	2 years
Ph.D.	NA	NA	NA	NA	4 years[2]
Applied Training	7 months	1 year[3]	1.5 years	2 years	NA
Total (beyond Gr. 12)	**10 months**	**3 years**	**7.5 years**	**9 years**	**11 years**

Source: Police College and University Calendars, 1994.

1   The College of Nurses in this province has stipulated that by the year 2,000 the minimum entry to practice requirement for nurses will be a four-year baccalaureate degree.
2   The time it takes to complete the requirements for a Ph.D. can vary considerably; however, typically most people require between 3 and 4 years.
3   Nursing applied training is included in the time required to obtain a nursing diploma.

---

13   This was recommended by the Task Force on Race Relations and Policing (1989: 98-100). Also, Vincent (1990: 79-80) notes that some of the police officers he interviewed expressed this opinion.

A comparison of the minimum entry to practice requirements for police officers and other major occupational groups is quite revealing (Table 6.3).[14] Police recruits in this province receive substantially less training than other major occupational groups despite the fact that a mistake by a police officer can, and sometimes does, lead to the loss of a human life. Nevertheless, typically, police recruits receive only *3 months* of in-class instruction before commencing regular duties. This compares unfavourably with the *6.5 years* of in-class instruction, on average, recruits in other occupations receive. The issue is brought into even clearer focus when one realizes that police recruits spend fully *70%* of their training period in an applied setting, whereas recruits in other occupations spend, on average, only *15%* of their training period in an applied setting.

To summarize, short duration and heavy emphasis on practical application are the hallmarks of police training. This situation moved Forcese (1992: 156-157) to remark:

> Generally the remarkable feature of police recruit training is its brevity. Were one to assume a single occupation, with rudimentary and straightforward job demands, then training of high school educated recruits for no more than twelve to twenty-seven weeks — or in some extreme instances, not at all — would be acceptable, but such brief pre-service training, followed by non-systematic supervised or probationary service of six to twelve months, usually referred to as an in-service training period, is deplorable for a demanding, stressful, and sensitive job such as policing.

Similarly, in reference to police training in Ontario, Steven Lewis (1992: 12) noted:

> The situation ... is grossly unfair to the police and to new recruits in particular. We have a society of immense diversity, with a complex proliferation of multiracial and multicultural sensibilities, and we don't prepare our police for dealing with it. These are areas where the exercise of judgment and the development of skills for conflict resolution become every bit as important as the grasp of sophisticated technology. If we really believe in investing in our justice system, then the people who are on the front-lines deserve the best training possible. It is ultimately a test of management. The management of a police force in the 1990s requires qualitative shifts in training, and without those shifts, things go wrong.

---

14   These occupations were selected for inclusion in this sample because they are widely viewed as being difficult and socially important roles and, in this respect, they are comparable to police work.

Clearly, police recruits need more training overall, and more training in spiritual skills in particular, before they will be qualified to effectively police a multicultural society.

Summary

The overall effect of the police recruit basic training programme at the Ontario Police College under study is that it does a thorough job of training minds in the *tactics* needed to win a "war on crime" and conditioning bodies to be fit to *fight* in a "war on crime." Unfortunately, the basic training programme does an inadequate job of training the police in spritual skills that are needed to interact sensitively and humanely with other people. The basic training programme would be excellent preparation for police recruits if crime control was their primary responsibility; however, this is not the case. Today's police officers' primary responsibility is providing social service — not fighting crime. As a result, graduates of the basic training programme may lack the spiritual skills needed to effectively police a multicultural society.

In short, police today need more training in inclusiveness (i.e., acceptance), but they actually receive more training in exclusiveness (i.e., detection, apprehension and detention); they need more training in non-violent conflict resolution (i.e., inter-personal communications and problem solving), but they actually receive more training in violent conflict resolution (i.e., firearms and defensive tactics). They need more training in empathy (i.e., victim sensitivity), but they actually receive more training in technics (i.e., police vehicle operations and C.P.I.C.). They need more training in police accountability (i.e., police ethics), but they actually receive more training in police powers (i.e., arrest). Finally, they need more formal training, but they actually receive more applied training.

7 Authority

Introduction

The police function in society is to reproduce order by enforcing the law. For this purpose Canadian police are authorized by law to use extraordinary power, including the use of lethal force, to enforce the law. More often, however, police rely on moral authority to obtain citizen cooperation with law enforcement. This arrangement creates an awkward tension between police legal authority and their moral authority. When police are forced to rely on legal authority to enforce the law, they risk losing moral authority; if police are able to rely on moral authority to enforce the law, they may not need to use legal authority.

This chapter analyses the relationship between the use of para-military hierarchies in police organizations and police authority. Also, the relationship between police moral authority and police legal authority is analysed. In particular, it considers what happens when police lose moral authority and are forced to rely on legal authority to enforce the law and reproduce order. This chapter concludes with the analysis of a case that involved a police officer who refused a lawful order from a superior officer because it conflicted with his religious beliefs.

Police Authority

The *Oxford English Dictionary* (1990: 72) defines "authority" as "the power or right to enforce obedience." An important feature of this definition is that authority is first, and foremost, *power*. For example, a police officer exercises authority whenever he or she makes an arrest or conducts a search. It follows that "police authority" *is the extraordinary power police have to enforce the law*. A key feature of this definition is the idea that police have *extraordinary* authority, to the extent that other citizens do not have this power. For example, "citizen's powers of arrest" outlined in section 494 of the Criminal Code are not nearly as comprehensive as "peace officer's powers of arrest" outlined in section 495 — police are authorized to arrest in many circumstances in which a citizen may not arrest. Another key feature of this definition is the idea that the authority police have is *original* not delegated. This was made clear by Lord Denning in *R.* v. *Metropolitan Police Commissioner* when he noted:

> I have no hesitation ... in holding that, like every constable in the land, he (the Commissioner of Police) should be, and is, independent of the executive... No Minister of the Crown can tell him that he must, or must not, keep observation of this place or that; or that he must, or must not, prosecute this man or that one. Nor can any police authority tell him so. The responsibility for law enforcement lies on him. He is answerable to the law alone. [1]

In short, police authority is a *privilege* of being a police officer and not a right. As we will see in Chapter 11, this privilege creates a reciprocal obligation for police to act responsibly and to be accountable for the consequences of their actions.

Para-Military Hierarchies

The existence of extraordinary authority for police creates the potential for abuse. To minimize the likelihood of this happening, Sir Robert Peel modeled the first public police organization on the British Military (Critchley, 1972: 51). In particular, the London police were organized into a "para-military" hierarchy with ranks and a central line of authority (ibid.).[2] Peel's innovation became so successful that every public police organization today is organized in a para-military hierarchy — indeed, the para-military hierarchy is *the* defining feature of public police organizations.

The para-military organizational structure[3] was, as the name implies, originally developed for use in military organizations or what Drucker (1988: 45) has called "command and control structures." Command and control structures were designed to maintain order in the typically chaotic conditions that occur during a battle. This was important because experience had demonstrated that the threat represented by an attacking army was much greater if the defenders were disorganized. For example, if a commanding officer gave an order to conduct a tactical manoeuver and one or more

---

1   *R.* v. *Metropolitan Police Commissioner, Ex parte* Blackburn [1 All England Reports (1968)].
2   Para-military (*Oxford English Dictionary*, 1990:863) means "ancillary to and similarly organized to military forces."
3   Eisler notes (1987: 105) that para-military hierarchies or "domination hierarchies" as she calls them have been common to all "androcratic" cultures throughout history. Drucker terms (1988: 45) this model "command and control."

subordinates refused to comply (i.e., were insubordinate) or simply questioned the command, the confusion and disorder that would result could compromise the safety of the entire unit. As a result, military organizations impose strict discipline at all times as part of their preparations for battle.

Canadian military law *still* authorizes the use of capital punishment for "deserters." Similarly, betraying their military origins, police organizations are authorized by law to impose a variety of punishments for police who breach the police code of discipline. Generally, the statutes that regulate policing in Canada create two categories of offences — "major" and "minor." Major and minor offences are analogous to the indictable and summary conviction offences, respectively, that are created by the Criminal Code of Canada. An important difference between criminal offences and the regulatory offences that regulate police behaviour are punishments. The maximum penalty for a criminal offence is "life imprisonment," whereas the maximum penalty for a regulatory offence for a police officer is dismissal. Of course, the existence of a code of discipline, complete with major and minor offences and commensurate punishments, ensures that police organizations are very effective at what they do.

Ultimately, the purpose of a para-military hierarchy is to *control* police power by organizing it into discrete and manageable units. The effect of a para-military hierarchy is to *distribute* power among the various levels of the police bureaucracy. More specifically, police bureaucracies are vertically differentiated into horizontal levels, or "ranks." Ranks are distinguished by their differential access to power: lower or "inferior" ranks have less power than higher or "superior" ranks (Figure 7.1). So, for example, Constables are subordinate to Sergeants (a.k.a. Detectives), who are subordinate to Staff-Sergeants (a.k.a. Detective-Sergeants), who are subordinate to Inspectors, who are subordinate to Staff Inspectors, who are subordinate to Superintendents, who are subordinate to Staff Superintendents, who are subordinate to Deputy Chiefs, who are subordinate to Chiefs (Figure 7.2). [4]

---

4   There is considerable variation among police organizations across Canada in the terms they use to describe their ranks. For example, the R.C.M.P. and some provincial and municipal police organizations have the rank of Corporal which is superior to a constable and inferior to a sergeant. Generally, these ranks are holdovers from the military origins of public policing. In addition, some police organizations have the special rank of cadet. Typically, cadets are not sworn peace officers. When they are not sworn peace officers, cadets are part of the civilian bureaucracy and not the police hierarchy.

Figure 7.1
Access to Power in Police Hierarchies

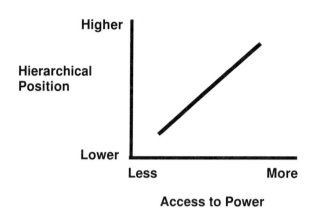

Police organizations use a variety of symbols to signify differences in rank. For example, police officers below the rank of Inspector wear blue shirts (i.e., blue-collar workers); whereas police officers above the rank of Staff Sergeant wear white shirts (i.e., white-collar workers). As well, all uniformed police are required to wear patches, badges and/or medals to signify their rank. These symbols ensure that the those who are "on the job" (i.e., members of the police subculture) can always quickly and easily determine a colleague's rank and, therefore, his or her authority. Of course, this is important to prevent insubordination or, when it happens, to remove ignorance as a defence.

An irony of the distribution of power in police organizations is that, in theory, every rank, with only two exceptions, is both super-ordinate and subordinate to other ranks. For example, Sergeants are both super-ordinate to Constables and subordinate to Staff Sergeants and Staff Sergeants are both super-ordinate to Sergeants and subordinate to Inspectors. The two exceptions to this situation are Constables, who are *always* subordinate to other ranks, and the Chief, who is always super-ordinate to other ranks. However, in practice, Constables exercise power vis à vis the public and, in theory, the Chief of Police is accountable to a civilian board or commission.

Figure 7.2
The Police Hierarchy

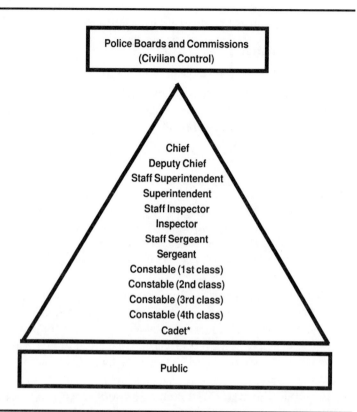

*   Not all police organizations have the Cadet rank and frequently when it is included cadets are not sworn peace officers. As a result, cadets may not be part of the police hierarchy. Also, there is considerable variation in the names police organizations assign ranks. For example, the RCMP and several provincial and municipal police organizations continue to use the rank of Corporal, a holdover from the military origins of modern policing.

In theory, all police officers, regardless of rank, have the same *legal* powers; however, in practice, their monopoly over *administrative* power ensures that senior ranks control not only their own legal power but also the legal power of *all* officers subordinate to their command. In effect, a para-military hierarchy concentrates or focuses power, much like a magnifying glass focuses light, at the top of the hierarchy. As a result of this arrangement and because, as we noted above, police have extra-ordinary legal power, senior police ranks, and especially the Chief of Police, have tremendous power.

The police subculture has several vulgar expressions that describe the hierarchical organization and distribution of power in police bureaucracies. For example, constables are fond of noting that "cadets are lower than whale-shit at the bottom of the ocean" and that "shit flows down hill." These bits of occupational "wisdom" demonstrate that the police "rank and file" are aware that power is correlated with position in a para-miltary hierarchy, and the lower you are the less power you have.

A consequence of the distribution of power in police bureaucracies is that interpersonal relationships are either between equals (i.e., subordinate/subordinate or super-ordinate/super-ordinate) or unequals (e.g. super ordinate/subordinate). As a result, the informal organization of police bureaucracies emphasizes peer relationships (i.e., constables with constables), whereas the formal organization of police bureaucracies emphasizes relationships between unequals (i.e., constables and sergeants). This compartmentalization and balkanization of police bureaucracies has important consequences for the functioning of these organizations. For example, information "flows" most effectively from top to bottom and within ranks in police organizations; it flows much less effectively from bottom to top and between ranks.

Another key feature of the distribution of power in police bureaucracies is that it is the reverse of the distribution of individuals (Figure 7.3). Typically, there are many more constables (i.e., relatively powerless) than chiefs (i.e., relatively powerful). Ironically, the effect of this arrangement is that the relatively powerful (at least vis à vis the public) but lowest ranking members of police bureaucracies — constables — sometimes feel powerless and, as a result, may resent their police superiors. Of course, no one likes to feel powerless and, because in reality constables are extra-ordinarily powerful, there is a temptation for them to find someone or some group to exercise power over. The obvious choice is the public. However, not all members of the public are uniformly powerless — politicians, doctors, lawyers, journalists, for example. They exercise other forms of power (such as political, economic and ideological power) that make them as powerful or more powerful than police. Consequently, police must be careful to target their power at those the public labels as "criminals."

In practice it is quite difficult for police to distinguish between "criminals" and "law-abiding citizens." This difficulty arises because most people have, at one time or another, engaged in behaviour that could be labelled "criminal." For example, many people have engaged in acts — impaired driving, nudity (i.e., nude sunbathing in public), indecent acts (i.e., sex in a public place), theft (i.e., shoplifting), keeping a gaming house (i.e., illegal gambling), possession of a drug or narcotic (i.e., smoking a "joint"), trafficking in a drug or narcotic (i.e., sharing a "joint" with a friend), mischief to property (i.e., damaging property), assault (i.e., fighting), causing a disturbance (i.e., being drunk or loud in public) — that could have been criminalized but, for one reason or another, were not. As a result, frequently the difference between a "criminal" and a "law-abiding citizen" is a moot point. Police know this better than most because as law enforcers they know that most crimes go undetected and many guilty people are never charged and many accused are never convicted. The police subculture implicitly recognizes this situation by the saying that "it doesn't matter if he did it (the crime for which he's charged) because he's sure to have done something else (another crime)."

Figure 7.3
The Distribution of People and Power in Police Hierarchies

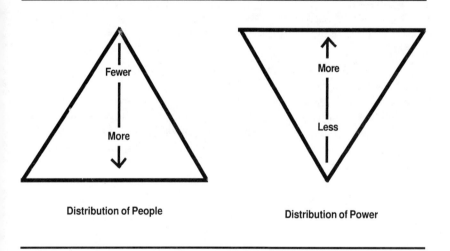

Distribution of People   Distribution of Power

The pervasiveness of what amounts to criminal behaviour in society means that police have a hard time recognizing the "enemy." This is no minor problem since the *raison d'étre* of a para-military hierarchy is to fight an enemy. As we saw in Chapter 4 (Roles), police (warriors) "need" criminals (enemies). However, in what is essentially a "guerilla" war, it is easy for police to make mistakes and target their power at the wrong individuals and groups. Contrary to the popular saying, not only do police *not* "always get their man," sometimes they even get the *wrong* man (or woman). When this occurs, police may experience a conflict between their legal authority and their moral authority.

Sometimes police are authorized by law and sometimes they are authorized by the community to enforce the law. For example, a police officer who conducts a search under the authority of a search warrant issued pursuant to section 487.(1) of the Criminal Code is exercising a "legal authority." In contrast, a police officer who conducts a search under the authority of a person's consent is exercising a "moral authority." As we will see in the discussion below, legal authority and moral authority are linked in a complicated relationship.

Significantly, while all authority involves the exercise of power, the opposite is not necessarily true; that is, the exercise of power is not always authorized. For example, a police officer who willfully and knowingly breaks the law may use power to do so but does not have the legal or moral authority to do so. This is an important distinction that is often over-looked by individuals who exercise power. Frequently, police officers and others who exercise authority assume that because they have power their actions are authorized. [5] On the contrary, when the use of power is not authorized by law or morality, typically, it alienates the individuals exposed to it. Similarly, when police rely on legal authority to enforce the law they may undermined their moral authority.

---

5   This is what Machiavelli meant when he stated that absolute power is absolutely corrupting.

Legal Authority

As we saw above, one type of authority police exercise is legal authority. Legal authority *is extraordinary power conferred by law.* For example, section 25 of the Criminal Code of Canada provides:

25 (1) Every one who is required or authorized by law to do anything in the administration or enforcement of the law

(a)   as a private person,

(b)   as a peace officer or public officer,

(c)   in aid of a peace officer or public officer, or

(d)   by virtue of his office,

is, if he acts on reasonable grounds, justified in doing what he is required or authorized to do and in using as much force as is necessary for that purpose.

(2)   Where a person is required or authorized by law to execute a process or to carry out a sentence, that person or any person who assists him is, if that person acts in good faith, justified in executing the process or in carrying out the sentence notwithstanding that the process or sentence is defective or that it was issued or imposed without jurisdiction or in excess of jurisdiction.

(3)   Subject to subsection (4), a person is not justified for the purposes of subsection (1) in using force that is intended or is likely to cause death or grievous bodily harm unless he believes on reasonable grounds that it is necessary for the purpose of preserving himself or any one under his protection from death or grievous bodily harm.

(4)   A peace officer who is proceeding lawfully to arrest, with or without warrant, any person for an offence for which that person may be arrested without warrant, and every one lawfully assisting the peace officer, is justified, if the person to be arrested takes flight to avoid arrest, in using as much force as is necessary to prevent the escape by flight, unless the escape can be prevented by reasonable means in a less violent manner.

This is an example of a *statutory* legal authority. Among other things, it authorizes a peace officer (eg., police officer) to use force to make an arrest — but only if the person being arrested resists.[6] Also, if a police officer uses force and the person dies, the officer's actions will be justified (i.e., he or she will have a defence to a criminal charge) if the officer believed on reasonable grounds that his or her life or the life of someone under his or her protection was endangered (subsection 3) or the person was killed while fleeing to avoid arrest for one of the more serious criminal offences and the officer did not have a less violent alternative (subsection 4).[7]

---

6   The arrest is authorized by section 495.(1) of the Criminal Code of Canada.

7   Generally, the more serious criminal offences are the indictable offences not mentioned in section 553 of the Criminal Code. These include Murder, Aggravated Sexual Assault, Robbery, and Theft over $1,000 among others.

It is a relatively simple matter to determine whether a particular authority exists in law because the authorization will be documented either in statutory or case law. As we will see below, this may not be true of moral authority. Also, because legal authority is documented, typically, it is relatively easy to determine if police actions were authorized by law and therefore justified. If police cannot point to a specific law that authorized their actions, then most likely they acted unlawfully.

In all these respects the use of legal authority by police is a rational process — logical and verifiable. Moral authority, on the other hand, appeals to emotion not reason. As a result, moral authority often conflicts with legal authority.

Moral Authority

Another type of authority police officers exercise is moral authority. Moral authority *is the extraordinary power conferred by a religious or spiritual conviction.* For example, Dr. Martin Luther King Jr.'s non-violent struggle to desegregate the American South earlier this century was motivated by his belief that racism is immoral. Dr. King stated:

> We the disinherited of this land,
> We who have been oppressed so long,
> Are tired of going through the long night of captivity,
> And now we are reaching out for the daybreak of freedom, justice and equality ...
> And we are not wrong ...
> If we are wrong,
> The Supreme Court of this nation is wrong,
> If we are wrong,
> The Constitution of the United States is wrong,
> If we are wrong,
> God almighty is wrong.

Similarly, Mohandas Gandhi's non-violent struggle to free India from British rule early this century was motivated by his belief that colonialism was "unjust." The Mahatma (as quoted in Merton, 1965: 71) noted:

> An unjust law is itself a species of violence. Arrest for its breach is more so. Now the law of non-violence says that violence should be resisted not by counter-violence but by non-violence ... This I do by breaking the law and by peacefully submitting to arrest and imprisonment.

A profound irony of the dynamics of authority is that, frequently, moral authority conflicts with legal authority. For example, Dr. King and Mahatma Gandhi were repeatedly arrested and imprisoned for breaking the law. Despite the personal hardships they and their followers endured, they persisted with their non-violent struggles against injustice and, eventually, they were instrumental in ending the injustice in their countries. Theirs is an example that has inspired many others to non-violently resist injustice wherever they find it.

Police in the United States, Canada, China, India and South Africa — in short, all over the world — have been instrumental in enforcing laws that repress human rights. Occasionally, usually after bitter conflict and much suffering, these "laws" have been repealed. Often when this has happened, the police have been excoriated for their role in oppressing human rights. This possibility — that what is "just" today may be "unjust" tomorrow — hangs like the Sword of Damocles over the heads of law enforcement officers everywhere. This possibility alone should be enough to cause police to proceed cautiously when enforcing the law; however, time and time again, police have demonstrated by their actions that they have not learned this important lesson. Clearly, as we noted in Chapter 6, "police ethics" is an area where police training needs improvement. Imagine how law enforcement would be transformed if every police officer behaved as if the person he or she arrested was Dr. King or Mahatma Gandhi!

A community can be policed with moral authority alone;[8] however, only in exceptional circumstances can a community be policed with legal authority alone (Turk, 1982). This is a result of the fact that the civilian population always vastly outnumbers the police population. Consequently, if social consensus breaks down and violent confrontation ensues, police are compelled to use extreme force to reproduce order. When this happens it has profound implications for the police use of authority.

The police use of legal authority is inversely correlated with police moral authority (Figure 7.4). As a result, when police have moral authority they seldom need to use legal authority to reproduce order; however, the opposite is also true, when police lose moral authority, they must rely more heavily on their legal authority. As we will see in Chapter 8, the exercise of authority routinely involves the use of force, and the use of force by police is alienating to the individuals subjected to it. The practical result of this situation is that police lose moral authority when they are forced to rely on their legal authority to reproduce order. This is a classic "Catch-22" situation:

---

8   Traditional farming communities are examples of communities that are policed with only moral authority.

police lose moral authority when they rely too heavily on the use of force (i.e., legal authority), but they are compelled to rely on the use of force when they do not have moral authority. If this cycle cannot be broken, eventually the community cannot be policed by consent and, consequently, police must routinely use lethal force to reproduce order. Many large American inner cities are prime examples of this situation. It remains to be seen if Canadian police can avoid this outcome.

Figure 7.4
Relationship between the Level of Moral Authority and the Need to Use Legal Authority

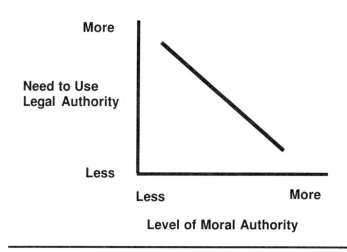

Police are sensitive to the nuances of authority. For example, the police subculture has an informal rule that "you don't lecture them if you charge them." This is a tacit acknowledgment by police that "authorities" — parents, teachers, legislators and police officers — may punish (i.e., exercise legal authority) *or* admonish (i.e., exercise moral authority), but not do both. As we will see in Chapter 9, a key element of police discretion is the officer's ability to match the type of authority they use to the situation.

In an ideal world, legal authority and moral authority would always coincide so that the two never conflict. For example, most people consider the arrest and imprisonment of a serial killer both a moral and legal imperative. However, because the law stigmatizes both moral wrongs (i.e., *malum in se*) and regulatory wrongs (i.e., *malum prohibitum*), frequently, police are required to enforce laws that have legal but not moral authority. As we will see in the example below, when this happens police may find that their function (i.e., enforcing the law) conflicts with their convictions.

Case Study

The potential for conflict between a police officer's morals and his or her legal duties was dramatically illustrated in 1987. In April of that year Constable Packard of the Metropolitan Toronto Police Service was assigned to guard an abortion clinic that had a history of unruly anti-abortion demonstrations. Constable Packard refused the order on the grounds that it violated his religious convictions.[9] Subsequently, he was tried, found guilty of "insubordination" and ordered to resign by a police tribunal. On appeal to the police commission the conviction was upheld but the sentence was reduced to a reduction in rank and salary.

At his trial, when asked if he would disobey a similar order in the future, Constable Packard (*Globe and Mail*, February 16, 1990: A1, A2) replied, "wrong is wrong, is wrong ... (but that he would weigh the decision) ... against my informed Catholic conscience." In making its ruling, the Chair of the police commission (*Toronto Star*, December 14, 1989: A10) noted:

> An alternative (to the suggestion that an employer is obligated to make reasonable accommodation of an employee's religious beliefs) is to hold that a police officer has voluntarily surrendered some of the rights of other people and accepted his duties and obligations to protect all of the people — whether his name be Morgentaler or otherwise.[10]

In this case, the police officer's religious convictions (i.e., morals) conflicted with his duty (i.e., legal responsibilities) as a police officer. This conflict was eventually resolved by the legal authorities imposing a punishment on the insubordinate officer. By doing so, police administrators reaffirmed the *primary* rule of para-military hierarchies which is: "when there is a conflict between your beliefs and your duty, you are expected to do your duty."

---

9   The officer in question was a practicing Roman Catholic.
10   The clinic in question was founded and operated by Dr. Henry Mortgentaler.

Summary

Ultimately, authority is power. Canadian police are conferred extraordinary authority by law and, to the extent that the law is moral, by morality. Police bureaucracies attempt to control police power by organizing it into a para-military hierarchy and by imposing discipline. As long as law and morality coincide, police can reproduce order by using their moral authority; however, when law and morality diverge, as they often do, then police must use their legal authority generally, and the use of force more particularly, to reproduce order. At these times policing is reduced to a naked act of aggression.

8 Use of Force

Introduction

As individuals and groups strive to improve their position in the Canadian social hierarchy, they are forced to compete with other individuals and groups whose interests conflict. The function of the police is to resolve these conflicts by enforcing laws that are designed to reproduce the status quo. For this purpose, Canadian police are authorized by law to use force, including lethal force, to resolve conflict. On several occasions in the recent past, when deadly force was used by or against Canadian police, these events catalysed major incidents of civil disobedience.

This chapter analyses the use of force by and against Canadian police. In particular, a "use of force response options" model used by police is analysed to identify the "logic" police use to resolve conflicts. As well, the use of deadly force by and against Canadian police is analysed. In particular, the role of factors such as a shooter's race, sex and intentionality are used to analyse the use of deadly force by and against Canadian police. This chapter concludes by analysing a case in which numerous police used force to "break-up" a large, boisterous house party.

Use of Force By and Against Canadian Police

There are few areas of public policy as important as the use of force by and against Canadian police. For example, the 1990 fatal shooting of a police officer in Quebec, by a native, sparked a major international incident. Similarly, the 1992 fatal shooting of a black man in Toronto, by a police officer, sparked street riots. In different ways, both incidents represented landmark events in the history of Canadian civil disobedience. It is not an exaggeration to state that the use of force by and against Canadian police is like a barometer of the health of the Canadian body politic. In short, the use of force by and against police is perhaps the most important issue in contemporary Canadian policing.

As noted in Chapter 3, industrial societies like Canada are politically, economically, and socially stratified (Lenski et al., 1991). The effect of this stratification is to concentrate most power in the hands of a small group of elites (ibid.). Inevitably, the large disparities between rich and poor in industrial societies forces individuals and groups to compete to improve their life chances (Dahrendorf, 1979; Turk, 1982). Predictably, this competition produces conflict which, if left unchecked, can and sometimes does undermine the status quo. To prevent this from happening, industrial societies use a system of laws and law-enforcers (i.e., police) to preserve and reproduce the status quo (Chambliss, 1973: 5; Turk, 1982).

Use of Force by Police

To assist them with their law enforcement mandate, Canadian police are authorized by section 25 of the Criminal Code of Canada to use force, including lethal force, to resolve conflict:

> 25.   (1) Every one who is required or authorized by law to do anything in the administration or enforcement of the law
>
> (a)   as a private person,
>
> (b)   as a peace officer or public officer,
>
> (c)   in aid of a peace officer or public officer, or
>
> (d)   by virtue of his office,
>
> is, if he acts on reasonable grounds, justified in doing what he is required or authorized to do and in using as much force as is necessary for that purpose...
>
> (3)   Subject to subsection (4), a person is not justified for the purposes of subsection (1) in using force that is intended to or is likely to cause death or grievous bodily harm unless he believes on reasonable grounds that it is necessary for the purpose of preserving himself or any one under his protection from death or grievous bodily harm.
>
> (4)   A peace officer who is proceeding lawfully to arrest, with or without warrant, any person for an offence for which that person may be arrested without warrant, and everyone lawfully assisting the peace officer, is justified, if the person to be arrested takes flight to avoid arrest, in using as much force as is necessary to prevent the escape by flight, unless the escape can be prevented by reasonable means in a less violent manner (R.S., c. C-34, s.25.).

Very simply, subsection (1) creates a legal justification for individuals, including police officers, who are "required or authorized by law" to use "as much force as necessary" in the "administration or enforcement of the law" if they "act on reasonable grounds." If a police officer is acting under the authority of subsection (1) and uses force "that is intended to or is likely to cause death or grievous bodily harm," then, to be justified, he or she must believe on "reasonable grounds" that it was necessary for the purpose of preserving him or herself or someone under his or her protection from "death or grievous bodily harm."

Section 25 of the Code is problematic for several reasons. First, the use of the expression "as much force as necessary" creates the impression that the use of force by police to resolve conflict is an expectation. Second, nowhere does this section answer the critical question: How much force is *too much* force? In a much-needed attempt to clarify the use of force under section 25 of the Code, police authorities in Ontario have developed a "Use of Force Model" (UOFM) (Figure 8.1) to help police decide how much force is appropriate.

UOFM is an attempt to create a standardized and systematic approach for police to use force. The model is based on the common-sense notion that the use of force is on a continuum beginning with little or no violence (i.e., verbal threats) and progressing to extreme physical violence (i.e., lethal assaults). The objective of UOFM is to help police strike a balance between the force being threatened or used by a citizen and the force being threatened or used by police. To accomplish this UOFM offers police a total of nine options for resolving conflict. Depending on the level of violence being threatened or used by the citizen, police are encouraged to use more or less force or, perhaps, not to use any force at all. So, for example, if a citizen is being compliant or passively resisting, UOFM recommends police use only their physical "presence" or "tactical communications" to resolve the conflict. Alternatively, if a citizen is being actively resistant, UOFM recommends police use "empty-handed techniques" or "soft-impact weapons" to resolve the conflict. If, on the other hand, a citizen is being "assaultive," UOFM recommends police use an "aerosol spray" or "hard-impact weapon" to resolve the conflict. Finally, if a citizen is threatening to inflict serious bodily harm or death, UOFM recommends police use the "police challenge," a "firearm" or, as a last resort, "disengage" from the conflict (Figure 8.1). While UOFM is an important first step to standardizing the use of force by Canadian police, it has several serious shortcomings.

An implicit feature of UOFM is that police should use a "graduated response" when using force. That is, police should assess the level of force being used or threatened by the citizen and respond with a slightly higher level of force. Also, if at any time the citizen increases the level of force, police should increase their level of force commensurably. The *intent* of this approach is to ensure that police always have the "upper hand" (i.e., always use or threaten more force than the citizen) in a police-citizen conflict. The *result* of this "approach" may be that, by trying to stay "one step ahead," police unintentionally escalate non-violent conflicts into violent conflicts, or low-intensity conflicts into high-intensity conflicts. In short, UOFM may have the unintended effect of *escalating* the level of violence in police-citizen conflicts.

Another problematic feature of UOFM is reflected in the range of options offered by the model. Of the nine options recommended for resolving conflict, six are violent conflict-resolution strategies, and only three are non-violent conflict-resolution strategies. Clearly, there is a inherent bias in UOFM for the use of violent conflict resolution techniques. This impression is reinforced by the fact that in the materials distributed for UOFM training, one of the non-violent options (i.e., "disengage") is given a smaller visual presence than each of the violent options.

Figure 8.1
Use of Force Response Options

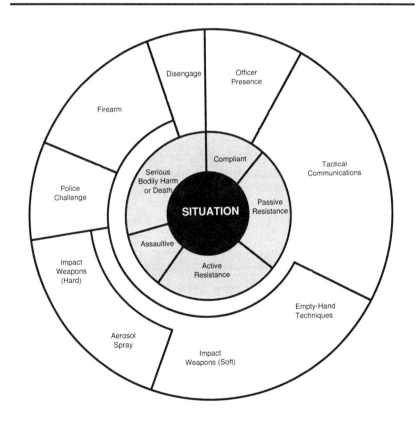

Source: Ontario Police College, 1994.

Profiled Behaviours	Use of Force Response Options

I. **Compliance** is "a cooperative and willing compliance in response to lawful police officer's request or direction."

II. **Passive Resistance** is "non-compliance to a lawful request or direction through verbal defiance but with little or no physical response (eg., refusal to leave the scene, failure to follow directive, taunting officers, advising others to disregard officer's lawful requests, etc.)."

III. **Active resistance** is an "increased scope and intensity of resistance beyond verbal defiance" that includes pushing or pulling away with intent to escape, or verbal refusal to respond to lawful commands.

IV. **Assaultive** is an "active, hostile resistance exhibited whether an actual assault has occurred or is about to occur on an officer or a citizen in response to the officer's attempt to gain lawful compliance or in an unprovoked assault (eg., kicking, punching spitting etc.)."

V. **Serious Bodily Harm/Death** is a "behaviour likely to cause death or serious bodily harm to an officer or a citizen (eg., choking, holding at gunpoint, brandishing an edged weapon, threatening and approaching with a weapon."

I. **Officer Presence** includes manner of arrival (eg., foot, cruiser), number of officers at scene, etc.

II. **Tactical Communications** includes both verbal (i.e., crisis intervention skills) and non-verbal (i.e., proxemics) behaviours (ibid., 4).

III. **Empty Hand Techniques** include "soft control" (i.e., restraining techniques and joint locks) and hard strikes (i.e., punches, and elbow, leg, and knee strikes).

IV. **Impact Weapon** when used for "soft control" include the use of batons in restraining techniques and joint locks.

V. **Aerosol Spray** includes oleoresin capsicum, orthochlorbenzalmalononitrite, and chloroacetophenone.

VI. **Impact Weapon** when used for hard control includes baton strikes and blocks.

VII. **Police Challenge** includes verbal commands such as: "Police, don't move!"

VIII. **Firearm** includes the drawing and discharging of service revolvers and pistols or the use of supplementary weapons such as shotguns and rifles.

IX. **Disengage** includes calling for back-up and creating time and distance.

It can be argued that UOFM is not intended to provide a full range of non-violent conflict resolution strategies. Why then is there no comparable "non-violent response options model"? This glaring omission reinforces the observation made in Chapter 6 that police training emphasizes the use of force in the resolution of conflict.

Another important feature of section 25 is that subsection 4 authorizes a peace officer to use force, including lethal force, to apprehend anyone who the peace officer has the power to arrest, but only if the offence is one for which the person could be arrested without warrant. Under "common law" (i.e., during the Agricultural Era), this was known as the "fleeing felon" rule. Essentially, the fleeing felon rule authorized any member of the community who had reasonable grounds to believe an individual had committed a criminal offence to use force, including lethal force, to apprehend the "felon."

An important difference between the use of force in the Agricultural Era and the use of force in the Information Era is that modern weapons, such as the semi-automatic pistols used by some police, are highly effective and efficient tools for inflicting lethal injuries. This contrasts with the relatively crude "weapons" (i.e., swords, knives and bows) that agriculturalists used to resolve conflict. One result of this situation has been that contemporary Canadian police kill relatively large numbers of people. For example, during the decade 1980-90, 101 Canadians were killed by firearms during "legal intervention" (Table 8.1). The overwhelming majority, or 81.2 percent (n=82), of those killed were shot in only three provinces: 34.7 percent (n=35) were shot in Ontario; 29.7 percent (n=30) were shot in Quebec; and 16.8 percent (n=17) were shot in British Columbia. This regional distribution of shootings of civilians by police closely resembles the overall distribution of the Canadian population in which 35.9%, 25.8%, and 11.4%, of Canadians live in Ontario, Quebec and British Columbia, respectively.[1]

The ongoing use of the fleeing felon rule in Canada,[2] combined with the partial abolition of capital punishment in Canada,[3] has created the contradictory situation in which Canadian police — on the basis of behaviour that may not be criminal and for which, even if it was judged to be criminal, the person could not be executed under Canadian law — can shoot and kill a fleeing felon. As we will see below, this situation has produced calls for the elimination of the fleeing-felon rule.

---

1   1986 Census.
2   The Supreme Court of the United States (*Tennessee* v. *Garner*) invalidated the use of lethal force to capture a non-violent fleeing suspect in 1985 (Geller and Scott, 1991: 456).
3   Canada has abolished capital punishment for "ordinary" crimes but not for some offences committed by soldiers during war (Amnesty International, 1989: Appendix 15).

Table 8.1
Firearm Death by Legal Intervention,[1] Canada and the Provinces/Territories, 1980-1990

Year	Canada	Nfld.	PEI	NS	NB	Que.	Ont.[2]	Man.	Sask.	Alta.	BC[3]	Yukon	NWT
1990	9				1	3	1				4		
1989	7					2				3	2		
1988	9					3	4	1			1		
1987	14					7	5				2		
1986	3					2				1			
1985	14				1	4	6		1		2		
1984	15					5	4	1	2		3		
1983	11					4	2	2		1	2		
1982	6	1					2			2	1		
1981	7					1	4	2					
1980	6					1	5						
TOTAL	**101**	**1**	**0**	**0**	**2**	**30**	**35**	**6**	**3**	**7**	**17**	**0**	**0**

Source: Canadian Centre for Health Information and Canadian Centre for Justice Statistics, 1992.

1   "'Legal intervention' includes injuries inflicted by the police or other law-enforcing agents, including military on duty, in the course of arresting or attempting to arrest lawbreakers, suppressing disturbances, maintaining order, and other legal action" [Canadian Centre for Health Information (C.C.H.I.) and Canadian Centre for Justice Statistics (C.C.J.S.), 1992]. The reliability of this data is suspect. For example, Hackler and Janssen (1985: 229) reported that seven police were murdered on duty in Ontario in 1984; whereas, the Canadian Centre for Justice Statistics (C.C.J.S.) reported only *five* police murders. Similarly, Chappell and Graham (1985) reported that there were three fatal police shootings in B.C. in 1982; whereas, the C.C.J.S. reported only one. Also, the Ontario Police Commission (1989: 17) reported that there were twenty-five fatal police shootings in Ontario between 1984-1988; whereas, the C.C.J.S. report only twenty-two.

2   The Ontario Police Commision (1989:17) reported that there were 25 fatal police shootings in Ontario between 1984 and 1988, inclusively.

3   Chappell and Graham (1985:97) reported that there were one and three fatal police shootings in B.C. in 1980 and 1982, respectively.

Shootings by Tactical Police

One might expect that, because of the dangerous nature of their assignments (i.e., "high-risk" incidents), tactical police would use *more* force when resolving conflict than their non-tactical counterparts.[4] This expectation is reinforced by the fact that tactical police receive extensive training in the use of specialty weapons that are not available for use by non-tactical police.[5] While the evidence is far from clear, it appears that the *opposite* may be true. For example, in the five-year period 1984-88, tactical

---

4   In the discussion that follows "high-risk incidents" will mean incidents involving barricaded or dangerous persons, hostage takings and high-risk searches.

5   Examples of the specialty weapons possessed by most tactical police units are: semi-automatic pistols, sub-machine guns, shot-guns, assault rifles, sniper rifles, tear-gas guns, percussion grenades, and smoke bombs (Ontario Police Commission, 1989).

police in Ontario responded to more than 2,620 high risk incidents (Table 8.2). Lethal, or life-threatening, force was used in only seven of those incidents, resulting in four fatalities and three woundings. During the same period non-tactical police, in an unknown number of incidents, shot fifty-five people, killing twenty-five of them (Ontario Police Commission, 1989: 17). Without knowing the precise number of "high-risk" incidents attended by non-tactical police it is impossible to know whether tactical police in Ontario resolve conflict more effectively (i.e., with less loss of life) than non-tactical police. [6] However, these figures suggest precisely that. If this speculation is borne out by future research, it will indicate that police services possess the skills needed to resolve many conflicts non-violently but use them selectively, thus leaving the overall impression that non-violent conflict resolution is a relatively low priority for police.

Table 8.2
Police Shootings in High Risk Situations, Ontario, 1984-1988.

Description	Non-Tactical	Tactical
High Risk Incidents	Not available	2620
Shootings	55	7
Fatalities	21	4
Woundings	34	3

Source: Ontario Police Commission (1989: 17).

If, as we have speculated, tactical police are less prone to using force than non-tactical police, then one is left to wonder why. One possible explanation may be that, typically, tactical police have more control of their interactions with civilians than non-tactical police. For example, in his study of tactical police effectiveness in the United States, Fyfe (1989: 473) concluded that "(t)here is evidence that attempts by police to manipulate time and involuntariness and to make more private highly volatile encounters between police and citizens, do reduce violence."

---

6   In order for non-tactical police to achieve an efficiency rate comparable to their tactical counterparts they would have to have attended 20,585 "high-risk" calls between 1984 and 1988. In view of the fact that responding to "high-risk" incidents is the primary responsibility of tactical units it appears unlikely that non-tactical police would have responded to this number of "high-risk" calls. Also, since 1979 the Emergency Task Force Unit (E.T.F.) of the Metropolitan Toronto Police Service (M.T.P.S.) has shot and killed only one person while responding to approximately 2,000 calls for service (M.T.P.S. - E.T.F., 1992).

Victim's Race in Police Shootings

There is a large and growing body of research in the United States examining the link between a person's race and their risk of being a victim of police deadly force. It clearly demonstrates that blacks are at a much higher risk than whites. For example, after a thorough review of the U.S. literature, Geller and Scott (1991: 454) noted that, "virtually all of the studies that have examined the race of civilian victims of shootings by the police have shown that blacks are shot in numbers significantly disproportionate to their percentage of the local general population." Similarly, Blumberg (1986: 236) concluded that, "(a)ll studies are in agreement that blacks are the victims of police deadly force in numbers disproportionate to their representation in the general population ... What the studies disagree about is the reason for this finding."

A variety of reasons have been proposed to explain the disproportionate numbers of blacks who are victims of the police use of deadly force in the United States. Some (Takagi, 1974: 32) have suggested that the results may be explained by systematic police racism. Others (Matulia, 1985: 7; Fyfe, 1981a; Alpert, 1989) have suggested that the disproportionate involvement of blacks in violent criminal activity may be the reason. Clearly, more research is needed to resolve this contentious issue.

Despite the major importance of this issue (i.e., the possibility of there being a link between a person's race and their risk of being a victim of police deadly force), this subject has received very little attention by Canadian scholars. Among the few Canadian studies conducted to date, Chappell and Graham (1985: 96) found in their study of thirteen fatal police shootings in British Columbia during 1970-1982 that 15.4 percent (n=2) of the victims were racial minorities. Similarly, in their study of seven fatal police shootings in Toronto during 1978-1980, Abraham et al. (1981) found that 28.6 percent (n=2) of the victims were racial minorities. Also, in a study of fourteen police shootings in Toronto during 1988-1991, Stansfield (1993) found that 28.6 percent (n=4) of the victims were racial minorities.[7]

Before it will be possible to assess the relative risks for different races to be victims of police deadly force in Canada, additional research will be needed. If this research demonstrates that blacks, and probably natives, are at a higher risk of being victims of police deadly force, then the issue will be whether this is a result of systemic police racism or other factors (i.e., the over-representation of these groups in violent crime).

---

7   Visible minorities comprised 17.3 percent and 25.2 percent of the Toronto population in 1986 and 1991, respectively (Samuel, 1992:34). No estimates of the visible minority population in Toronto in 1980, and in British Columbia in the 1970s, are available; however, Samuel (ibid., 25) has noted that visible minorities comprised 10.2 percent of the British Columbia population in 1986.

Table 8.3
Victim's Race in Police Shootings, Canada

Researcher(s)	Location Studied	% Shot by Police/ % of Population	
		Racial Minorities	Whites
Abraham et al. (1981)	Toronto	28.6/17.3[1]	71.4/82.7[1]
Chappell & Graham (1985)	British Columbia	15.4/10.2[2]	84.6/89.9[2]
Stansfield (1993)	Toronto	28.6/21.3[3]	71.4/78.7[3]

1   Samuel (1992:34) notes that visible minorities comprised 17.3 percent of the Toronto population in 1986. Since Toronto's visible minority population has been steadily increasing since the 1970s, this number actually overestimates the visible minority population and underestimates the white population in Toronto during the period of Abraham et al.'s study (i.e., 1978-1980).
2   Samuel (1992: 25) notes that visible minorities comprised 10.2 percent of the British Columbia population in 1986. Since British Columbia's visible minority population has been steadily increasing since the 1970s, this number actually overestimates the visible minority population and underestimates the white population in British Columbia during the period of Chappell and Graham's study (i.e., 1970-1982).
3   This estimate was derived from the 1986 and 1991 census.

Characteristics of Police Who Use Deadly Force

There appear to be no significant differences in the rates at which black and white police officers in the United States use deadly force (Blumberg, 1986: 235). Female police officers, however, are less likely than their male colleagues to use deadly force (ibid., 234). Also, in his study of police shootings in Kansas City between 1972 and 1978, Blumberg (1985) found that younger, less experienced police officers were significantly more likely to become involved in a shooting. The usefulness of this finding was diminished, however, by Alpert's (1989) finding, in his study of police shootings in Miami during 1980-1986, that there was no significant relationship between an officer's age, years of experience, and the likelihood that he or she would become involved in a shooting; however, he (ibid., 487) also found that younger, less experienced officers were more likely to unintentionally discharge their firearms.

The race and sex of Canadian police who use deadly force has been a foregone conclusion, until recently (i.e., since the late 1980s). This is because, except for marginal representation, women and racial minorities have been all but excluded from Canadian policing. So, for example, with one exception, all of the police officers in the shootings that the author studied were white males.[8] However, as Canadian police forces become more racially and sexually diverse this may change. If Canada follows the American example, one can expect that female police officers will continue

8   One of the police officers in the author's (Stansfield, 1993) study of police shootings in Toronto during 1988-1991 was a black man.

to be disproportionately under-represented in fatal shootings, but black police officers will become proportionately represented. A harbinger of things to come may have occurred in Toronto in 1991, when a black police officer shot a black suspect (*Toronto Star*, 20 September 1991: A1).

Restricting Police Use of Force

The relatively large numbers of people who have been shot by Canadian police in recent years has resulted in a call for restrictions on the police use of force. Ontario was the first Canadian jurisdiction to respond to these calls when, in 1993, the *Police Services Act* in that province was amended to prohibit police officers from using their guns "unless they believe, on reasonable grounds, that to do so is necessary to protect against loss of life or serious bodily harm." For all practical purposes, this change eliminated the fleeing-felon rule in Ontario with the result that police in that province now may only use lethal force in "defence of life" situations. Attempts to amend section 25(4) of the Criminal Code to eliminate the fleeing-felon rule in the remainder of Canada, thus far, have met with no success.

There is evidence that a large proportion of the incidents involving the police use of deadly force in Canada occur in fleeing-felon situations. For example, Chappell and Graham (1985) found in their study of thirteen fatal police shootings in British Columbia between 1978-80 that 38.5 percent (n=5) of the victims were shot while fleeing. Similarly, the Stansfield (1993) found in his study of fourteen police shootings in Toronto between 1988-91 that 57.1 percent (n=8) of the victims were shot while fleeing. Also, Savage and Ault (1984: 167-8) found in their study of 260 police shootings in Canada[9] between 1967-83 that a "majority" of the shootings occurred in "flight without other resistance" incidents; however, they also noted (ibid.) that virtually all of these incidents involved the use of warning shots or shots at a civilian vehicle. These results contrast with the findings in Abraham et al.'s (1981) study, in which they found that all the police shootings occurred while the victim was confronting police (Table 8.4).

An alarming feature of the use of lethal force by Canadian police is the number of "accidental" shootings. For example, Chappell and Graham (1985) found that 27 percent (n=3) of the victims in their study were shot accidentally. Similarly, Stansfield (1993) found that 28.6 percent (n=4) of the victims in his study were shot accidentally. Also, Savage and Ault (1984) found that 8 percent (n=22) and 5 percent (n=3) of the shootings they studied were accidental. Only Abraham et al. (1981) found that there were no accidental shootings among the cases they studied.

---

9   Savage and Ault (1985) studied two unidentified Canadian police forces.

Table 8.4
Police Shootings Classified by Circumstance, Canada

| | | Circumstances of Shooting | | | | | |
| | | Confrontational | | Fleeing Felon | | Undetermined | |
Study	Location	Intentional	Accidental	Intentional	Accidental	Intentional	Accidental
Abraham et al. (1981)	Toronto (n=7)	7	0	0	0	0	0
Chappell and Graham (1985)	British Columbia (n=13)	6	0	2	3	2	0
Stansfield (1993)	Toronto (n=14)	6	0	4	4	0	0

The incidence of accidental shootings by police disclosed by some Canadian studies resembles data in the United States where Geller and Scott (1991: 457) have noted "studies show that relatively high levels of police gun discharges occur accidentally in many cities: 9 percent in Chicago ... 27 percent in Boston ... almost 13 percent in New York City during 1971-1975 ... and 24 percent in 1987."

Attempts to restrict the police use of deadly force have met with stiff resistance from police in what appears to be a sincere but naive belief that these policies compromise their personal safety. On the contrary, after reviewing the results of the adoption of "restrictive policies" in several large American cities, Geller and Scott (1991: 465) concluded:

> The empirical research suggests with remarkable unanimity but, admittedly, with less data than is desirable, that restrictive policies seemed to have worked well where they have been tried. Their adoption usually is followed by marked decreases in shootings by police, increases in the proportion of the shootings that are responses to serious criminal activity, greater or unchanged officer safety, and no resultant adverse impact on crime levels or arrest aggressiveness.

Significantly, American police have been prohibited from using lethal force to capture non-violent fleeing suspects since 1985 (ibid., 456). It would appear that it is only a matter of time before the fleeing-felon rule will be eliminated from Canadian law — a change that is long overdue.

Use of Force Against Police

Despite their near monopoly on the legitimate uses of force in civil society, 103 Canadian police officers were murdered on-duty between 1961-91 (Canadian Centre for Justice Statistics, 1992) (Table 8.5). The overwhelming majority — that is, 83.5 percent — (n=86) of those killed were shot in just four provinces: 33 percent (n=34) were shot in Ontario and Quebec each; 9.7 percent (n=10) were shot in British Columbia; and 7.8 percent (n=8) were shot in Alberta. As noted above in the discussion about shootings by police, the regional distribution of shootings of police closely resembles the current overall distribution of the Canadian population where 35.9 percent, 25.8 percent, 11.4 percent, and 9.4 percent of Canadians live in Ontario, Quebec, British Columbia and Alberta respectively. [10]

The most dangerous incidents for Canadian police during this period were: an "in-progress" robbery (23.3 percent); investigating a complaint (13.6 percent); apprehending/questioning a suspect (10.7 percent); intervening in a "domestic dispute," stopping a vehicle (9.7 percent); delivering/executing a court order (4.9 percent); pursuing a vehicle, chasing an escapee (3.9 percent); investigating a burglar alarm, intervening in a non-domestic complaint, approaching a stolen car, other types of incidents (2.9 percent); and questioning a pedestrian, performing duties at a psychiatric hospital, performing duties in a police station, being attacked without provocation (1.9 percent) (ibid.) (Table 8.6). These results resemble data in the United States where between 1979-88 the most dangerous incidents for American police were: robberies in-progress/pursuing robbery suspects (15 percent); investigating suspicious persons/circumstances, traffic pursuits/stops, attempting other types of arrests [11] (14 percent); "man with a gun," bar fights (10 percent); ambush situations (9 percent); arrests in drug related matters (8 percent); family quarrels (6 percent); burglaries in-progress/pursuing burglary suspects (5 percent); handling, transporting, custody of prisoners (4 percent); mentally deranged (2 percent); and civil disorders (.01 percent) (F.B.I., 1988: 17).

When a Canadian police officer is murdered on duty, the cause of death almost invariably is a wound caused by a firearm. For example, 96.1 percent (n=99) of the 103 Canadian police officers murdered on duty between 1961-91 were shot (ibid.). Once again, these results resemble data in the United States where 93 percent of police murders during 1979-88 were caused by firearms (F.B.I., 1988: 12, 41). Of the four Canadian police officers who were not killed by firearms, two were stabbed to death and two were killed by the use of motor vehicles (ibid.).

---

10   1986 Census.
11   "Other types of arrests" included all arrests other than burglary, robbery or drug arrests.

Table 8.5
Canadian Police Officers Murdered While on Duty, 1961-1991

Year	Canada	Nfld.	PEI	NS	NB	Que.	Ont	Man.	Sask.	Alta.	BC	Yukon	NWT
1991	3					1	2						
1990	2					1				1			
1989	0												
1988	0												
1987	3				1					1	1		
1986	4					3		1					
1985	5					3				1	1		
1984	6					1	5						
1983	1						1						
1982	1						1						
1981	5					2	2		1				
1980	3						2				1		
1979	1					1							
1978	6				2		2	1	1				
1977	5					2	2			1			
1976	3					2				1			
1975	2			1		1							
1974	6				2	1				1	2		
1973	5					1	4						
1972	3					1	2						
1971	3					2		1					
1970	3							1	2				
1969	5					2	2	1					
1968	5					2	3						
1967	3					1	1				1		
1966	3						1		1	1			
1965	2						1			1			
1964	2	1				1							
1963	0												
1962	11					4	3				4		
1961	2					2							
TOTAL	103	1	0	1	5	34	34	5	5	8	10	0	0

Source: Canadian Centre for Justice Statistics, Homicide Project, July 1992.

Table 8.6
Canadian Police Officers Murdered on Duty by Circumstances, 1961-1991

TYPE OF INCIDENT	%
During Robbery	24
Investigating a Complaint	14
Apprehending/Questioning Suspect	11
Domestic Dispute	10
Stopping a Vehicle	10
Delivering/Executing Court Order	5
Escapee	4
Pursuit of Vehicle	4
Residence, Non-Domestic Complaint	3
Investigating Burglary Alarm	3
Approaching Stolen Car	3
Other	3
Questioning Pedestrian	2
Psychiatric Hospital Duty	2
Unprovoked	2
In Police Station	2
Pursuit on Foot	1
TOTAL	103

Source: Homicide Survey Canadian Centre for Justice Statistics, September 1992.

The majority of Canadian police are shot and killed with either a rifle or a revolver. For example, of the ninety-four Canadian police officers murdered on duty by firearms between 1961-87: 39.4 percent (n=37) were shot with a rifle; 31.9 percent (n=30) were shot with a revolver; 14.9 percent (n=14) were shot with a shotgun; 3.8 percent (n=6) were shot with a pistol; 3.2 percent (n=3) were shot with a machine-gun or a handgun of an unspecified type; and 1.1 percent (n=1) were shot with a firearm of an unknown type (ibid.) (Table 8.7). Surprisingly, 11.1 percent (n=11) of the police who were shot and killed between 1960-91 were shot with their own, or a colleague's firearm (ibid.). This statistic is particularly shocking because it indicates that more than one in ten police who were shot and killed during this period may have survived if they had not been carrying a firearm.

Table 8.7

Canadian Police Officers Murdered While on Duty, by Type of Firearms, 1961-1987

Total Police Firearm Deaths	Rifle	Shotgun	Machine-Gun	Revolver	Pistol	Handgun	Not Stated
94	37	14	3	30	8	3	1

Source: Homicide Survey, Canadian Centre for Justice Statistics, 1992.

Of the ninety-four Canadian police officers murdered on duty by firearms between 1961-87: 41.5 percent (n=39) were shot in the head; 38.3 percent (n=36) were shot in the upper torso; 11.7 percent (n=11) were shot in the lower torso; and 8.5 percent (n=8) were shot in an unknown part of the body (Table 8.8) (ibid.). The relatively large number of fatal upper torso wounds in police shootings is surprising in light of the pervasive use of body armour among Canadian police. However, this may be a consequence of the relatively recent adoption of body armour. If this speculation is correct, then it may be expected that, barring a change in the targeting strategies used by individuals who shoot police (i.e., away from the upper torso to the head), one can expect fewer fatal police shootings in the future.

Table 8.8

Canadian Police Officers Murdered While on Duty, by Location of Primary Bodily Injury[1] Due to Firearms, 1961-1987

Total Police Firearm Deaths	Head Injuries[2]	Upper Torso Injuries[3]	Lower Torso Injuries[4]	Not Stated
94	39	36	11	8

Source: Homicide Survey, Canadian Centre for Justice Statistics, 1992.

1   **Primary Bodily Injury**: In cases where more than one location for bodily injury was reported, the first listed was selected as the primary location.
2   **Head Injuries:** include head, face and neck.
3   **Upper Torso Injuries:** include chest, heart, shoulders, back and side.
4   **Lower Torso Injuries:** include abdomen, stomach, buttocks and lower chest/abdomen.

Police Shooting Police

As improbable as it may seem, *police shooting police* is quite common in the United States. Geller and Scott (1991: 452-453) note that:

> In New York City, from 1971 through 1975, nine shootings of police involved mistaken identity exchanges of shots between uniformed police and plainclothes or off-duty officers at crime scenes. Three resulted in death (Fyfe 1978). Five of 26 New York City officers wounded (but not killed) by gunshots in 1987 were accidentally shot by a fellow officer. Nine of the 26 accidentally shot themselves (NYPD, 1988). In 1988, 53 New York City officers were shot and either wounded or killed (13 officers received minor injuries from gunshot pellets in one incident). Of those five were shot by fellow officers, two of them fatally (NYPD, 1989). Eleven percent of the Chicago officers shot between 1974 and 1978 were shot by fellow officers, and overall, 38 percent were shot either by themselves or their colleagues (Geller and Korales 1981a: 93-100, 141-155). For the ten-year period 1974-1983, these rates were 9 and 43 percent.

To date, there has been only one Canadian study (Savage and Ault, 1984) that investigated shootings of police. Of the thirty-five shootings of police they studied, Savage and Ault (ibid., 151) found: 74 percent (n=26) were intentional discharges by civilians; 5.7 percent (n=2) were unintentional discharges by other police; and 20 percent (n=7) were accidental discharges that were self-inflicted. If future studies reproduce these findings, it will provide a powerful argument *for* restricting police use of deadly force to increase *police* safety.

Other Findings

Despite the relatively large numbers of police officers who are murdered while on duty, Canadian police kill more civilians than vice versa. For example, between 1980-90, 30 Canadian police officers were slain while on-duty (ibid.). During the same period, 101 Canadians were shot and killed by police (Canadian Centre for Health Statistics, 1992). Expressed as a ratio of police fatalities to civilian fatalities, Canadian police kill approximately three civilians for every police officer who is killed. Lee (1981) notes that the Canadian ratio is comparable to the United States but much higher than in Europe where police typically kill approximately one civilian for every police officer that is killed. Bearing in mind that Canada is a liberal democracy founded on the principle of natural justice, it must be asked: Is this imbalance a "reasonable limit" on the "right to life, liberty and security of the person"?[12]

---

12   Section 7 of the Canadian Charter of Rights and Freedoms guarantees every person the "right to life, liberty and security of the person." These rights are qualified, however, by section 1 of the Charter which provides that the State has the right to impose "such reasonable limits prescribed by law as can be demonstrably justified in a free and democratic society."

Extensive analysis of the large data base of police shootings in the United States has made it possible to identify the stereotypical circumstances in which a police shooting occurs. Geller and Scott (1991: 453) note:

> The most common type of incident in which police and civilians shoot one another in urban America involves an on-duty, uniformed, white, male officer and an armed, black, male civilian between the ages of 17 and 30 in a public location within a high-crime precinct at night in connection with a suspected armed robbery or a "man with a gun" call.

While it is much too early to specify with precision the features of a "Canadian police shootings stereotype," a general outline is beginning to emerge. The most common type of incident in which Canadian police and civilians shoot one another seems to involve an on-duty, white, male officer and a male civilian in Ontario, Quebec or British Columbia. More research is needed to focus this picture more sharply.

Case Study

About midnight on March 8, 1988, members of the Winnipeg City Police were in the downtown core of the city in pursuit of two native men who were "joyriding." [13] Two constables, Cross and Hodgins, arrested one suspect and the other suspect was arrested a short time later by another group of police officers. A few moments after the second suspect was arrested and, knowing that both suspects were already in custody, Constable Cross attempted to stop and question another native male, J.J. Harper, who was walking home after an evening of socializing that included the consumption of a large quantity of alcohol. The Aboriginal Justice Inquiry of Manitoba (1991: 11) that reviewed this incident noted:

> Upon seeing Harper, he (Cross) approached him and asked for identification. According to Cross, Harper replied that he did not have to tell Cross anything. Cross said Harper then started to walk past him. Cross reached out, placed his hand on Harper's arm and turned him around. At that point, Cross said, Harper pushed him, causing him to fall backward onto the sidewalk. As he fell, he grabbed Harper, pulling him down on top of him. Cross testified that while he was on his back, he struggled with Harper and felt a tugging at his holster and, therefore, he reached

---

13 Section 335.(1) of the Criminal Code creates a summary conviction offence commonly known as "joyriding" for everyone who takes a motor vehicle or vessel without the owner's consent for the purpose of operating it.

down to grab his revolver. He said the gun came out of the holster with his and Harper's hands on it. He testified that he and Harper both were tugging at the gun when it went off. The blast hit Harper in the middle of the chest.

J.J. Harper died a short while after being shot by Constable Cross.

In many ways, this tragic incident is an archetypal story about police use of force. First, this incident pitted a minority, aboriginal male against a white, male police officer; as noted in Chapter 4 (Roles), there is a long history of conflict between Canadian police and minorities. Second, this conflict was about authority — the Constable expected the victim to cooperate with his *moral* authority (i.e., by identifying himself); the victim refused because the Constable did not have *legal* authority. Third, this incident demonstrates how a routine police-civilian interaction can become conflictual, quickly escalate out of control and, because police carry firearms, produce a result (death) that is entirely disproportionate to the original incident (a disagreement). Finally, this incident demonstrates how, because police are authorized to use force including lethal force to resolve conflict, inevitably some police-civilian encounters result in the death of either a police officer or, more frequently, in the death of a civilian.

Summary

Canadian police are authorized by law to use force, including lethal force, to resolve conflict. Attempts to systematize the use of force by some Canadian police have produced a situation in which police training in the use of force emphasizes violent conflict resolution strategies rather than non-violent conflict resolution strategies, and police-civilian conflicts tend to be escalated rather than de-escalated. This may explain the relatively large numbers of police and civilians who have been shot and killed by one another over the past thirty years.

The most striking feature about the deadly use of force by and against Canadian police is how little is known. Among the disquieting features of the studies done to date are the relatively large numbers of police who are disarmed and shot with their own or a colleague's firearm. Similarly, some studies indicate that a relatively large percentage of all police shootings are accidental shootings that occur in fleeing-felon situations. Before these and other curious features of the Canadian data can be explained, more research will be needed.

9 Discretion

Introduction

Discretion is an unavoidable feature of law enforcement and therefore policing. The question is not whether police need to exercise discretion when enforcing the law, it is to what extent. To this end the law specifies the criteria police must follow when exercising discretion. Police however, sometimes use "extra-legal" criteria to inform their discretion.

This chapter analyses police discretion by identifying the legal and extra-legal criteria police use to inform their discretionary decisions. As well, the concepts of discrimination and stereotyping and their relationship to discretion are considered. This chapter concludes with the analysis of a case in which a native woman was arrested by police and transported back and forth across Canada so that she could appear as a witness at the trial of her attacker.

Police Discretion

The *Oxford English Dictionary* (1990: 333) defines "discretion" as "the freedom to act ... as one wishes." An implicit feature of this definition is that discretion is power (Ericson, 1981: 10) and, in particular, it is the power to choose. It follows that police discretion *is the power police have to choose among two or more law enforcement alternatives*. An important feature of this definition is that a decision is not discretionary unless there are at least two options. For example, section 494.(3) of the Criminal Code provides that "any one other than a peace officer who arrests a person without a warrant shall forthwith deliver the person to a peace officer." Note that this section requires a citizen who makes an arrest to deliver the person into the custody of a peace officer forthwith — failure to do so is a criminal offence. This is an example of a *non-discretionary* decision because a citizen who makes an arrest has no legal alternative but to deliver the person into the custody of a peace officer. In contrast, the police decision of which automobile to stop and investigate — in, for example, a routine spot-check for drunk drivers — is a discretionary decision because there is more than one alternative.

A concept related to discretion is "discrimination." The *Oxford English Dictionary* (1990: 334) defines "discrimination" as "a distinction made with the mind or action." An implicit feature of this definition is that every decision, including discretionary decisions, involves an act of discrimination (Black, 1978: 184).[1] For example, when an police officer makes a decision to charge someone with an offence (i.e., a discretionary decision), the officer discriminates (i.e., makes a distinction) on the basis of some criteria such as: Are there "reasonable grounds" to believe the person committed an offence?

In Canada, some forms of discrimination are legal and some are illegal or "extra-legal." For example, section 15.(1) of the Canadian Charter of Rights and Freedoms provides:

> Every individual is equal before and under the law and has the right to the equal protection and equal benefit of the law without discrimination and, in particular, without discrimination based on race, national or ethnic origin, colour, religion, sex, age or mental or physical disability.[2]

In effect, this section specifies the "prohibited grounds" of discrimi-nation in Canada.[3]

In addition to the list of "prohibited grounds" of discrimination identified in section 15.(1) of the Charter, there is a large group of "grounds," that, while not expressly prohibited by law, are implicitly prohibited by police regulations and procedures. For example, a police officer who witnesses a minor motor vehicle collision and fails to respond because the officer is about to go "off-shift" is guilty of "neglect of duty." Despite the fact that "extra-legal" criteria are prohibited, police have been known to use them when enforcing the law (Vincent, 1990; Westley, 1970; Ericson, 1981; 1982; Reiss, 1971; Kirkham, 1976).

---

1   Defined in this way discrimination is a "neutral" action and does not necessarily have the pejorative overtones often associated with it. For example, a police officer who chooses to stop and investigate only brightly coloured automobiles discriminates between automobiles on the basis of colour. In Ontario, as in most jurisdictions in information societies, some, but by no means all, forms of discrimination are prohibited by law.

2   As well as the "prohibited grounds" of discrimination identified in section 15.(1) the Charter of Rights, each jurisdiction in Canada has authority to define "rights." For example, in Ontario, when providing a "service" such as policing, discrimination on the basis of a person's race, religion, creed, colour, age, ancestry, marital status, family status, place of origin, ethnic origin, sex, sexual orientation or handicap is prohibited (R.S.O.).

3   Note that the Charter does not apply to disputes between private indiviuals or activities in the private sector (MacIntosh, 1989: 29).

A simple test to determine if a criteria is "legal" or "extra-legal" is to imagine how a judge would react if a police officer testified that a particular criteria was the main reason he or she arrested and charged an accused. For example, how would a judge react if a police officer told the court that the the accused was arrested because the person is a particular race or sex? Clearly, this would be an unacceptable situation and would invite the court's censure! On the other hand, the way a criteria is presented to the court may make the difference between whether it is legal or extra-legal. For example, if a police officer said the reason the accused was arrested was because he or she had a "bad attitude," this would invite the court's censure; however, if the police officer said the reason was because the accused demonstrated "a lack of remorse" by his or her attitude, most courts would accept this justification, assuming that all the necessary legal criteria were also present.

In theory, it might be desirable for police to enforce all the laws all the time; however, in practice, police do not even detect most offences let alone apprehend and charge every offender, and the courts would soon be overwhelmed if they did. This demonstrates that full enforcement of the law is an unrealistic ideal and that police, crowns and judges must use discretion to achieve partial enforcement of the law.

The fact that full enforcement is not possible nor even desirable tells us that the law is intended as a *guide*, not as a rigid set of rules that always must be enforced. Evidence of the guiding role of law comes from two very different sources. First, when police want to disrupt "production," perhaps to strengthen their bargaining position during contract negotiations, they use their discretion to issue warnings instead of tickets (i.e., charges). This demonstrates that police do exercise discretion when enforcing the law and perhaps, more importantly, that police are willing to use discretion as a "tool" to produce outcomes that meet their needs. Similarly, when non-police unions want to disrupt the workplace without going on strike, they instruct workers to "work to rule." Of course, the effect of working to rule is that production slows. Both of these examples are powerful evidence that the law is intended as a guide, not as a rigid and inflexible set of rules.

Once it is understood that police must exercise discretion when enforcing the law, then the real question becomes which *criteria* do they use to determine whom to charge with an offence. For example, police use criteria such as the "seriousness of an offence" and the "availaiblity of evidence" to determine when to lay a charge. Generally, the criteria police use to decide when to lay a charge can be divided into four groups: criteria relating to the offence, criteria relating to the offender, criteria relating to the police officer and criteria relating to the setting in which the offence was committed (Table 9.1).

Table 9.1
Criteria Police May Use to Determine Whom to Charge with an Offence

Description	Criteria	Group At Risk
Offender	Age	teenagers and young adults
	Sex	males
	Marital Status	singles
	Employment Status	unemployed
	Attitude	defiant and uncooperative
	Ecomonic Status	poor
	Religion	non-Christians
	Race	visible minorities
	Ethnicity	minorities
	Type of Auto	muscle car and decrepit autos
	Sexual Orientation	gays
	Alcohol/Drug Use	users and addicts
	Social Status	low
	Appearance	unconventional, eg., long hair, dread locks, tatoos, skin heads
	Criminal History	prior criminal record
Officer	Experience	2-5 years
	Sex	male
	Officer's Attitude	authoritiarian or prejudiced
	Departmental Policies	yes
	Assignment	uniform
Setting	Location	public place
	Time of Shift	start
	Time of Day	evenings
	Time of Week	weekends
	Time of Month	end
	Time of Year	non-holiday periods
	Weather	good
Offence	Seriousness of Offence	serious
	Availabilty of Evidence	available
	Victims	present
	Witnesses	present

Some of the criteria relating to the *offence* that may influence an officer's decision about whether or not to lay a charge are: the seriousness of the offence, the availabilty of evidence, and the presence or absence of victims and witnesses. Generally, police are more likely to lay a charge when the offence that has been committed is relatively serious. That is to say, that police discretion varies as a function of the seriousness of an offence (Figure 9.1). For instance, all else being equal, police are more likely to charge Criminal Code offences and especially indictable offences than provincial offences and summary offences in the Criminal Code. As a result, typically, discretion does not become an issue unless the offence is relatively minor (eg., theft under $1,000, mischief to property, causing a disturbance). For example, if, on the one hand, the offence is very serious, such as murder, then police have little or no discretion about whether to lay a charge. They are expected to lay a charge and may be guilty of neglecting their duty if they do not. If, on the other hand, the offence is a relatively minor one, such as speeding, then police have considerable discretion about whether or not to lay a charge. In practice, the overwhelming majority of offences police charge are relatively minor provincial offences such as speeding and liquor offences, the less serious criminal offences such as thefts under $1,000, and minor assaults with the result that police routinely use discretion when deciding whether or not to lay a charge.

Figure 9.1
Police Discretion Versus Seriousness of the Offence

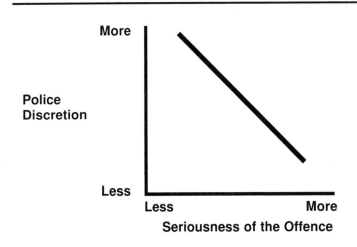

Another important criteria relating to the offence that may influence the police decision to lay a charge is the availability of evidence. Generally, police are more likely to lay a charge if they have good direct evidence of the offence. That is to say, that police discretion varies as a function of the availability of evidence (Figure 9.2). As a result, typically, discretion does not become an important issue unless the offence is relatively minor *and* there are "reasonable grounds" to believe an offence has been committed. For example, even if the offence is relatively minor such as theft under $1,000, police cannot lay a charge unless they have "reasonable grounds" to believe that an offence was committed. If police lay a charge when they do not have reasonable grounds to believe an offence was committed, they may be guilty of "malicious prosecution."[4] In practice, obtaining enough evidence to ensure that there are reasonable grounds that the accused committed the offence can be quite difficult. Consequently, police will occasionally resort to other criteria to help them decide whether or not to lay a charge.

Figure 9.2
Police Discretion Versus Availability of Evidence

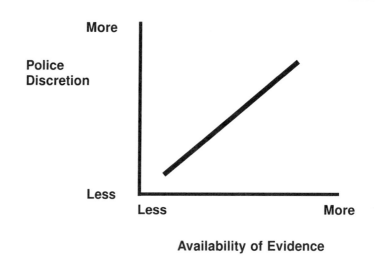

---

4   Malicious prosecution is a civil "tort".

One final criteria relating to the offence that may influence the police decision to lay a charge is the presence of witnesses or involvement of a victim. Generally, police are predisposed to lay a charge when witnesses and/or a victim is present for two reasons. First, the presence of a witness or involvement of a victim often means that there is direct "eyewitness" evidence of the offence. Second, when a witness is present or a victim is involved police lay a charge to appease the witness/victim and reduce the likelihood that the witness/victim will complain. Police refer to this as "covering your ass."

Some of the criteria relating to the *offender* that may influence a police officer's decision about whether or not to lay a charge are the offender's age, sex, marital status, family status, employment status, social status, attitude, religion, race, ethnicity, sexual orientation, alcohol and/or drug use, appearance and criminal history. Generally, young, poor, single, unemployed minorities (i.e., blacks, aboriginals and gays) who have a prior record of convictions and who defy police authority or who are uncooperative are at the highest risk to be charged with an offence. Police are more likely to charge people who fit this stereotype than those who do not because their experience and/or the police subculture teaches them that these people are more likely to be offenders.

Some of the criteria relating to the *police officer* that may influence his or her decision about whether or not to lay a charge are the officer's age, experience, sex, attitude, the department that he or she works for and assignment. Generally, young, less experienced, and prejudiced male police officers who work in bureaucratic police organizations are most likely to lay a charge. Young, inexperienced police officers are more likely to lay a charge because typically these individuals are still striving to be promoted whereas their more experienced colleagues may have abandoned all hope of ever being promoted.

Some of the criteria relating to the *setting* that may influence an officer's decision about whether or not to lay a charge are the location, time of shift, time of day, time of week, time of month, time of year and the weather. Generally, police are most likely to lay a charge in a public place, at the start of a shift, on a weekend (including Fridays), near the end of the month, during a non-holiday period and in good weather. These conditions are preferred by police for a variety of reasons. For example, police are most likely to lay a charge at the end of the month because that is when performance results that are used to calculate organizational quotas are submitted. Similarly, police are most likely to charge at the start of a shift to avoid working overtime and are least likely to charge during major holidays such as Christmas.

Inevitably, as police go about their day-to-day work of deciding who to charge with an offence they generate statistical profiles of the "average" criminal that become "stereotypes." The *Oxford English Dictionary* (1990: 1195) defines a "stereotype" as "a person or thing that conforms to an unjustifiably fixed ... mental picture." For example, a belief that all people from a particular racial or ethnic group are criminals is unjustified and, therefore, is a stereotype. Most people, including most police officers, have stereotypes about criminals (Table 9.2).

Table 9.2
Common Criminal Stereotypes

"Men are criminals"
"Women are prostitutes"
"Italians are Mafiosi"
"Jamaicans are drug traffickers"
"Gay men are child molesters"
"Arabs are thieves"
"Natives are drunks"
"Vietnamese are extortionists"
"Chinese are illegal gamblers"
"Bikers are gangsters"
"Young people are trouble makers"
"Old men are child molesters"
"Sikhs are terrorists"
"Iranians are terrorists"
"Palestinians are terrorists"

Stereotypes about criminals are formed when, either through direct personal experience or, more often, indirectly through the media, we receive information about who is committing crimes. This information is then used to construct a "profile" of the average or typical criminal.[5] It follows that if this information is biased or distorted, then the criminal stereotype will also be biased or distorted. Obviously, the techniques used to produce this information play an important part in determining the accuracy of criminal stereotypes.

---

5   To determine your criminal profile, close your eyes and imagine the "typical" criminal: what does this person look like? how old are they? what is the person's race and sex? If you find this task difficult, imagine that this person sells drugs or molests children. What images come to mind? If you are like most people, these words invoke powerful *archetypal* (see Chapter 4) images: these images are our stereotypes. The criminal archetype in the United States and, to an increasing extent in Canada also, is a young, urban, poor, black male (Reiman, 1984: 48).

A key source of the information used to form stereotypes about criminals comes from police. When police decide who, what, where, when, why and how to investigate and charge an offence, they indirectly produce the information (i.e., arrest rates) used to construct criminal stereotypes. Significantly, police not only *produce* this information, they also *consume* it.[6] For example, police use criminal stereotypes to formulate crime control/ prevention strategies and generally to guide their law enforcement actions. As a result, if police criminal stereotypes are biased and distorted, the information they produce will be biased and distorted, and the criminal stereotypes that result will be biased and distorted.[7]

When police use criminal stereotypes to guide their law emforcement activities, they risk creating a "self-fulfilling prophecy."[8] A self-fulfilling prophecy can occur when police have a belief (i.e., a stereotpye) that most, if not all criminals, belong to a particular group. Consequently, police use their discretion to target members of this group with the predictable result that they find members of this group committing crimes. When police arrest and charge these individuals they produce statistics that reinforce the stereotype about who is doing crime. Armed with these "objective" statistics, police target members of this group.

A very clear stereotype about criminals exists in the United States (cf Pearce, 1976; Reiman, 1984), where, Reiman (1979: 48) notes, the "Typical Criminal" is:

> [F]irst of all, a *he*. Second, he is a *youth* — most likely under the age of 20. Third, he is predominately *urban* — although increasingly *suburban*. Fourth, he is disproportionately *black* — blacks are arrested ... at a rate three times that of their percentage in the national population.

The only thing needed to make this a *Canadian* criminal stereotype, is to include natives in addition to blacks (Aboriginal Justice Inquiry of Manitoba, 1991; Royal Commission on the Donald Marshal Jr. Prosecution, 1989: Vol. 3, 4). Of course, saying that criminals are disproportionately young black and native men who are poor and live in cities begs the question: What exactly does this mean?

---

6   If law enforcement was a scientific experiment instead of a social service, the "data" (i.e., arrest rates) it generates would be rejected because it is invalid and unreliable. However, because it is a social service these deficiences are conveniently overlooked.

7   Of course, this is another example of a "Catch-22": groups who have a reputation for being criminals are targeted by police with the result that some members of the group are caught committting crimes which provides additional evidence that members of this group are criminals.

8   Social scientists refer to this situation as the naturalistic fallacy.

There is compelling evidence that criminal stereotypes *are* biased and distorted. For example, Reiman (1984: 50) notes:

> [T]he Typical Criminal is not the greatest threat to which we are exposed. The acts of the Typical Criminal are not only the acts that endanger us, nor are they the acts that endanger us the most. We have a greater chance *by far* of being killed or disabled by an occupational injury or disease, by unnecessary surgery, by shoddy emergency medical services, and much else, than by aggravated assault or even homicide! Yet even though these threats to our well-being are far graver than that posed by our poor, young, urban, black males, they do not show up in the F.B.I.'s Index of serious crimes! And the individuals who are responsible for them do not turn up in the arrest records or prison statistics.

As well as including many forms of behaviour that pose a less serious threat than many behaviours that are not included, crime rates are distorted because most crimes go unreported (Radizinowicz and King, 1977).

Very simply, stereotypes are unreliable because they are *indiscriminate*; that is, they do not distinguish between individuals. Rather, they assume that if one member of a group has a certain characteristic (i.e., is a criminal) then all members of that group must also possess the same characteristic. Clearly, this is wrong; however, it is much easier for police to unthinkingly pre-judge (i.e., stereotype) than it is to laboriously evaluate (i.e., discriminate) each individual on his or her merits. As a result, people, including police, have a tendency to abdicate responsibility for evaluating people on *their merits* and, instead, judge them on the basis of stereotypes. When stereotypes are used in this way they can be very destructive, but the potential for damage is greatest when police stereotype because police have extraordinary power.

Case Study

On June 7, 1990, in Iqaluit in the North West Territories a 26-year-old Inuk woman, Kitty Nowdluk-Reynolds, was raped and viciously beaten.[9] Ms. Nowdluk-Reynolds' injuries were treated at a local hospital where she was interviewed by two members of the R.C.M.P. Based on the description provided by Ms. Nowdluk-Reynolds, the R.C.M.P. arrested her attacker, Inusiq Shoo, and charged him with aggravated sexual assault. Subsequently, on June 13th, Ms. Nowdluk-Reynolds implemented plans she had made before the attack and moved to Surrey, British Columbia (in suburban

---

9   Royal Canadian Mounted Police Public Complaints Commission Report, *re: Kitty Nowdluk-Reynolds*, 1993.

Vancouver), with her husband. On July 3rd a judge in Iqaluit issued a subpoena requiring Ms. Nowdluk-Reynolds to appear in court in Iqaluit as a material witness at her attacker's preliminary inquiry.

On July 10th the victim was served with a subpoena at her home in Surrey by Constable Anderson of the R.C.M.P. Contrary to Department of Justice practice, Ms. Nowdluk-Reynolds was not provided with a letter instructing her how to obtain travel assistance. In any event, despite encouragement from Corporal Juby of the R.C.M.P. to attend, the victim was not present in court at the preliminary hearing on July 27th and, as a result, a warrant for her arrest as a material witness was issued.

On August 27th Constable Davidson of the R.C.M.P. attended at Ms. Nowdluk-Reynolds' residence, placed her under arrest and advised that she was going to be transported in custody to the N.W.T. to testify against her attacker. The now extremely distraught Ms. Nowdluk-Reynolds was transported in handcuffs to the R.C.M.P. Detachment Surrey where she was lodged in a cell. At the police detachment a social worker, Betty Smith, and a correctional officer, Mr. Mortimer, attempted to calm the victim and inform her of her right to counsel.

On August 29th Ms. Nowdluk-Reynolds was transported to a court in Cloverdale, British Columbia, where she was given clothing, personal effects and allowed to see the duty counsel. Duty counsel promised to investigate the situation and report back. Despite this, Ms. Nowdluk-Reynolds did not receive legal advice from the duty counsel or any other lawyer before appearing in court. In court she was remanded into the custody of Lakeside Correctional Centre.

At Lakeside Correctional Centre Ms. Nowdluk-Reynolds was stripped-searched, de-loused, photographed, fingerprinted and lodged in a cell with other female prisoners.[10] Ms. Nowdluk-Reynolds had no visitors at either the R.C.M.P. Detachment Surrey or at Lakeside Correctional Centre. When her husband, Robert Callaghan, attempted to visit her at Lakeside Correctional Centre he was refused permission because he could not establish a family relationship.[11] At no time while Ms. Nowdluk-Reynolds was at Lakeside Correctional Centre did anyone attempt to explain what was going to happen to her. On September 2nd Ms. Nowdluk-Reynolds was transported in handcuffs from Lakeside Correctional Centre to Vancouver International Airport where she was placed on a flight to Yellowknife with a stop-over in Edmonton.

---

10   This is a standard admissions process for all new inmates and does not imply that the victim's personal hygene was problematic, although, as we will see, her personal hygene does become problematic as a direct result of the actions of the authorities.

11   The victim and her husband were living "common-law" at the time.

In Yellowknife Ms. Nowdluk-Reynolds was lodged in a cell at the local police detachment. Ms. Nowdluk-Reynolds' cell was adjacent to male prisoners and, despite her requests, she was not allowed to shower. The next morning, on September 3, Ms. Nowdluk-Reynolds was scheduled to fly to Iqaluit; however, her police escort, Constable Testo, overslept and, as a result, Ms. Nowdluk-Reynolds missed her flight. Subsequently, on September 3rd, another police officer, Constable Journeay, escorted the victim *sans* handcuffs on a flight from Yellowknife to Ottawa with stopovers in Edmonton and Toronto.[12] In Ottawa, Ms. Nowdluk-Reynolds was lodged overnight in a cell at the city jail.

Finally, on September 4th, Ms. Nowdluk-Reynolds was transported from Ottawa to Iqaluit. At Iqaluit, Ms. Nowdluk-Reynolds was lodged in a cell at the local police detachment until she could be transported to court. Once again her request to be allowed to shower was denied. Ms. Nowdluk-Reynolds was transported to court, along with other inmates, in the rear of a prisoner van. Among the other prisoners was the man, Inusiq Shoo, who sexually assaulted her. Predictably, Ms. Nowdluk-Reynolds became extremely distraught when she was confronted by her attacker.

At the courthouse in Iqaluit, Ms. Nowdluk-Reynolds was interviewed for approximately ten minutes by a Crown Counsel. As a result of this meeting, Ms. Nowdluk-Reynolds understood that she would be testifying at her attacker's trial and that once her testimony was complete she would be allowed to go to her mother's home in Iqaluit.

In court, defence counsel sought a two-day adjournment of the hearing. Crown counsel advised that Ms. Nowdluk-Reynolds was present in court, under arrest, and would only be released once she testified. The judge suggested releasing the victim and adjourned the proceedings until the next day (i.e., September 5th) and, at that time, having Ms. Nowdluk-Reynolds return to court and testify. Ms. Nowdluk-Reynolds "erupted in an emotional and angry outburst" when the judge left the courtroom. Subsequently, she was transported back to a cell at the police detachment where, once again, she was not allowed to shower. After Ms. Nowdluk-Reynolds had left the court, the Crown Counsel, defence counsel and judge agreed to adjourn the matter until the next day and have her testify then. At no time while she was in court in Iqaluit was a lawyer appointed to act on Ms. Nowdluk-Reynolds' behalf notwithstanding that she was charged with a criminal offence and lawyers were present in the courtroom. Also, at no time did anyone from the Crown's office or the police attempt to explain to her what was happening.

---

12 The detour Edmonton-Toronto-Ottawa detour was necessitated when the police officer transporting the victim overslept and missed their flight to Iqaluit. No apology for this incident was offered to the acused.

On September 5th the accused waived his right to a preliminary inquiry and was committed to stand trial at a later date. As a result, the court ordered Ms. Nowdluk-Reynolds' release from custody and withdrew the charges for failing to respond to the subpoena. No one from the police attempted to explain to her what had happened.

Ms. Nowdluk-Reynolds arrived back in Vancouver at 10:30 p.m. on September 5th. Despite the fact she had been assured by the R.C.M.P. in Iqaluit that R.C.M.P. at the Vancouver Airport would arrange transportation to her home, police at the airport were unaware of the arrangements and simply helped her to get on a bus. Before arriving home, Ms. Nowdluk-Reynolds was forced to wait, alone, for 45 minutes at a dark, deserted location to transfer buses.

This case graphically illustrates how matters can go terribly wrong when police[13] exercise discretionary powers. The Commission (ibid., 46) noted that Ms. Nowdluk-Reynolds:

> [W]as taken from her home, placed in handcuffs, jailed for five days and then escorted from Vancouver to Edmonton to Yellowknife, and then back to Edmonton, to Toronto, to Ottawa, and finally to Iqaluit. During this time she was kept in jail cells at RCMP Detachment Surrey, Lakeside Correctional Centre in Burnaby, B.C., RCMP Detachment Yellowknife, Ottawa City Jail, and RCMP Detachment Iqaluit.

Throughout this ordeal, Ms. Nowdluk-Reynolds was denied her constitutional right to retain and instruct counsel and was prevented from practicing basic personal hygiene.[14] In short, she was treated *inhumanely* by the very people sworn "to serve and protect" her.

Ms. Nowdluk-Reynolds was effectively stripped of her freedom, dignity and humanity. Was it simply a coincidence that she was poor, female and coloured or were her race, sex, and socio-economic status the key criteria police used to inform their discretion?[15] The Commission (ibid., 31) that investigated her complaint was unable to determine if Ms. Nowdluk-Reynolds' race was a factor in her treatment at the time of her arrest and did not consider the issue otherwise. Whatever the answer to this question might be, it is clear that police in this case showed:

---

13   This is not to suggest that police were the only irresponsible actors in this case. The Commission (ibid., 44) noted:
    No one in the criminal justice system, inquired as to whether or not she was physically or emotionally capable of fulfilling the obligation imposed by the subpoena, or financially able to make her way from Surrey, British Columbia, to Iqaluit, Northwest Territories. Seemingly, no one cared.
    Nevertheless, it is clear that police were leading actors in this tragedy.
14   Imagine how the victim must have felt when she was "treated" this way. At least one police officer in this case feared that the victim might commit suicide (ibid., 20).
15   The victim (ibid., 30) believed her race influenced her treatment when she was arrested.

- "Poor judgment" when deciding to transport Ms. Nowdluk-Reynolds in the same vehicle as her attacker (ibid., 39);

- "Lack of judgment" when they failed to explain to her the significance of the subpoena (ibid., 24);

- "Lack of consideration" and "conduct ... less than appropriate" when she was given shampoo and a wash cloth and told she could take a "sponge bath" in a basin in her cell and for failing to consider her for release so that she could visit with her family (ibid., 38).

In all of these areas police in this case were required to exercise discretion. By allowing expediency, not responsibility, to dictate their decisions these officers ensured that the victim "was twice a victim (ibid., 44)."

Summary

Ultimately, police *must* have the discretion to decide whether or not to lay a charge. The question is which criteria will police use when enforcing the law, not whether they will use discretion. Very simply, the criteria police use can be classified into four groups: criteria relating to the offence, criteria relating to the offender; criteria relating to the officer, and criteria relating to the setting in which the offence was committed. A few of these criteria, such as the seriousness of the offence and the availability of evidence are appropriate criteria as demonstrated by the fact that they are authorized by law; however, many other criteria police use, such as the sex, race and sexual orientation of the offender, are prohibited by law and therefore should not be used by police.

10 Corruption

Introduction

Canadian police are delegated extraordinary authority to enforce the law. In particular, they are authorized to use discretion to decide when and how to enforce it. Inevitably, some police misuse their authority by using this extraordinary power for their own personal benefit or advantage. When this happens, it is a corruption of police authority.

This chapter analyses police corruption by defining this phenomenon and classifying several scenarios as corrupt or not. Also, the role of "minor perks" in police corruption is considered. This chapter concludes with the analysis of a case in which a police officer used his position to organize and run a pay-for-sex service.

Police Corruption

Corruption is an important issue in policing because it threatens to undermine police moral authority and, by doing so, it attacks the legitimacy of the criminal justice system and the wider social order. Evidence of the importance of police corruption comes from cases like the one described later in this chapter in which the corrupt actions of a police constable nearly forced the resignation of the Chief of Police of the largest municipal police service in Canada. It goes without saying that there are very few organizations where the corrupt behaviour of the least powerful member of the organization could undermine the credibility of the most powerful member.

Black's Law Dictionary (1979: 311) defines "corruption" as "(a)n act done with an intent to give some advantage inconsistent with official duty and the rights of others." The key features of this definition are the ideas that corruption involves an abuse of power to obtain an unauthorized benefit or advantage. It follows that police corruption *occurs when a police officer uses the power of his or her position to obtain a benefit or advantage.* The key features of this definition are the obtaining of "a benefit or advantage" and the use of the power of the police position.

The fact that police corruption is prohibited by law is strong evidence that legislators treat this issue very seriously. For example section 120 of the Criminal Code states:

120. Everyone who

(a)   being a justice, police commissioner, peace officer, public officer or officer of a juvenile court, or being employed in the administration of criminal law, corruptly

    i.   accepts or obtains,

    ii.   agrees to accept, or

    iii. attempts to obtain, for himself or any other person any money, valuable consideration, office, place or employment with intent

    iv. to interfere with the administration of justice,

    v.   to procure or facilitate the commission of an offence, or

    vi. to protect from detection or punishment a person who has committed or who intends to commit an offence, or

(b)   gives or offers, corruptly, to a person mentioned in paragraph (a) any money, valuable consideration, office, place or employment with intent that the person should do anything mentioned in subparagraph (a)(iv) or (vi),

is guilty of an indictable offence and liable to imprisonment for a term not exceeding fourteen years.

This section creates indictable offences for police officers and others who corrupt their authority by accepting bribes and for anyone who bribes a police officer or anyone else mentioned in the section. Note that the section only applies to those individuals who exercise extraordinary authority and obtain or attempt to obtain a benefit or advantage for themself or another. As well, all federal and provincial laws that authorize the formation of police services provide punishments for police corruption.

Following are three scenarios (Table 10.1) that will help to clarify what constitutes police corruption. [1] Scenario A is a clear example of police corruption. The two key factors in this scenario are the police officer's decision to accept the "bribe" (i.e., a benefit or advantage) and the implicit understanding that the bribe was offered to influence the officer's discretion (i.e., the power to charge the driver). It would make no difference if the

---

1   Read each scenario, decide whether it is an example of police corruption and justify your answer.

police officer accepted the bribe *and* charged the driver, since the only reason the bribe was offered was to influence the police officer's discretion — the driver would not have made the offer if she thought she would still be charged. Similarly, it makes no difference that the police officer did not solicit the bribe, since the driver's offer was *contingent* on the police officer being in a position to help her — the driver would not have offered the bribe to just anyone who stopped her car. To avoid being corrupted, the police officer in this example should have refused the bribe and then used his or her discretion to decide the appropriate charges, which could include speeding and bribery (section 120 (b) C.C.C.).

Table 10.1
Police Corruption Scenarios

Scenario A	Scenario B	Scenario C
A police officer stops a driver for speeding and asks to see her documents. When she gives the officer the documents there is a $100 bill tucked inside. When the officer shows her the money and offers to return it, she says, "No, that's okay, you keep it." The officer keeps the money and lets the driver go with only a warning.	A police officer stops at a donut shop to order a coffee and donuts. When the officer offers to pay, the waiter pushes the officer's money back across the counter and says, "No, its free for you you." The officer accepts the free refreshments and leaves without paying.	While conducting a routine investigation into a "Break and Enter" at the home of an elderly couple, a police officer is offered "refreshments" (i.e., coffee and donuts). The officer accepts the refreshments and then continues her work as before.

At first glance scenario B may not appear to be an example of police corruption. However, a more thorough analysis reveals that it is. In this case, the police officer accepts the refreshments [2] (i.e., a benefit or advantage) with no apparent obligation (i.e., there appears to be no expectation to use the power of his or her position for the benefit of the proprietor). However, as we will see below, it can be demonstrated that the restaurant proprietor's offer of the "perk" is based on the expectation that he or she will benefit from the power of the police officer's position.

---

2   Note that the value of the benefit is irrelevant. The issue is: Was the benefit offered/accepted for the purpose of influencing the police officer's discretion (i.e., power)?

Consider two donut shops operating a short distance from one another and a nearby police station that has a total complement of 100 police officers (Figure 10.1). Assume that" donut shop A, like many fast-food businesses, has a "free coffee and donuts" policy for "emergency service workers" (i.e., police, ambulance attendants and firefighters) and donut shop B does not.[3] Also, assume that all of the police at this hypothetical police station, "buy" their coffee and donuts at donut shop A and never at donut shop B. As well, for the purposes of this example, we will assume that each officer buys one serving of coffee and donuts every day and each serving has a wholesale value of 10¢. Thus, over the course of a year, the police in our example will consume approximately $3,650 worth of free coffee and donuts!

Figure 10.1
Police Station Proximity to Potential Sources of Corruption

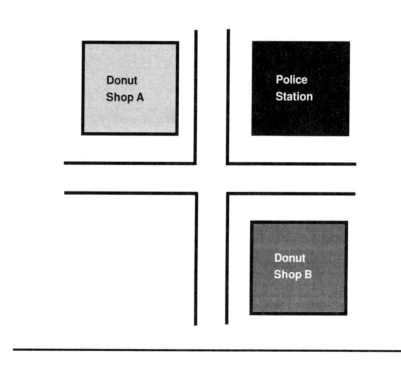

---

3   Most police consider these "freebies" to be "perks" of being a police officer similar to the perks business people enjoy.

Frequent and irregular visits by police to donut shop A will produce several collateral effects. [4] First, a variety of "undesireable" individuals such as criminals (eg., robbers) and disruptive patrons will be less likely to patronize donut shop A because of the intermittent and unpredictable presence of police there. Second, when these individuals begin to patronize donut shop B other customers, especially families, will switch their patronage to donut shop A because it is a seen to be a safer environment. Clearly, this will put donut shop B at a competitive disadvantage vis à vis donut shop A. To remain competitive, eventually donut shop B will be forced to offer police free refreshments.

In theory, donut shop B pays the same taxes as donut shop A and therefore is entitled to the same level of police service. However, in practice, if donut shop A but not B has a free refreshments policy for police, then donut shop A will receive premium police service while donut shop B receives merely ordinary police service. In effect, for the price of a cup of coffee and a donut, donut shop A receives the equivalent of a full-time police presence — a $50,000 per year value. This analysis explains why most fast-food restaurants and many businesses offer police free or deeply discounted goods and services. Very simply, businesses that do not participate in this informal arrangement have difficulty competing.

Significantly, the "perks" offered by fast-food resaurants are available only to emergency service workers (i.e., those with special powers) such as police. For example, if an off-duty and out-of-uniform police officer ordered coffee and donuts in donut shop A, then he or she would be required to pay. This demonstrates that the benefit is offered to influence police authority and not because the proprietor has altruistic intentions. In short, the perk is intended to finesse police into using their extraordinary power to the benefit of the proprietor — making this a *prima facie* case of police corruption.

Obviously, this example is an over-simplification. Nevertheless, it clearly demonstrates that police power has a *real* effect even when it is latent in a transaction (Shearing and Leon, 1973). Also, this example demonstrates how the actions of a single police officer can combine with the similar actions of many colleagues to produce a result that is entirely out of proportion to any single individual's actions — the whole of police power is greater than the sum of its parts. Police organizations are often insensitive to this fact and, as a result, occasionally they collude in the corruption of their own officers. For example, most large police associations publish newsletters that advertise "discounts" for police.

---

4   These effects are unintended by police perhaps but clearly they are intended and desired by proprietors who offer police and other emergency workers these "perks".

Finally, scenario C is *not* an example of police corruption. It can be distinguished from scenario B, which it closely resembles, by the fact that the police officer did not use the power of her position to obtain the refreshments (i.e., benefit or advantage). For example, it is customary in many cultures to offer a guest a refreshment — indeed to fail to do so may be considered rude. Similarly, a guest who refuses a refreshment may be considered impolite. This is true whether the guest is a police officer or a neighbour. Since the police officer's powerful position is not the reason the refreshments are offered, it is not corrupt for the officer to accept them. If, however, the elderly couple made it known that they expected preferential treatment in exchange for the refreshements and the police officer accepted, then this would also be an example of police corruption.

A comparison of scenarios B and C reveals that the value of the benefit or advantage that is offered/accepted is irrelevant when determining whether an act is corrupt. Similarly, the person's intent in offering the bribe to a police officer is irrelevant when determining whether or not it is a corrupt act. As noted at the outset of this discussion, the only issues that are relevant when considering whether a police officer's actions are corrupt are — Did the officer use the power of his or her position? Did the officer obtain a personal benefit or advantage? If these conditions are satisfied then the behaviour is corrupt.

Another example of low-level, less serious police corruption are the free rides offered to police by many public transit services. Obviously, police benefit from this practice because they literally "ride free." Similarly, transit companies benefit because an intermittent police presence in their place of business increases the safety of their service and attracts customers. The losers in this arrangement are the taxi cab companies that pay equal taxes but do not receive equal police services.

Most police would reject an obvious "bribe." However, because the bribes in the examples described above are disguised as "perks" and distributed in relatively small amounts among large numbers of police, many police accept them. As a result, low-level, less serious police corruption is widespread. This makes it difficult for police recruits to resist these forms of corruption with the result that many are quickly indoctrinated in the corrupt practices of their more experienced colleagues. Those who refuse to participate risk being ostracized by their colleagues. This problem would not be so serious if it ended with just free coffee and donuts and free rides on subways and buses, but sometimes it does not.

Sherman (1981: 323) has argued that police "graft" (i.e., corruption) is a continuum that begins with "minor perks," proceeds to "bribes" for regulatory offences such as traffic enforcement, and ends with "pay-offs" for narcotics offences. If this is correct, then "minor perks" like free coffee and donuts is just the first step in a process that can lead to much more serious forms of corruption such as bribes and pay-offs. In short, the acceptance and toleration of low-level, less serious forms of police corruption results in an enabling environment in which more serious forms of corruption can flourish. Whether or not more serious forms of police corruption will occur depends on a variety of factors that includes a police officer's morals and ethics (ibid., 322).

Typically, the more opportunities police have to commit corrupt acts, the more corruption there will be in a police organization. Stated differently, the level of corruption in a police organization is inversely correlated with the risk of individual police officers being caught (i.e., the "opportunity") committing a corrupt act so that as the risk of being caught increases the level of police corruption decreases and vice versa, assuming that all other factors are constant (Figure 10.2). This suggests that an effective strategy for reducing police corruption is to increase the risk that corrupt police will be caught and punished. For this purpose all large police organizations maintain an internal unit that is responsible for investigating police deviance and corruption (see Chapter 11).

Figure 10.2
The Risk of Being Caught Committing a Corrupt Act Versus the Level of Corruption in a Police Organization

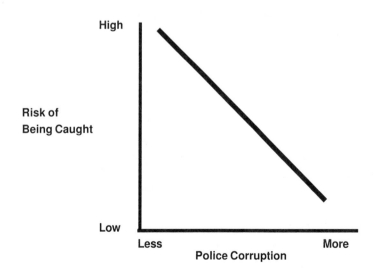

Typically, the risk of police being caught committing a corrupt act is inversely correlated with the strength of the Code of Silence (see Chapter 12) in a police organization, so that, as the Code of Silence gets stronger, the risk of getting caught decreases, and vice versa, if all other factors are held constant (Figure 10.3). This suggests that police corruption could be reduced by weakening the Code of Silence and, as a result, increasing the risk that police would be caught committing corrupt acts. This however, ignores other factors that may, and usually do, influence police corruption.

Figure 10.3
Strength of the Code of Silence Versus Level of Police Corruption

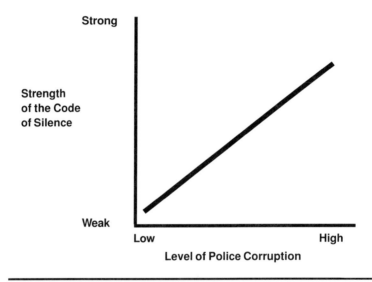

Typically, police corruption is positively correlated with the "incentive"[5] (i.e., greed) for committing a corrupt act, so that as the incentive increases the level of corruption in a police organization increases also and vice versa, assuming that all other factors are held constant (Figure 10.4). This suggests that police corruption can be reduced by decreasing the incentive police officers have for committing corrupt acts. Since incentive is determined by the levels of "graft" that are available in a community minus the level of police compensation (i.e., salaries and benefits), this suggests that one way to decrease the incentives for police to commit corrupt acts is to increase

5   The incentive for committing a corrupt act equals the graft that is available minus the police officer's salary and benefits.

police salaries and benefits to a point where they exceed the graft that is available. This, however, ignores the large sums of money that are available from the traffic in illicit drugs. It appears unlikely that police corruption can be controlled by increasing police compensation in jurisdictions where graft is available from the traffic in illicit drugs.

Figure 10.4
Incentive for Police to Be Corrupt Versus the Level of Corruption in a Police Organization

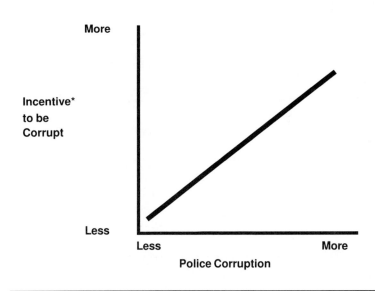

*   Incentive = Graft - Police Salaries and Benefits

Perhaps most importantly, police corruption is negatively correlated with police moral authority — so that as police corruption increases, police moral authority decreases and vice versa, assuming that all other factors are held constant (Figure 10.5). This suggests that police corruption is a serious threat to the status quo. If police corruption is allowed to flourish, in time it will undermine police moral authority so that police will be required to rely more heavily on their legal authority. As we saw in Chapter 7, at its most basic level, police legal authority is the power to use force. Consequently, when police are forced to rely on their legal authority, they inevitably alienate those parts of the community exposed to their use of force. For this reason police organizations prohibit and punish a wide range of behaviours that can be loosely described as corruption.

Figure 10.5
Police Moral Authority Versus the Level of Police Corruption

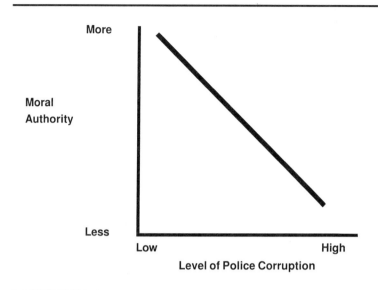

Given the potentially devastating effects of police corruption, one might assume that police organizations go to extraordinary lengths to prevent police corruption. However, as we saw in Chapter 5 (Selection), the police selection process does not systematically select the spiritual skills police need to resist being corrupted. Similarly, as we saw in Chapter 6 (Training), less than one percent (i.e., 3 hours) of police basic training is devoted to training police in the ethics they need to resist being corrupted. Clearly, police organizations could and should to do more in this important area.

The following case study illustrates how a single corrupt police officer can undermine the moral authority of an entire police organization.

Case Study

In 1989 Constable Gordon Junger of the Metropolitan Toronto Police Service (M.T.P.S.) formed an "association" with a prostitute, Roma Langford. In the spring of that year, the two began living together at Langford's residence. In July, the M.T.P.S. Internal Affairs Unit received a report that the couple were cohabiting. In the fall of that year the couple started a pay-for-sex "escort agency" and began advertising for customers and employees in a local publication.

In December 1989 Langford contacted Internal Affairs and advised them that Junger was engaging in discreditable conduct and dereliction of duty that included possession of narcotics and use of the police computer system (C.P.I.C.) to check out prospective employees of the escort service. Subsequently, with Langford's co-operation, investigators from Internal Affairs set up a videotaped "sting" operation. Junger attended a meeting in a hotel room with an undercover police officer who offered to purchase his sexual services. Junger was subsequently arrested when he accepted the undercover police officer's offer. A search of Junger's residence revealed a small quantity of hashish. He was charged with possession of a narcotic.

Subsequently, a secret agreement was reached between Junger and the M.T.P.S. that stipulated the following conditions:

- Junger would resign from the police service;
- All charges would be withdrawn;
- All physical evidence relating to the investigation would be destroyed;
- The M.T.P.S. would provide a non-derogatory letter of reference.

This case is a clear example of police corruption. Junger used the power of his position as a police officer to obtain a variety of benefits and advantages for himself and his partner. For example, Junger used his privileged access to a confidential police computer system to obtain information he wanted to evaluate prospective employees for his company.

Perhaps the most interesting feature of this case occurred when the "secret" agreement between Junger and the M.T.P.S. became public. When this happened, the Ontario Civilian Commission on Police Services appointed a panel to conduct an inquiry into the incident. The panel (1992: 8) concluded:

> [I]f the Chief of Police ... had responded vigorously and openly when he discovered the full details of the Junger resignation agreement, instead of keeping them confidential, the reaction to this whole matter would have been different ... [as well] ... [h]ad the force been less defensive and the Board less complacent at the outset, the public would have been assured that the issues were being addressed.

The emphasis on secrecy in this case was a tacit admission by police that they appreciate the serious threat to their moral authority represented by police corruption. Ironically, police efforts to protect their moral authority undermined police moral authority in this case.

Summary

By threatening to undermine police moral authority, police corruption represents a serious threat to the status quo. As a result, police organizations attempt to prevent corruption by prohibiting and punishing a variety of behaviours and, in particular, by prohibiting police from accepting gratuities. Despite this, police routinely accept gratuities in the form of free meals and services. Consequently, low-level, less serious corruption is widespread in Canadian police organizations. The pervasiveness of these forms of corruption creates an enabling environment in which more serious forms of corruption can flourish. Whether police corruption does flourish depends on a variety of factors that include the strength of the Code of Silence in an organization, the incentive to commit a corrupt act, the opportunity to commit a corrupt act, the risk of being caught committing a corrupt act, and a police officer's personal ethics and morals.

11 Accountability

Introduction

Canadian police are delegated extraordinary authority to enforce the law. Occassionally, police misuse this power and by doing so corrupt their authority. When this happens there is need for a process to hold police responsible for the consequences of their actions. This process is known as police accountability.

This chapter analyses police accountability by classifying the various processes used to hold police accountable according to "locality" and "formality." Also, the full range of formal processes that are used to hold police accountable are identified and described. This chapter concludes with the analysis of a case in which a police constable was found guilty of misconduct and forced to resign by a civilian review process.

Police Accountability

"Who will watch the watcher?" This is the perennial question associated with the use of para-miltary mercenary (i.e., public) police. You will recall from Chapter 2 (History of Policing) that prior to the Industrial Revolution police were part-time volunteers who, when they were not acting as police, were ordinary citizens with ordinary powers; that is, farmers. As long as "the police were the public and the public were the police," accountability was not an issue. However, once Peel created a full-time mercenary public police with extraordinary powers, police accountability became an important issue. Over the ensuing two hundred years a variety of processes have been developed to make police accountable. As a result, today we have an *ad hoc* system of police accountability that, as we will see, is both complicated and prone to conflict.

The Oxford English Dictionary (1990: 9) defines "accountable" as "responsible; required to account for one's conduct." Very simply, to be accountable is to be responsible for the consequences of one's actions. It follows that police accountability means *the process by which police are held responsible for the consequences of their actions*. A key feature of this definition is the idea that actions produce consequences and someone *must* logically be responsible for these consequences. It follows that if an individual exercises extraordinary power, his or her actions can produce extraordinary results and, therefore, he or she must be extraordinarily accountable. As we will see below, Canadian police *are* extraordinarily accountable.

The extraordinary power police exercise is a privilege not a right. This can be demonstrated by simply noting that police who misuse and corrupt their authority can be compelled to resign. Despite this, some police behave as if their extraordinary power is a right, not a privilege. Evidence of this is seen in the way some police react when their authority is challenged. For example, it is an unwritten rule in the police subculture that a person who resists arrest by attempting to flee on foot or in an automobile may be beaten when captured in order to "teach" the person a "lesson." The Rodney King beating by members of the Los Angeles police following a lengthy automobile pursuit was a vivid demonstration of this "rule."

When police view their extraordinary power as a right and not as a privilege, they may resent and resist attempts to hold them accountable. An example of police resistance to accountability is the informal and unwritten rule in the police subculture that when accused of wrong-doing, one should "look concerned, act surprised, and deny everything!" An example of police resentment of accountability, as discussed in the case study at the end of this chapter, occurred when members of the Metropolitan Toronto Police Association "worked to rule" by refusing to issue traffic tickets in 1984 to protest the implementation of a civilian review process of police behaviour. However, it would be wrong to attribute the widespread police dissatisfaction with the accountability process to immaturity by saying that police simply "threw a temper tantrum" in this instance when they did not get their way. Most police accept that accountability is necessary, even desirable. For instance, the panel struck by the Ontario Civilian Commission on Police Services (1992: 4) noted:

> [P]eople ... must have confidence in the integrity of their police. Police officers occupy a position of trust. They have authority and responsibilities beyond those of a private citizen ... Those who are responsible for the quality of policing must be accountable to the public. Our whole system is predicated on accountability ...

The real question then is not *whether* police should be accountable, but *how* they should be accountable.

Police accountability processes can be classified according to two factors, "locality" and "formality" (Table 11.1). Formality describes the form of the accountability process — systematic and structured processes are *formal* and unsystematic and unstructured processes are *informal*. Locality describes the locus of administrative control of the accountability process — processes administered by the police bureaucacy are *internal* and processes administered by non-police bureaucracies are *external*. Criminal law is an example of a formal/external accountability process because criminal procedure is specified in the Criminal Code and adminstered by an independent judiciary. Print and electronic media are examples of informal/external accountability processes because there is no systematic and structured procedure for the media to hold police accountable, and these processes are administered by the media. Police disciplinary proceedings are examples of internal/formal accountability processes because these procedures are specified in the statutes that authorize police services such as Part V of the *Police Services Act*[1] in Ontario, and they are administered by police bureacracies. The police subculture is an example of an informal/internal accountability process because there are no systematic and structured procedures for police to hold their peers accountable, and the process is administered by the police rank and file. Special cases are *hybrid* processes like the Public Complaints process specified in Part VI of the *Police Services Act*[2] of Ontario. This process has elements of both an internal and external review of police actions. For example, this process allows both civilian and police participation in the investigation and adjudication of public complaints.

Table 11.1

Police Accountability Processes Classified According to Formality and Locality

	Formal	Informal
Internal	Disciplinary Proceedings	Police Subculture
External	Criminal Code	Media

---

1   R.S.O. 1990, c. p. 15.
2   ibid.

While there are some inter-provincial variations and differences between the provinces and the federal government, typically there are seven formal ways that Canadian police can be held accountable for their actions (Table 11.2). For example, Canadian criminal law provides that everyone[3] in Canada who commits a criminal offence can be prosecuted for the offence. If, after a public trial at which "hearsay"[4] evidence is inadmissible, it can be demonstrated that a person is guilty "beyond a reasonable doubt" (Figure 11.1c), then the person can be convicted and, depending on the offence, sentenced to two, but not more, of the following punishments: the imposition of a fine, a term of imprisonment or a term of community supervision. As well, the court can order the person to pay the victim "restitution."[5] In this respect, Canadian police are accountable to a formal, independently administered criminal law process in the same way as other Canadian citizens.

Another way Canadian police can be held accountable for their actions is by a constitutional process. For example, Canadian courts are authorized by the Charter of Rights and Freedoms to issue writs, such as *habeas corpus*,[6] that require government employees generally, and police more particularly, to justify their actions. If, after hearing evidence that may include hearsay, the court is satisfied on a "balance of probabilities" that police actions were not justified, the court can remedy the situation by ordering the police to release someone who has been "wrongfully imprisoned," for example. In this respect, Canadian police are accountable to a formal, independently administered constitutional law process in the same way as other employees of the municipal, provincial and federal governments.

Yet another way Canadian police can be held accountable for their actions is by a civil process.[7] For example, civil courts[8] in Canada are authorized by common law to determine whether a "tort"[9] such as "wrongful

---

3 The only exceptions are foreign diplomats and their families and children under 12 years of age.
4 Black's Law Dictionary (1978: 649) defines "hearsay" as "(e)vidence not proceeding from the personal knowledge of the witness, but from the mere repetition of what he has heard others say." Generally, "hearsay" is not admissible as evidence at a criminal trial; however, there are several exceptions to this rule.
5 Black's Law Dictionary (1978: 1180) defines "restitution" as "the act of making good or giving equivalent for any loss, damage or injury."
6 Black's Law Dictionary (1978: 638) defines *habeas corpus* as "(a) writ directed to the person detaining another, and commanding him to produce the body of the prisoner, or person detained."
7 Note that Quebec's civil law is based on the Napoleonic Code, whereas, elsewhere in Canada, civil law is based on English common law.
8 This is true everywhere in Canada except Quebec where common law based on the French Napoleonic Code is still the practice in non-criminal matters.
9 Black's Law Dictionary (1978: 1335) defines "tort" as "(a) private or civil wrong or injury, other than breach of contract, for which the court will provide a remedy in the form of an action for damages."

Table 11.2

Formal Police Accountability Processes

Process	Criminal Law	Police Disciplinary Proceedings[1]	Public Complaints Law[2]	Human Rights Laws[3]	Charter of Rights and Freedoms	Civil Law	Government Inquiries
Source	federal	provincial	provincial	provincial/ federal	constitutional	common law	federal and provincial
Form of Process	1) accusatory— adversarial	1) conciliatory 2) accusatory— adversarial	1) conciliatory 2) accusatory— adversarial	1) conciliatory 2) accusatory— adversarial	1) adversarial	1) adversarial	1) inquisitory
Burden of Proof	"beyond a reasonable doubt"	"clear and convincing evidence"	"clear and convincing evidence"	"balance of probabilities"	"balance of probabilities"	"balance of probabilities"	not applicable
Remedies	1) punitive (fines, imprisonment, community supervision) 2) restorative	1) punitive (fines, dismissal, demotion, reprimand)	1) punitive (fines, demotion, dismissal, reprimand)	1) compensatory 2) remedial 3) restorative	1) remedial— has the force of law	1) compensatory 2) punative— damages only	1) remedial— does not have the force of law
Rules of Evidence	hearsay inadmissible	hearsay admissible	hearsay admissible	hearsay admissible	hearsay admissible	hearsay inadmissible	hearsay admissible
Applicability	all members of the public	police only	police only	employment, housing, services, contracts, unions and professional associations	government employees only	all members of the public	all members of the public
Form of Hearing	public	public	public	public	public	public	public

NOTE: Restitutive means the remedy provides for financial compensation to be paid to the complainant. Remedial means the remedy provides a mechanism for correcting the conditions which lead to the tort. Punitive means the remedy provides for a financial penalty (i.e., fine) or other form of penalty to punish the offender..

1   This example is based on the provisions of Part V of the *Police Services Act*, R.S.O. 1990, c. P. 15. Readers interested in similar provisions in other provinces, territories or at the federal level should consult the relevant statutes.

2   This example is based on the provisions of Part VI of the *Police Services Act*, R.S.O. 1990, c. P. 15. Readers interested in similar provisions in other provinces, territories or at the federal level should consult the relevant statutes.

3   This example is based on the provisions of the Human Rights Code. Readers interested in similar provisions in other provinces, territories or at the federal level should consult the relevant statutes.

imprisonment" has occurred and to compensate a plaintiff who has sustained damages as a result of the malicious or negligent actions of a defendant, such as a police officer. If, after hearing evidence that may not include hearsay, the court is satisfied on a "balance of probabilities" that the police committed a tort, then the court may order the police to compensate the paintiff for his or her injuries. As well, a civil court can award punative damages to the plaintiff. In this respect, Canadian police are accountable to a formal, independently administered civil law process in the same way as other Canadian citizens.

A fourth way Canadian police can be held accountable for their actions is by an "administrative process" such as a human rights action. For example, the Human Rights Commission in Ontario is authorized by provincial law to appoint a "board of inquiry" to determine if a violation of the *Human Rights Code*[10] has occurred. If, after hearing evidence that *may* include hearsay, the board of inquiry is satisfied on a "balance of probabilities" (Figure 11.1a) that the police denied a person their human rights, then the board may order the police to do one or more of the following: take whatever actions are necessary to restore the victim to his or her original position, compensate the victim for the infringement of the victim's rights, or engage in a remedial process designed to prevent the reoccurrence of the problem. In this respect, Canadian police are accountable to formal, independently administered human rights law process in the same way as other agencies that offer "services" to the public.

A fifth way Canadian police can be held accountable for their actions is by another "administrative process" such as a government inquiry or commission. For example, both federal and provincial law authorize the appointment of a commission or inquiry to investigate matters affecting the public interest. Recent examples of these types of administrative processes were the *Aboriginal Justice Inquiry of Manitoba* and the *Royal Commission on the Donald Marshall, Jr., Prosecution.* After hearing evidence that may include hearsay, a commission or inquiry can "recommend" changes to the government.[11] In this respect, Canadian police are accountable to formal, independently administered inquiries in the same way as other Canadian citizens.

---

10 R.S.O. 1981, c. 53.
11 Inquiry recommendations do not have the force of law.

Figure 11.1 a, b and c
Misconduct Assessment Criteria

(a)

On a Balance of Probabilities

(b)

Clear and Convincing Evidence

(c)

Beyond a Reasonable Doubt

A sixth way Canadian police can be held accountable for their actions is by yet another "administrative process" such as the "disciplinary proceedings" set out in *Part V* of the *Police Services Act*[12] in Ontario. This process authorizes a Chief of Police in Ontario to investigate and "hold a hearing to determine whether a police officer ... is guilty of misconduct." If, after a public hearing that may include hearsay evidence, misconduct is proved on "clear and convincing evidence" (Figure 11.1b),[13] the Chief may impose any of the following punishments: dismissal, demotion, suspension, fine or reprimand. In this respect, police in Ontario are accountable to a formal, internally administered review process that is similar to the accountability that exists among self-regulating professionals such as doctors, lawyers and accountants.[14]

The seventh, and final, way in which Canadian police can be held accountable for their actions is by an "administrative process" such as the "public complaints" process set out in Part VI of the *Police Services Act*[15] in Ontario. This process authorizes the Police Complaints Commissioner to conduct an investigation and "order a hearing by a board of inquiry if he or she believes it to be necessary in the public interest." If, after a public hearing that may include hearsay evidence, misconduct is proved on "clear and convincing evidence," the board of inquiry may impose any of the following punishments: dismissal, demotion, suspension, fine or reprimand. In this respect, Ontario police are accountable to a formal, quasi-independent review process that has no equivalent in other areas of Canadian society.

The most notable feature of the system of police accountability in Canada is that, typically, it is an *ad hoc* system — a patchwork quilt that has been improvised as circumstances demanded. As a result, in some jurisdictions police can be held accountable to seven different processes. The sheer complexity of this "system" is enough to invite criticism; however, it should also be noted that ordinary Canadian citizens are accountable to at least three of these processes and government employees are accountable to five of these processes unless they belong to a self-regulating profession

12　R.S.O. 1990, c. P. 15.
13　Black's Law Dictionary (1978: 227) defines "clear and convincing proof" as "(t)hat measure or degree of proof which will produce in mind of trier of facts a firm belief or conviction as to allegations sought to be established; it is intermediate, being more than mere preponderance, but not to the extent of such certainty as is required beyond reasonable doubt as in criminal cases."
14　Technically, police disciplinary proceedings *are not* a "peer review" process because the principal actors are not peers (i.e., the Chief or his or her designate is not the same rank as a constable). Despite this, police disciplinary proceedings resemble the peer review process in self-regulating professions to the extent that they are administered by police practitioners.
15　R.S.O. 1990, c. P. 15.

such as medicine or law, in which case they are accountable to six of these or similar processes. Only police, however, are accountable to an additional, formal, quasi-independent review process (i.e., public complaints).

Clearly, Canadian police are extraordinarily accountable. The question is: Do police powers justify this extraordinary accountability? As noted at the beginning of this chapter, Canadian police exercise extraordinary authority including the power to use lethal force — no other group in Canadian society has this power. Obviously, this extraordinary police power justifies their extraordinary accountabilty. What is less obvious is why the present system of police accountability is so complicated. Surely, the current system could be streamlined and simplified without compromising the extraordinary level of accountability Canadians expect of their police.

Case Study

On February 15, 1984, Constables Terry Weller and Derek Cregeen attended at a drug store in response to a report that a man had attempted to purchase goods with a stolen credit card. Upon their arrival the officers found Robert Neely in the custody of store security officers. There was considerable disagreement about what happened next.

Neely alleged that when the police arrived they escorted him into a security room and closed the door. Once inside, Constable Weller asked Neely his name, which he refused to answer. According to Neely, at this point, Constable Weller stated, "We can do this the hard way or the easy way" and then grabbed Neely by the lapels of his jacket and kneed him in the groin. Allegedly, Constable Weller then punched Neely in the abdominal area twice and threw him to the floor with a twisting motion so that Neely fell to his left and then onto his back. Finally, according to Neely, Constable Weller lifted his right boot and brought it down on Neely's left ribs twice. Constable Weller denied using any force whatsoever on Neely and suggested that his injuries must have been sustained during a scuffle he had with the store security officers prior to the arrival of police.

Whatever their origin, Neely sustained the following injuries: a ruptured testicle; torn ligaments in three areas of his left knee; clinically observable tenderness in the right upper side of his abdomen and over the lower ribs. Neely was hospitalized for twelve days as a result of his injuries (*Toronto Star*, January 29, 1988: A17).

In finding Constable Weller guilty of "misconduct" (i.e., assault), the Board of Inquiry [16] directed him to resign and noted that based on the testimony of the store security officers and the two medical practitioners who treated Neely, they were led (ibid., 24) "to the irresistible conclusion that the injuries were caused by Constable Weller in the security office as alleged by Mr. Neely." Constable Weller's repeated attempts to appeal the Police Complaint Board's decision were unsuccessful.

To protest Constable Weller's forced resignation and the Police Complaints Board's authority, the Metropolitan Toronto Police Association initiated a twelve-day job action during which association members refused to issue traffic tickets (*Toronto Star*, January 29, 1988: A17). This conflict was not resolved until the Chief of Police, Jack Marks, met with association members and, in an unreported agreement, agreed to re-employ Constable Weller as a civilian member of the police service. Also, in an apparent belief that a criminal court would exonerate Constable Weller, a member of the police association charged him with assault. However, the criminal proceedings were stayed by the Attorney General, Ian Scott, when it was revealed that the police officer who laid the charge did not have reasonable and probable grounds to believe that Constable Weller had committed the offence (*Globe and Mail*, April 22, 1988: D12).

This case demonstrates several important features of the present system of police accountability. First, the system may give rise to the perception that police are placed in "double jeopardy" (Hamilton and Shilton, 1992: 68) because they can be held accountable in several different ways. Second, because each form of police accountability has a different set of "rules" and "procedures" (i.e., a different burden of proof), it creates the possibility the processes will conflict and yield contradictory results. For example, if Constable Weller had been tried and acquitted by a criminal court after he had been found guilty by the Board of Inquiry and forced to resign, it would have created the appearance that the police complaints process is arbitrary and unfair. [17] Finally, the reaction of the police association and the Chief of

---

16 *Neely* v. *P.C. Weller* (October 15, 1985) (Metropolitan Toronto Police Complaints Board of Inquiry).

17 Clearly, this was the police association's strategy when they had Constable Weller charged with criminal assault (*Toronto Star*, Feb. 2, 1988: A7). This possibility existed because at the time the burden of proof in the Police Complaints process was "on a balance of probabilities" whereas the burden of proof in a criminal trial is the more difficult "beyond a reasonable doubt." Consequently, it was possible that a police officer could be found guilty by one process and acquitted by the other on the basis of similar facts. An attempt was made to remedy this situation by raising the burden of proof in the Police Complaints process to "clear and convincing" evidence; however, this standard is still lower than "beyond a reasonable doubt." As a result, the same problem could still arise.

Police in this case demonstrates that the ways in which police are held accountable is one of the most contentious, if not important, issues in policing.

Summary

Canadian police have been delegated extraordinary powers to enforce the law. Occasionally, police misuse this power and, by doing so, corrupt their authority. When this happens it is necessary to hold police responsible for the consequences of their actions. For this purpose, each Canadian province and territory has a system of police accountability that is a combination of formal and informal and internal and external processes. The formal police accountability system is characterized by an ad hoc design, complexity, conflict and, in some cases, an extraordinary level of police accountability. This extraordinary accountability is justified by the extraordinary power police exercise. What is *not* justified is the unecessary complexity of the present police accountability system

12 Secrecy

Introduction

The heavy emphasis on police accountability and the relatively severe consequences for police misconduct ensure that the police subculture places a high priority on secrecy. Similarly, the threat posed by criminals who learn police law enforcement strategies ensures that police organizations also place a high priority on secrecy.

This chapter analyses police secrecy by identifying two major types, the official "oath of secrecy" and the unofficial "code of silence." [1] Also, the relationship between the code of silence and factors such as corruption and penalties for violating the code are discussed. This chapter concludes with the analysis of a case in which four police officers were sentenced to jail and another was forced to resign when one of them broke the code of silence.

Official Secrecy

Police organizations fear that if criminals learn their law enforcement strategies they may lose the war on crime. As a result, police organizations, like military organizations, maintain strict rules to keep their "secrets." The Oxford English Dictionary (1991: 1092) defines "secret" as "kept or meant to be kept private, unknown, or hidden from all but a few." It follows that police secrets are formal, official police information that is withheld from the public. A key feature of this definition is the idea that secrecy is a formality and is official policy in police organizations. That is, police organizations have written rules and regulations that authorize secrecy. This

---

1   A variety of terms, including "code of silence" (Barker and Roebuck, 1973), "rule of silence" (Westley, 1970), and "secretive" (Vincent, 1990), have been used to describe the police subculture's emphasis on secrecy. In this discussion we will follow Barker and Roebuck's example.

is important because it means that police organizations authorize police to withhold information from the public. As we will see below in the discussion of unofficial secrecy, this has important implications for honesty in the police subculture.

A perennial problem faced by police organizations is, "How to keep classified information secret?" Police organizations have developed a few simple, yet effective, strategies to accomplish this goal. One key strategy is to require all new members to swear an "oath of secrecy." A typical police oath of secrecy is contained in the regulations of the *Police Services Act* [2] of Ontario:

> I solemnly swear (affirm) that I will not disclose any information obtained by me in the course of my duties as a police constable, except as I may be authorized or required by law.

A key feature of this oath is that it makes no distinction between "classified" and "unclassified" information. In effect, all police information is classified, and, therefore, secret. For example, all information obtained from the Canadian Police Information Computer (C.P.I.C.) and all findings of ongoing investigations are classified information. The tendency police organizations have to classify all information as secret aggravates the problem of how to keep information secret. When "leaks" occur, as they inevitably do, police organizations respond by aggressively enforcing the rules they have for maintaining the confidentiality of police information.

All police organizations maintain rules and regulations that prohibit police officers from disclosing police information to the public. For example, the *Police Services Act* [3] of Ontario provides that:

> **108**. (2) A person shall preserve secrecy in respect of all information obtained in the course of his or her duties and not contained in a record as defined in the *Freedom of Information and Protection of Privacy Act*, and shall not communicate such information to any other person ...
>
> **111**. A person who contravenes ... subsection 108(2) (confidentiality) is guilty of an offence ...

These sections create an offence for members of police organizations who communicate police information to another person. The intention of this section is to punish police officers who divulge police information to the public. Naturally, this has important implications for how police behave.

---

2   R.S.O. 1990, c. P.15, Reg. 144/91, s.4.

3   Police in other Canadian jurisdictions have similar requirements.

Comprehensive secrecy is necessary in police organizations because, as noted in Chapter 4 (Roles), the war on crime is viewed by police as a "guerrilla war" in which the enemy (that is, criminals) are camouflaged and therefore difficult, if not impossible, to recognize. Police recognition of the enemy is further complicated by the fact that, as noted in Chapter 9 (Discretion), almost everyone has at one time or another engaged in behaviour that could have been classified as criminal but was not caught. This combination of pervasive criminal behaviour in society and a camouflaged enemy that is hard to distinguish from ordinary citizens results in police distrusting everyone who is not a member of the police subculture or family. This distrust is revealed in the informal police expression "everybody lies, all the time."

The police passion for secrecy extends far beyond information obtained by police law enforcement activities. Typically, even administrative information about police budgets is a closely guarded secret. Police justify the classification of administrative information as secret by linking it to their law enforcement activities. For example, "If we release budget information to the public, organized criminals might use this information to defeat our battle plans." This linkage between police law enforcement activities and their administrative activities makes it very difficult for civilian administrators to hold police organizations accountable.

Clearly, the police pre-occupation with secrecy can only be justified by a war metaphor and not by a social service metaphor. However, given, as noted in Chapter 3 (Functions), that police spend the majority of their time involved in providing social services and not enforcing laws, then the police preoccupation with secrecy is patently unjustified. Why then do police organizations exaggerate their need for secrecy?

Police organizations exaggerate the perceived need for secrecy because, within their world, information is power (Turk, 1982: 15) and, by keeping information secret, police protect their power (Manning, 1977: 135). Police struggle to protect their power because, ultimately, their extraordinary power is what makes them unique — reduce their power and you reduce them. In short, police organizations will use every legitimate technique to protect their privileged positions and power and, when legitimate techniques are not enough, the police subculture improvises informal, unofficial techniques such as the "code of silence."

Unofficial Secrecy

One of the first "rules" a police recruit learns when he or she joins the police subculture is secrecy (Westley, 1970: 11). Police organizations have formal, official rules and regulations to ensure that important organizational information remains secret and the police subculture has an informal and unofficial rule or "code of silence" to ensure that important subcultural information remains secret. Very simply, the "code of silence" is an informal, unofficial rule that requires police to keep subcultural information secret. An important feature of this definition is the idea that the police subculture authorizes and condones secrecy. This is important because it means that police may withhold information from anyone who is not a member of the police subculture, including the public, the courts, and even police managers. In effect, the "code of silence" is like a "cloak" that "hides" police actions from outside scrutiny.

Relatively little is known about the "code of silence" outside the police subculture. For obvious reasons, police are reluctant to discuss this topic. Despite this, numerous American studies (Westley, 1970; Barker and Roebuck, 1973; Manning, 1978; Reiss, 1971) and several Canadian studies (Vincent, 1990; Ericson, 1981; 1982) have unequivocally established the existence of a police "code of silence." As well, several high profile cases [4] involving police both in the United States and Canada demonstrated the existence of a police code of silence. In short, the police "code of silence" is real, not imaginary.

The purpose of the code of silence is to protect police from accountability. This begs the question: Why do police feel the need to be shielded from accountability in the first place? The answer is that typically the consequences for police misconduct are much worse than for misconduct in other occupations. For example, as noted in Chapter 11 (Accountability), the consequences for police who engage in misconduct can include admonitions, demotion, fines, dismissal and imprisonment. Few other occupations have such severe consequences for misconduct.

---

4   The books, *Prince of the City* and *Serpico*, and films of the same name, detail the experiences of two New York City police officers, Robert Lucci and Frank Serpico respectively, who breached the code of silence. Similarly, the case of *R. v. Hanneson et al.* (see Case Study below) and the Moorish Road Incident, a 1979 case in Toronto when police refused to identify colleagues who were videotaped committing criminal acts, confirmed the existence of a code of silence in Canadian policing.

The police subculture is not unique in having a code of silence — to the contrary, most social groups including most occupational groups, have such a code. What makes the police code of silence unusual is its strength. Generally, the strength of a code of silence is positively correlated with the severity of the punishment that may be imposed for misconduct revealed by a breach of the code (Figure 12.1). It follows that the code of silence is very strong in the police subculture (and, ironically, in criminal subcultures) because the consequences that can be imposed for misconduct (i.e., perjury) committed by members of these subcultures are usually very serious (i.e., imprisonment). For example, in the case study discussed below, four police officers lost their jobs and were imprisoned when a colleague disregarded the code of silence and told the truth. In contrast, the code of silence is very weak in student subcultures because, typically, the worst consequence that can be imposed on a student caught cheating is expulsion.

When a police officer "breaks" the code of silence the police subculture must respond in order to demonstrate its commitment to the value (i.e., police solidarity) represented by the code. Typically, the police subculture responds by imposing a "penalty" against the officer who disregards the code. This is another factor that influences the strength of the code. Generally, the strength of the code of silence is positively correlated with the severity of the penalty that the police subculture may impose for a breach of the code (Figure 12.2). The police subculture imposes relatively severe penalties on members who breach the code. For example, the police officer in the case study below was harassed and threatened when he disregarded the code of silence and told the truth. [5] Westley (1970: 111) notes that ostracism is another tactic the police subculture uses to punish members who breach the code of silence:

> The stool pigeon, the squealer, the one who tells, is anathema to almost any social group. He is an outcast among police. To him is applied the most powerful sanction the group has available — the silent treatment. This is powerful because it deprives the unfortunate man of information vital to his continued success and necessary to his happiness, and because he works alone. This is the penalty for a serious abrogation of the rule of silence. It is a penalty for a threat to the secrecy of the group.

---

5   Perks notes (personal communication, November 17, 1995) that he was harassed and implicitly threatened by some colleagues while others supported him. A typical threat was to suggest that he might not receive "back-up" when needed.

Figure 12.1
Strength of the Code of Silence Versus Punishment for Misconduct

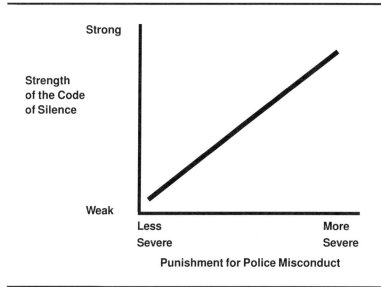

Figure 12.2
Strength of the Code of Silence Versus Subcultural Penalties

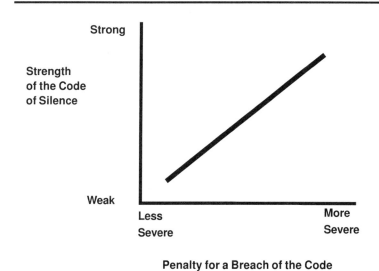

Contrary to what Westley suggests here, ostracism is not the most powerful penalty the police subculture can impose. There are documented instances [6] when much more serious penalties were imposed by members of the police subculture against colleagues who violated the code of silence.

The existence of the code of silence and the legal requirement that witnesses generally, and police witnesses more particularly, "tell the truth, the whole truth and nothing but the truth" when testifying ensures that occasionally police lie. For example, police lie to protect colleagues (Westley, 1970: 114), to procure evidence (Klockars, 1991: 424) and to obtain convictions (Manning, 1978: 242). For this purpose, police use their notebooks to "script" [7] occurrences so that when the "story" is told in court it seems as if the accused has been transported to "Disneyland." [8] For example, the Commission (1991: 39) that enquired into the fatal shooting of J.J. Harper by Constable Cross [9] concluded:

> We believe that officers collaborated in preparing their notes, that at least one set of notes was rewritten completely, and that Cross was assisted over a lengthy period of time in preparing his written statement.

When police lie in the course of a legal proceeding, they may commit "perjury." Perjury is a serious threat to the moral authority of the criminal justice system because it threatens to undermine confidence in the system. As a result, the Criminal Code provides strict penalties for people who commit perjury. For example, the Criminal Code provides:

> **131.**(1) Subject to subsection (3), everyone commits perjury who, with intent to mislead, makes before a person who is authorized by law to permit it to be made before him a false statement under oath or solemn affirmation, by affidavit, solemn declaration or deposition or orally, knowing that the statement is false.
>
> **132.** Everyone who commits perjury is guilty of an indictable offence and liable to imprisonment for a term not exceeding fourteen years ...

---

6   Frank Serpico was a New York City police officer who broke the code of silence. Subsequently, he was seriously wounded during a struggle with a criminal while his colleagues watched without trying to help.

7   Scripting refers to the practice of two or more police collaborating to produce a single version or "script" of the same event. This script is then recorded by each police officer in his or her notebook. The script may not be written until long after the incident and may be re-written several times before it is used in court. This practice is a closely guarded secret in the police subculture because the use of scripts could undermine police credibility. Courts are reluctant to accept statements that are not made at the time of the incident on which they are based and that are not the product of a single individual's recollection.

8   Disneyland is a reference to the popular cartoon characters produced by the Disney Corporation. The expression is intended to convey the idea that the scripted story is so unlike reality (i.e., what actually happened) that the accused will think he or she is in a fantasy (i.e., Disneyland).

9   For additional information relating to this incident, see the case studies at the end of Chapters 8 (Use of Force) and 13 (Stress).

These sections create an indictable offence punishable by a maximum of fourteen years imprisonment for everyone who commits "perjury." Generally, police receive more severe sentences for perjury than other people because they have a privileged position both in society and in the criminal justice system. As a result, this section is a powerful incentive for police to disregard the code of silence and tell the truth. Despite this, as we will see below, some police are still willing to commit perjury.

Case Study

At approximately 3:30 a.m. on May 4, 1985, an off-duty police officer, Sergeant Gary Hanneson, observed a man, Michael Stoewner, riding his bicycle away from Hanneson's house. [10] Hanneson suspected that Stoewner had attempted to break into his house and began to pursue him. While pursuing Stoewner, Hanneson observed two on-duty police officers, Constables Rick Turpin and Derek Perks, in a police car and informed them about his suspicions. Subsequently, Turpin and Perks apprehended Stoewner and returned him to Hanneson's house for identification. Hanneson proceeded to beat Stoewner in the back seat of the police car. Two other police officers, Constables Herb Van Den Broek and Wayne Seymour, were also present when Stoewner was beaten.

Stoewner suffered a broken nose and a chipped tooth. As well, he was charged with "assault" and "break and enter." These charges were later withdrawn when it was discovered that there was no evidence to indicate that he had attempted to break into Hanneson's house. Subsequently, Stoewner charged Hanneson with assault.

Initially, Turpin, Perks, Van Den Broek and Seymour corroborated Hanneson's story which was that Stoewner was injured when he attempted to assault Hanneson during the pursuit. However, on May 16, 1985, Perks met with his supervisors and advised them that Stoewner's injuries were sustained when Hanneson beat him in the back of the police car. [11]

Subsequently, Turpin, Van Den Broek and Seymour were charged with attempting to obstruct justice and Hanneson was charged with assault. All four police officers were eventually convicted and sentenced to imprisonment. Hanneson received three years, Turpin received 9 months and Van Den Broek and Seymour each received 6 months (*Toronto Star,* July 1, 1989: A17).

---

10   R. v. Hanneson et al., [49 C.C.C. (3d) 467].
11   Ibid., 474.

This case demonstrates several important features of the police code of silence. First, contrary to police denials, the code of silence is a very real part of the police subculture and exerts a powerful influence on police behaviour. For example, even though they did not assault Stoewner, Turpin, Van Den Broek and Seymour were willing to commit a criminal offence and jeopardize their own careers by lying, in order to protect Hanneson. The court of appeal acknowledged this when it noted:

> With respect to the other three appellants there is something to be said for the argument that they found themselves in a very difficult position. They found themselves, by chance, involved in a situation not of their making and subjected to pressure emanating from a senior officer to "stick together."[12]

Also, this case demonstrates that the code of silence is viable only if every police officer is willing to participate.[13] Most likely, none of the police in this incident would have been held accountable and punished if they had all lied;[14] however, once Perks decided to breach the code and tell the truth, the others were compromised. This explains why the code of silence is enforced so strongly in the police subculture.

Finally, this case demonstrates the harsh consequences that may be imposed when police engage in misconduct. The Court of Appeal acknowledged this when it noted:

> It is argued on behalf of all of the appellants (Hanneson, Turpin, Van Den Broek and Seymour) that the sentences imposed are too severe. While conceding that the sentences involved were very serious it is said that because of the consequences of conviction the jail terms need not be more than symbolic. All of the appellants have been suspended without pay from the police force. With the determination of this appeal these suspensions will no doubt culminate in dismissal. All had served for relatively long periods with the police force and the loss of office is, in itself, a significant penalty. The pension entitlement will be lost. These appellants, like most police officers, found their friends within the ranks of the police force. These convictions have resulted in the loss of those friendships.

---

12 Ibid.

13 Co-operation does not always involve active participation in a "cover-up." Co-operation may be as simple as testifying that you did not observe or hear anything (i.e., "See nothing, hear nothing, and say nothing!").

14 Recall that unless there is compelling evidence to the contrary, the courts are predisposed to accept police testimony when it contradicts other citizens' testimony. Clearly, if all five police told the same story and contradicted the suspect, the police would be believed.

Even Constable Perks did not escape this incident unscathed. Perks was harassed and threatened by some of his police colleagues after this incident.[15] This was his "punishment" for breaching the "code of silence." Again, this explains why the "code of silence" is so strong in the police subculture.

Summary

Like military organizations, police organizations have secrets they want to safeguard from criminals. For this purpose, police organizations require police recruits to swear a formal "Oath of Secrecy." Very simply, the "Oath of Secrecy" requires police to maintain the secrecy of the police organization's information. As well as the formal oath of secrecy, the police subculture has an informal, unwritten rule known as the "Code of Silence" that prohibits police from disclosing the police subculture's secrets to outsiders. The "Code of Silence" is intended to shield police from accountability when they enforce the law. Police feel the need to have a code of silence because the consequences of police misconduct are much more severe than in other occupations. As a result, the code of silence is very strong in the police subculture and the penalties for police who breach the code are quite severe.

15   Perks eventually decided to leave police work altogether although he denies that this incident was a factor in his decision (Personal communication, November 17, 1995).

13 Stress

Introduction

Policing is widely recognized as one of the most stressful occupations in modern communities. Numerous studies have reported that police officers suffer from high rates of a variety of stress related disorders including suicide, premature death from natural causes, and hypertension. In an attempt to solve this problem police organizations have developed employee assistance programmes that are designed to help police officers cope with distress. It remains to be seen whether these programmes can overcome the stresses of an occupational environment that pits police against a large and disaffected underclass.

This chapter uses a "Stress Styles" model to analyse police stress. In particular, the major sources of police stress are identified and techniques for managing police stress are discussed. This chapter concludes with the analysis of a case in which a senior police officer committed suicide hours before he was scheduled to testify before a government inquiry into a fatal police shooting.

Stress Styles

As noted in Chapter 5 (Selection), every person is compounded of a body (physical level), mind (mental level), and spirit (Soul and Spiritual level) (Wilber, 1986a). Good health is the result of a balance between each of these three levels. In order for the different levels in the compound individual to be healthy they must be exercised regularly and vigorously. The body is exercised by respiration, perspiration, digestion, and elimination. The mind is exercised by cognition, conceptualization and abstraction. The spirit is exercised by meditation, contemplation and prayer. When the balance between the various levels of the compound individual is disturbed, the result is disease, dysfunction and distress.

The internationally renown stress researcher, Hans Selye (1975: 14), defined "stress" as "the non-specific response of the body to any demand made upon it" and "stressors" (ibid., 13) as the factors that produce stress. Very simply, we are stressed whenever we are forced to adapt to changing conditions. For example, riding a roller coaster, stepping outside on a cold winter day, and turning on the lights in a darkened room all produce stress because they require adaptation. Riding a roller coaster is a stressor because the sudden changes in speed and direction force us to adjust our balance; stepping outside on a cold winter day is a stressor because the sudden change in temperature forces our bodies to adapt; and turning on the lights in a darkened room is a stressor because the sudden change in lighting conditions forces our eyes to adapt.

Despite the fact that stressors force our bodies to adapt, stress is not intrinsically "good" or "bad." Indeed, Selye (ibid., 19-20) noted that stress is an unavoidable part of living and that "[c]omplete freedom from stress is death." This gives rise to the question: If stress is not necessarily bad, why then are stress-related disorders nearing epidemic proportions? The answer to this question lies in an appreciation of the different types of stress.

First and foremost, stress is a matter of perception. That is, what is stressful (i.e., a stressor) for one person may not be stressful for another. For example, some people enjoy a roller-coaster ride, whereas other people find riding a roller-coaster a very unpleasant experience. Selye (ibid., 18) termed the stress we enjoy or find pleasant, *eustress*, and the stress we do not enjoy or find unpleasant, *distress*.

Another important characteristic of stress is that the intensity of a stressful experience can vary from "very high" to "very low." For example, the feelings of excitement or anxiety produced by riding a roller-coaster are very different from the feelings of relaxation or depression produced by a hot bath or learning about the death of a loved one, respectively. In this discussion we will call high and low intensity stress, *hyperstress* and *hypostress*, respectively.

By combining the "intensity" of the stress experience (i.e., hypostress or hyperstress), with the "quality" of the stress experience (i.e., eustress or distress), four different "stress styles" can be identified: relaxation, anxiety, depression, and excitement (Figure 13.1). For example, when someone says they are "stressed-out" or "under a lot of pressure," they are "anxious." That is, their stress level is very high (i.e., hyperstress) and it is an unpleasant experience (i.e., distress). Conversely, when someone says they are "calm" or "mellow," they are "relaxed." That is, their stress level is low (i.e., hypostress) and it is a pleasant experience (i.e., eustress). Also, when someone says they are "up" or "thrilled," they are "excited." Their stress level is high (i.e., hyperstressed) and it is a pleasant experience (i.e., exciting). Conversely, when someone says they are "down" or "bummed out," they are "depressed." That is, their stress level is low (i.e., hypostressed) and it is an unpleasant experience (i.e., distressful).

Confusion about what stress is and the different ways stress can be manifested may explain why so many people, including many police officers, feel that they are "stressed-out" and that their stress is "out of control." Many people do not know how to manage and control their stress with the result that their stress literally is "out of control." Fortunately, learning how to manage stress is relatively simple and with regular practice most people can become experts at managing their stress. Unfortunately, very few people learn how to manage their stress and fewer still become expert in the use of stress management skills. Consequently, stress-related disorders are at epidemic levels in modern society and, because policing is a particularly stressful occupation, many police officers suffer from the adverse effects of prolonged and intense distress.

Figure 13.1
Stress Style

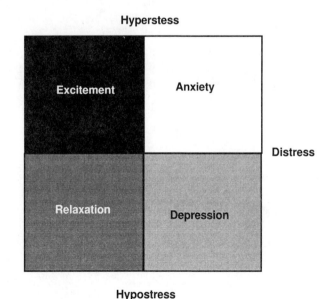

Source: Lockhart and Stansfield, 1989.

Police Stress

Recall that the police function in society (see Chapter 3) is to enforce laws that reproduce order and that the social order in Canada is stratified so that a small group of elites control most of the wealth, power and privileges and a much larger group are relatively poor, powerless and disadvantaged. The combination of a stratified social order that induces competition (and therefore conflict between individuals and groups) and the police duty to resolve conflict by enforcing the law ensures that police are often at the centre of social conflict.

In effect, police are like the oil in an automobile engine. The function of the oil is to lubricate the surface of the metal parts (rich and poor) so that friction (conflict) is minimized and the engine (society) functions smoothly (social order is maintained). As long as the oil is changed regularly (new police recruited) and the operating conditions are favourable (little or no crime), the engine will run smoothly and the oil will not break down ("burnout"). However, if the oil becomes contaminated by dirt (i.e., corrupted) or the engine parts are forced to exceed their limitations (new social conditions produced by technological change), then the oil may break down. When this happens the alternatives are to return to the old operating conditions (i.e., return to industrial conditions) or to use a new type of oil (private policing) better adapted to the new conditions. As long as the old oil (i.e., public policing) is used in the new conditions (i.e., informationalization), it will continue to "wear out" and need regular replacing. In effect, this is the situation for public police in Canada. As Canada is transformed from an industrial society into an informational society, public police are being asked to do more with less. The inevitable result is that police experience high levels of distress/anxiety and suffer from burn-out.

Police Stressors

Generally, police stressors can be classified into four categories: (1) organizational and administrative practices, (2) the criminal justice system, (3) the public, (4) and stress intrinsic to police work itself (Gaines, 1993: 541). Some of the organizational and administrative practices that cause police stress are: lack of administrative support, excessive paperwork, undesirable or inappropriate assignments, and conflict with supervisors (Kroes, 1985). Similarly, the criminal justice system causes police stress when the courts hand down lenient decisions and when they require police to appear in court on "off" days (ibid.). Also, the public causes police stress when it demonstrates a lack of support for police, when it demonstrates apathy towards law enforcement and crime prevention, and when it reacts negatively to police (ibid.). Finally, shift work, boredom, work overload, and danger are other ways that police work causes stress (ibid.) (Table 13.1).

Despite widespread reports of the danger of policing, police work is not as dangerous as many other more mundane occupations such as farming and mining (Robin, 1963: 231). This is ironic because police regularly identify "dangerous assignments" as a major source of stress in police work (Kroes, 1976: 29). [1] A possible explanation for this apparent anomaly may be that the danger of police work is, typically, both unpredictable and uncontrollable. For instance, while it is uncommon, occasionally, police are ambushed. [2]

Table 13.1
Police Stressors by Category

Organizational and Administrative Practices	Criminal Justice System	Public	Police-specific Stressors
lack of support	lenient court rulings	apathy	dangerous situations
rules and regulations	required to appear in court on 'day-off'	negative reactions	work underload (i.e., boredom)
conflict with supervisors		lack of support	shift work
inequities in pay/status			isolation
inappropriate assignments			work overload
unnecessary or excessive paper work			inadequate resources

Source: Kroes et al., 1974; Kroes, 1985.

1   It is noteworthy that in his study of 219 Canadian police deaths between 1983 and 1987, Stenning (1991) reported that the homicide rate for male police was, at 9.675 per hundred thousand, more than twice the rate for comparable males in the general population. Before any conclusions should be drawn from this result, it would be necessary to replicate this finding.
2   The Canadian Centre for Justice Statistics Homicide Project (1990) reported that three or 3.3% of the ninety-one police officers murdered on duty in Canada between 1961 and 1989 were ambushed.

Table 13.2

Average Annual Rates of Death for Canadian Police, 1983-1987 *

	Force 1	Force 2	General Pop.
Homicide	4.75	14.60	3.94
Suicide	15.85	4.87	28.97
Motor Vehicle Accident	17.43	43.79	27.36
Other Accidents	4.75	14.60	26.13
Circulatory Diseases	14.26	97.30	90.17
Cancer	19.02	38.92	77.12
Other Illnesses	3.17	19.46	50.85
Total - All Deaths	79.23	233.54	304.54

*   Rates per 100,000 population based on a sample of 215 male police officers between the ages of 20-59 who died between 1983-87 while employed by either of two large (i.e., more than 1,000 members) Canadian police services (Stenning, 1991).

The inability of police to predict and control the danger they encounter appears to be unique among occupations. With the possible exception of correctional officers, no other occupation is subjected to this type of random, arbitrary violence. It is known that prolonged exposure to unpredictable and uncontrollable danger increases anxiety (i.e., hyper-distress). Recognition of this situation has motivated police managers in many jurisdictions to decrease the normal age of retirement for police officers to twenty-five years experience. Despite this early retirement option, stories abound in the police subculture about police who die from "natural" causes a short time after retiring.

Effects of Police Stress

The numerous stressors inherent in the police occupational environment ensure that, in addition to air traffic control, dentistry, and medicine, policing is one of the most stressful occupations in contemporary society (Selye, 1976; 1978). Numerous studies have reported an unusually high incidence of psychosomatic disorders among police. For example, in their study of mortality and morbidity data for people admitted to hospitals and psychiatric facilities in Tennessee during the period 1972-74, Fell et al. (1980: 143) reported that police were "more prone to developing serious medical disorders than the majority of other occupations" particularly with respect to "premature death from stress-related causes" and for admission to medical hospitals for stress related disorders. Similarly, in his study of illness frequencies for nine psychosomatic disorders among Australian police during the year 1979, Davidson (1980: 41) reported that illness occurred more frequently in police than in a comparable group in the general population. In particular, police were 12 to 22 times more likely to experience hypertension and tension headaches than a comparable group in the general population (ibid.).

In addition to the numerous studies demonstrating that policing is a very stressful occupation, there are several studies that contradict this assertion. For example, in their study of stress levels among police and office workers, Lester and Mink (1979: 554) reported that there were "few differences between the stress of being a policeman in a small town and that of an office worker."[3] Similarly, in his study of stress levels among 23 occupational groups, French (1975: 60) reported that police are not an extreme group in the stress they experience.[4]

In one of the few Canadian studies to date that investigated police deaths caused by psychosomatic disorders, Stenning (1991) reported that police had lower death rates from "circulatory diseases," "cancer" and "other illness" than a comparable group in the general population (see Table 13.2). If this result is replicated by future studies, it would suggest that the stress of Canadian policing has been over-estimated.

Another stress-related disorder that police suffer from is suicide. For example, in their study of suicide rates among residents of Wyoming during the period 1960-1968, Nelson and Smith (1970: 295) reported that police were the occupational group at the highest risk of suicide.[5] Similarly, in a study that compared suicide rates among police in New York City and London for the period 1960-73, Heiman (1975a: 270) reported that the suicide rate for New York City police was almost twice the rate of a comparable group in the general population. Also, in a study of suicide rates among 130 occupational groups in Tennessee during the period 1972-74, Fell et al. (1980: 142) reported that police had the third highest rate.[6] As well, in a review of police shootings in Chicago and New York City, Geller and Scott (1991: 452-453) found:

---

3   The usefulness of this result was limited by the fact that the study used small sample sizes (N=15) and differences between the mean ages of the police and comparison samples (ibid.).

4   Here again, the usefulness of this result was limited by differences in the mean ages of the police and comparison samples (ibid.).

5   The police suicide rate was 203.66 per hundred thousand population. This was nearly twice the suicide rate for the next highest occupational group — physicians (ibid.).

6   Police had a suicide rate of 72 per hundred thousand population as compared to a rate of 22 per hundred thousand for the sample at large (ibid.).

In both New York City and Chicago, an alarming proportion of the police officers who were shot over the past two decades were shot either by themselves or by their colleagues. Fyfe (1980a: 77) found that, during the five years from 1971 through 1975, 30 New York City officers were killed in the line of duty, while 25 officers shot and killed themselves. In 1987, nine of the 12 New York City police officers who died took their own lives, all by gunshots (NYPD 1988). In 1986, those figures were eight out of ten. In 1970, it was seven out of fifteen (New York City Police Academy 1971). In Chicago over the period 1974-1978, 51 out of the 187 police officers who were shot (27 percent) shot themselves (Geller & Korales 1981a). During the ten-year period 1974-1983, of the 294 Chicago officers who were struck by bullets, 100 (34 percent) shot themselves...

The large body of evidence which indicates that American police commit suicide at a rate much higher than comparable groups in the general population has been contradicted by only a few studies. For example, in their study of suicide rates among police in Los Angeles between 1970-76, Reiser and Dash (1978: 20) reported that the police suicide rate was "significantly below the Los Angeles County and national averages." This anomalous result may be explained by Kroes' (1976: 28) contention that police suicide rates are "artificially low" because colleagues record police suicides as "accidental deaths" to ensure the victim's family receives survivor's benefits.

It is not yet clear whether Canadian police commit suicide as frequently as their American counterparts. However, Stenning (1991) reported that for the period 1983-87, the police suicide rate was less than half the suicide rate for a comparable group in the general population (see Table 13.2).[7] Also, typically, Canadian police commit suicide when they are "off-duty" (ibid.). Here again, if this result is replicated by other studies, it would suggest that Canadian policing is not as stressful as previously believed.

Like the Samurai who used a ritualistic form of suicide known as harikari,[8] police warriors have developed their own suicide ritual. In his study of 93 police suicides in New York between 1934 and 1940, Friedman (1968) reported that "(n)ine out of every 10 suicided officers used firearms — their service revolvers. Of this group, 82 percent of the wounds were in the head."[9] Typically, police commit suicide by inserting the service revolver in the mouth and pulling the trigger — this practice is euphemistically known in the police subculture as "swallowing your piece."

---

7   The police rate was 10.36 per hundred thousand as compared to a suicide rate of 28.97 for a comparable group in the general population.

8   The Samurai were a warrior caste in Japan during the last century. Harikari was performed by the Samurai warrior using his knife to disembowel himself.

9   As reported by Danto (1981: 129).

Managing Police Stress

Once policing was identified as one of the most stressful occupations, police managers began to design and develop stress management or Employee Assistance Programmes (E.A.P.) for police personnel. Typically, E.A.P.s combine several stress management strategies into a comprehensive approach to managing police stress. Most large Canadian police services now have E.P.A.s for their police personnel. For example, several police services (i.e., Calgary, Toronto) have full-time staff psychologists.

Several approaches have been used for classifying police stress management programmes. For example, Farmer and Monahan (1980) suggested that these programmes emphasize either intervention or prevention. Similarly, Kroes (1985: 157) suggested that stress management programmes either (1) reduce or eliminate stressors, (2) teach individuals more effective coping skills, or (3) provide distressed individuals with outside help. However they are classified, most authorities (Farmer and Monahan, ibid., 56; Kroes, ibid., 159) prefer to "manage" police stress by preventing it rather than intervening after it has occurred. For example, Kroes (ibid.) notes:

> [E]limination is by far the most effective, simplest to accomplish, and, yet, the one most rarely used. The other two approaches generally require either formal training or a one-on-one situation, which is time consuming and often expensive, as it takes time to train and counsel one policeman. Further, these approaches are inefficient, in that only a few officers can be helped at a time. With the first approach (elimination), however, the expended is toward the stressor itself, so that when it is reduced it affects all officers.

One of the few strategies that has been used to prevent police stress has been the use of psychological tests to identify and screen-out "at-risk" applicants (Somodevilla et al., 1981: 290). As we learned in Chapter 5 (Selection), these tests are now in widespread use in Canadian policing. While this approach is useful for preventing individuals who are prone to developing stress-related problems from entering policing, it does nothing to assist police who develop these problems after they are "on the job."

Most efforts to manage police stress have been focused at teaching police more effective coping skills. A few of the specific skills that police have been taught to manage their stress are: increased self-awareness (Kroes, 1985: 167), stress inoculation, deep muscle relaxation, breathing exercises, improved nutrition, improved physical fitness (Axelberde and Valle, 1981:282), and biofeedback (Somodevilla et al., 1981).

Kroes (1985: 167) suggests that teaching police increased self-awareness is an effective strategy for helping police to manage their stress. Selye (1978: 8) appeared to agree with this approach when he noted:

> Every policeman must learn to measure the stress level at which he personally can function best and then not to go either above or below that. By careful self-observation, he can gradually develop an instinctive feeling that tells him when he is running above or below the stress level that corresponds to his own nature. In practice, no refined chemical tests or monitors can do more for him.

As well as the plethora of skills police have been taught to manage their stress, considerable effort has been invested in providing distressed police with outside help. Typically, these programmes involve the use of either peer counseling (Terry, 1985: 397; Depue, 1981) or professional (i.e., psychological and psychiatric) counseling (Terry, 1985: 398; Wagner, 1981). A common problem encountered by these programmes has been satisfying police that their problems will be treated confidentiality (Depue, 1981: 309). For example, in the case study discussed below, the victim refused to seek help within the police department because he feared this would harm his chances for promotion. Police rightfully fear that evidence of mental or psychological instability will limit their advancement within the police organization.

Case Study

Following the fatal shooting of J.J. Harper by Constable Cross on March 8, 1988, in Winnipeg, [10] Inspector Ken Dowson was assigned responsibility for investigating the shooting. As senior officer in charge of the Crime Division, Dowson was responsible for ensuring that the shooting was thoroughly investigated. However, an independent inquiry that examined the shooting concluded (ibid., 63) that "the lines of supervision and communication (appeared to be) so ineffective that no one actually took responsibility for determining all the facts of (the) case." As well, the inquiry concluded (ibid., 113) that the investigation was "inadequate" at best, and a "cover-up" at worst.

---

10   For additional information about this incident, see the case study at the end of Chapter 8 (Use of Force).

Notwithstanding that Constable Cross was exonerated by an internal police review board and an inquest, an independent inquiry concluded (ibid., 39) that "it was Cross, through his unnecessary approach and inappropriate attempt to detain Harper, who set in motion the chain of events which resulted in Harper's death." As well, the independent inquiry concluded (ibid., 21) that Constable Hodgins' evidence was not reliable because she gave conflicting testimony at different times and that she lied to support Constable Cross.

In September 1989, just a few hours before he was to testify before the inquiry to answer questions about his role in the investigation, Dowson committed suicide by shooting himself in the head with his service revolver. Dowson left behind a suicide note that stated the investigation "was screwed up from the beginning ... I've never seen so many things go wrong ... And then the media took over and it's gone downhill from there. The effect on all of us has been devastating (*Toronto Star*, November 1, 1989: A3)." At a subsequent inquest, Dowson's family doctor testified (ibid.) that "the officer had suffered from anxiety attacks for years, but felt that he would be rejected for promotions if he sought help within the police department."

Both Constable Cross and Hodgins experienced acute stress reactions after the shooting. The inquiry noted (ibid., 21):

> It was apparent during the course of her testimony that the (events relating to the shooting) have affected Constable Hodgins deeply. She testified to that fact, and spoke of the emotional and psychological devastation that followed that night. She had trouble performing her work and stated that what occurred at the inquest is beyond her recollection. Her doctor informed us in a letter that she has been diagnosed as suffering from post-traumatic stress disorder.

Similarly, Constable Cross became profoundly depressed after the shooting and contemplated suicide. Also, he needed to be heavily sedated before he could testify at the inquiry.

This case is a potent reminder that police stress is real and not imagined. The extraordinary police power to use force including lethal force to resolve conflict makes it possible that even relatively minor incidents involving police (i.e., stopping a pedestrian) can escalate out of control and produce consequences (i.e., death) that are far out of proportion to the original incident. In this case, two people died and at least two others experienced acute stress reactions, not to mention the intense distress that others must have experienced, as a result of one police officer's "unnecessary" and "inappropriate" actions. Few other occupations produce the intense stress reactions caused by policing.

Summary

The stratified nature of Canadian society and the expectation that police will enforce laws that reproduce the status quo ensures that police are always at the centre of social conflict. When this is combined with the inherent danger of police work and the frustration many police experience as a result of unfulfilled role expectations, it is a recipe for police distress. In particular, Canadian police are prone to experiencing high levels of anxiety. The predictable result of this situation is that many police officers experience stress-related disorders such as hypertension, ulcers, early death from natural causes and suicide.

In an attempt to help police officers cope with the distress of police work, police authorities have developed and implemented employee assistance programmes. It remains to be seen whether these programmes will have the desired effect or whether police stress will prove to be an intractable problem associated with having a stratified social system.

14 Community Policing

Introduction

Community policing initiatives have been developed and deployed in large urban centres throughout Canada. All of this activity may lead one to conclude that community policing is the most important initiative in the history of public policing. Community policing has acquired this extraordinary importance because of the turmoil caused by the transformation of Canada from an industrial society into an informational society. As this process proceeds, social order is being redefined with the result that the mechanism for reproducing order — policing — has been thrown into crisis. Public police have responded to this situation by developing police programmes that are intended to promote community participation in law enforcement. This response is commonly referred to as community policing.

This chapter analyses community policing by comparing it to the now "archaic" form of vigilante policing that was used to reproduce order in agricultural communities prior to the Industrial Revolution. Also, research results evaluating the effectiveness of community policing programmes are discussed. This chapter concludes with the analysis of a case in which the Chief of a large Canadian police service who attempted to implement community policing was forced to resign when members of the police subculture undermined his authority.

Community Policing

Some observers have argued that community policing is the panacea needed to cure an increasingly troubled police-community relationship. For example, in Canada, Normandeau and Leighton (1990: 46) declared that:

> A review of the current status of community policing in Canada shows
> that this new approach has now become part of the conventional wisdom
> ... in most progressive police services. There is thus a growing
> consensus across Canada that community policing is the most
> appropriate policing approach to the past, present, and the future.

Similarly, in the United States, Trojanowicz and Bucqueroux (1990: 3) noted that:

> Community policing is the first major reform in policing since police
> departments embraced scientific management principles more than a
> half-century ago. It is a dramatic change in the way police departments
> interact with the public, a new philosophy that broadens the police
> mission from a narrow focus on crime to a mandate that encourages
> the police to explore creative solutions for a host of community
> concerns ...

Other observers have criticized community policing as a cynical attempt by police authorities to protect police power and prestige. For example, Klockars (1991: 531) noted that:

> The modern movement toward what is currently called "community
> policing" is best understood as the latest in a fairly long tradition of
> circumlocutions whose purpose is to conceal, mystify, and legitimate
> police distribution of nonnegotiably coercive force.

Here then are two widely different and largely incompatible views of community policing. Which is right? Is community policing simply a cynical attempt by a powerful special interest group to protect its privileged position or is it a sincere attempt by dedicated professionals to enhance the service they provide to the community? Like most dichotomies, the answer lies somewhere between these two extremes.

Vigilante Policing in the Informational Age

As noted in Chapter 2 (History), prior to the Industrial Revolution and the widespread introduction of public policing, farming communities reproduced order by a form of policing we have called "vigilante" policing. Very briefly, vigilante policing consisted of part-time police volunteers who were "recruited" from within the community (Critchley, 1972). In the country, vigilante policing employed strategies such as "hue and cry," "posse," and "frankpledge" to reproduce order (ibid.). In towns, in addition to these other strategies, "watch and ward" replaced frankpledge (ibid.). Very simply, during the Agricultural Era policing was a community responsibility.

Vigilante policing is now largely of historical interest, although this form of policing is still practiced in a few isolated areas of Canadian society. For example, a few "modern" farmers such as Mennonites, Dukhobors and Amish still adhere to a traditional farming lifestyle.[1] As a result, the social structure in these modern farming communities bears a strong resemblance to the social structure in "traditional" (i.e., pre-industrial) farming communities. For example, typically the extended family is the basis of the social structure in these communities and police, education, and health care "services" are provided from within the resources of the community, not the State. To the extent that these communities retain a traditional farming lifestyle, they also retain traditional vigilante police practices.

Another example of vigilante policing in modern communities are "grass roots" vigilante groups such as the Guardian Angels and Nation of Islam police. These groups are composed of community volunteers who have no special powers and work as part-time vigilantes. Vigilante police have formed in the poor areas of many of North America's large information centres in response to public police ineffectiveness (Naisbitt, 1984: 171). Essentially, public police have been unable to ensure individual safety and security in these communities and the communities have responded by developing their own "vigilante" police services. Interestingly, some Canadian public police have actively resisted the establishment of vigilante police (Carriere and Ericson, 1989 25; *Toronto Star*, January, 20, 1992: A18).

While the use of vigilante policing is relatively rare today, its ongoing use by "traditional" farming communities and in poor neighbourhoods in large informations centres is a poignant reminder of how policing was practiced in the past. As well, traditional vigilante policing offers a point of reference for assessing current developments of the police form, particularly community policing. As we will see below, contemporary community policing bears a striking resemblance to the vigilante policing that was used by agricultural communities.

---

1   Typically, these communities rejected the technological inventions of the Industrial Revolution such as the internal combustion engine and electricity and, as a result, retain a traditional farming lifestyle.

Community Policing in Informational Communities

The emergence of an informational society in Canada during the second half of the twentieth century has strained "traditional" social structures to the breaking point. Nowhere is this more apparent than in the criminal justice system generally, and public policing in particular. In many places, public police have been accused of ineffectiveness, insensitivity, incom-petence and irrelevance. For example, in Ontario the Task Force on Race Relations and Policing (1989: 153) noted that "it (is) abundantly clear that members of visible minorities believe they are treated quite differently from the majority community by the police." Also, the Aboriginal Justice Enquiry of Manitoba (1991: 610) observed:

> Our hearings indicated that, unfortunately, in many cases, the relationships between Aboriginal communities and the R.C.M.P. are seriously deficient. There are strong feelings of mistrust, if not hatred, directed towards R.C.M.P. members in some areas. Many police officers are seen as being arbitrary and antagonistic toward Aboriginal people.

As well, in his Report on Race Relations in Ontario, Stephen Lewis (1992: 3) noted:

> There was another emotion that was palpable, and it was fear. Mostly, of course, it was from members of the Black community, and in particular, mothers. The eight shootings over the last four years, and the sense, real or imagined, of unpredictable police encounters with Black youth has many families very frightened. I will admit to you that nothing left so indelible an impression on me as the expressions of apprehension and fear. I can't even begin to imagine it about my own children. Nor could you. We must find a way out of the present tension because it's intolerable, in this society, to know that, as one woman put it: "Mothers see their sons walk out the door; they never sleep until they see their sons walk back in."

Similarly, the Royal Commission on the Donald Marshall Jr., Prosecution (1989: 193-4) noted:

> The conclusion we have reached is that the system (criminal justice) does not work fairly or equally. Justice is not blind to colour or status. There is a widespread lack of understanding within the system of the appropriate roles of the Attorney-General, the prosecutor and the police.

This atmosphere of dislike and distrust is the context in which contemporary community policing initiatives have been developed.

Faced with accusations of incompetence and inadequacy, public police in large urban centres across Canada have responded by developing and deploying "community policing" programmes. While community policing is an inherently ambiguous concept (Manning, 1984) that has at least four possible meanings (Manning, 1993: 422), Leighton (1991: 487) has suggested that the "central principle" underlying the concept "is a full partnership between the community and their police in identifying and ameliorating local crime and disorder problems."[2] An implicit assumption of this approach is that there is an inverse correlation between public participation in policing, and crime rates, disorder and fearfulness in the community (ibid.).

The community policing "approach" provides a sharp contrast to the traditional or "professional" policing approach (Table 14.1). For example, traditional public policing emphasizes the use of randomized, motorized patrols to rapidly react to incidents and enforce the law, whereas community policing emphasizes the use of directed foot patrols, mini-stations, teams, and zones to proactively identify and solve problems and keep the peace. While there are many other differences between traditional policing and community policing, this discussion will be limited to consideration of just a few of the most important community policing "tactics."

An important tactic used in community policing programmes is "team" policing. Forcese (1992: 119) notes that "team" or "zone" policing is:

> The method used for community-based policing services, (and) depends upon decentralization and de-specialization. Zones or sub-communities are identified, and police personnel are assigned responsibility for that area on a continuing and stable basis. Working with members of the community, establishing better contacts, the emphasis is upon identifying problem areas and preventing crime rather than reacting after the fact.

An implicit feature of zone policing is the recognition that, unlike the homogeneous communities of the past, contemporary communities are heterogeneous. Consequently, contemporary communities can be subdivided into a virtually infinite number of smaller communities that are distinguished by race, culture, religion, language, sexual orientation, technological development and age, to mention a few. Faced with this diversity, a policing strategy must be equally differentiated to be effective. Zone policing is intended to deliver a differentiated police service.

---

2   Italics in original.

Table 14.1

Approaches to Policing

ISSUE	TRADITIONAL APPROACH	COMMUNITY-BASED APPROACH
Objective/Mission:	To enforce the criminal law, solve crime, and apprehend criminals	To ensure peace, order and civility, provide services to the community; and facilitate a sense of security
Police Role:	law enforcement officers	peace officers
Outcome Orientation -	police work	client/customer, service delivery
Authority/Mandate: Source -	delegated from elected representatives; exclusive	delegated from elected representatives and community; multiplex
Accountability -	exclusive; formal/legal; often co-opted	multiple; formal/legal and informal with community; usually independent
Priority Setting -	by police chief	by police governing authorities with community through consultations, etc.
Responsibility for Crime/ Order Problems -	exclusive property of police	shared/partnership with community as client
Main Strategy:	incident solving (of discrete incidents seen as unrelated to other similar incidents)	problem solving (of patterns among similar incidents and their underlying causes) and therefore of future similar incidents, i.e.,crime prevention
Criteria for Success: Effectiveness -	lower crime rates; higher clearance rates	absence of crime, disorder and incivility; reduction in repeat calls for service from repeat addresses, offenders and victims; reduced fear; greater community satisfaction
Efficiency -	more rapid response time	problem identification and solution, in partnership with the local community
Tactics/Police Response: Style -	Reactive — uniform/ standard tactics	Proactive; flexible tactics that are tailored to community needs and the nature of crime or disorder problems
Response to Calls -	undifferentiated; rapid response to all calls	differential response; target "hot spots" victims, places, offenses, offenders/recidivists
Predominant Tactic -	random, motorized preventive patrol	tailored to community and problem type; eg., dedicated neighborhood foot and/or car patrol, directed patrol, zones, mini-stations, flexible shifts, integrated teams, civilianization, volunteers, community liaison committees, etc.
Relationship to Community -	distant, few contacts (usually limited to victims, witnesses and offenders)	close, many contacts (facilitated by the above tactics)
Source of Intelligence -	internal; suspects, victims	public, community
Use of Technology (Cars, Radios, Computers) -	over reliance, technology driven	balanced, flexible, not technology driven (i.e., as a means to a tactic)
Relationship to Other Community Services -	lead role	partnership; recognizes limits to police mandate and expertise; inter-agency links (eg., housing, employment, education, victim support, agencies)
Organization and Control: Management Style -	para-military	participatory/democratic
Authority/ Command Structure -	centralized; hierarchical	decentralized; flatter, more "horizontal"

Table 14.1 (continued)

Approaches to Policing

ISSUE	TRADITIONAL APPROACH	COMMUNITY-BASED APPROACH
Scope of Officer Responsibility -	narrow; little discretion	broad; delegated; wide discretion and autonomy
Control -	invisible to public; informal internal discipline and formal/ bureaucratic control (rules and regulations)	visible to public; formal internal discipline and external/public complaints mechanisms
Loyalty -	to superior via chain of command (i.e., the "Brown" model)	to Charter, Criminal Code, common law, and the community (i.e., the "Blue" model)
Functional Units -	specialized	integrated (including investigation)
Role Definition -	specialized, with many specialist roles/units	generalist constable, with minimal complementary specialist roles/units
Human Resources -	generic police officer rotated through specialist positions	open to lateral entry, civilianization, part-time staff, career specialization, etc.
Corporate Culture: Professional Culture -	blue collar (below officer rank); policing as a career	white collar (all ranks); policing as a vocation
Subculture -	policing as separate from the community; self-image as being superior to clients	police as members of the community; self-image as partners with the community in crime and disorder control

Source: Leighton, 1991: 490-491.

For zone policing to be effective police service must be de-centralized. To accomplish this "neighborhood" or "storefront" police substations have been created and staffed with "constable generalists." Typically, these mini-police stations are located in high visibility locations (eg., store fronts) in the community making it easier for police to interact with the community and vice versa. Also, unlike traditional constables, constable generalists have an expanded, proactive role that emphasizes preventing crime by solving community problems before they become "criminogenic." An implicit assumption of this approach is that more police-community interactions will produce better police-community relations; however, the opposite may also be true: more police-community interactions may simply provide an opportunity for more problematic police-community interactions with the result that police-community relations may actually get worse.[3]

Another important tactic of most community policing programmes is the use of an approach known as "problem-oriented policing." Eck and Spelman (1993: 451) note that:

---

3   See Hodgson (1993: 259).

> Problem-oriented policing is a department-wide strategy aimed at solving persistent community problems. Police identify, analyse, and respond to the underlying circumstances that created incidents.

Problem-oriented policing is intended to provide an alternative to "incident driven" or reactive policing by identifying the "root causes" of crime and devising solutions for them and, in this way, stopping crime before it starts (ibid.). An implicit assumption of problem-oriented policing is that the causes of crime are amenable to police intervention. Clearly, this functionalist perspective of policing and crime is at odds with the conflict perspective which, by emphasizing social stratification, implicitly maintains that the causes of crime are beyond the limited control of police (see Chapter 3).

When problem-oriented policing fails the result may be crime. When this happens, and reactive police strategies do not "work," sometimes community police co-operate with television broadcasters to produce "Crime Stoppers" programmes. Crime Stoppers programmes re-enact major unsolved crimes and offer financial rewards for information leading to the arrest of offenders. These programmes are intended to induce people to become paid police informants. At one level, police informants are useful for helping police identify criminals. At an entirely different level, the presence of police informants in a community may cause fear and uncertainty among those predisposed to committing a crime with the result that these individuals will be inhibited from doing so.

Another major plank in the community policing platform are Neighborhood Watch programmes. These programmes are informal, part-time, volunteer, surveillance networks. They are intended to provide police with additional "intelligence" information by organizing communities into surveillance networks. When a member of one of these networks detects suspicious activity, he or she is expected to notify police. In theory, by organizing communities in this way and linking them through telecommunications devices to the formal police surveillance system, police are able to blanket a community with surveillance and gather invaluable intelligence on the activities of criminals. In practice, the usefulness of these programmes has been limited by the heterogeneous and transient nature of post-modern communities that makes the community and, therefore, community networks inherently unstable.

A key component in both traditional reactive and newer proactive (i.e., community policing) police programmes is sophisticated telecommunications technology. This technology is intended to extend the formal public police surveillance and alarm system deep into the community. Public police and other emergency services use a special telephone exchange (i.e., 911) to provide citizens with an automated emergency alarm system.

These formal systems are designed to work hand in hand with informal surveillance systems such as neighborhood watch programmes so that there is an unbroken surveillance continuum — surveillance systems detect criminal activity and alarm systems alert police who apprehend offenders. Very simply, this highly sophisticated surveillance system is the beginning of what Foucault (1979) has termed the "carceral continuum" — a seamless network of disciplinary power that envelopes society. Needless to say, the ominous images this inspires are entirely at odds with the benevolent rhetoric used to describe community policing.

At first glance community policing appears to be an original solution crafted to satisfy the specific security needs of informational communities. However, upon closer examination it can be seen that these programmes are rooted in the vigilante police form that was used by traditional agricultural communities [4] to reproduce order (Table 14.2). For example, "crime stoppers" is a high-tech version of "presentments"; "neighborhood watch," "neighborhood substations" and "zone policing" are up-dated versions of "watch and ward"; and automated emergency response systems are high-tech versions of "hue and cry" (Table 14.3). In the world of policing, at least, it appears that "what goes around, comes around."

Table 14.2
Police and Social Forms

Date	10,000 B.C.—1750 AD.	1750—1950	1950—Present
SOCIAL FORM	Agricultural	Industrial	Informational
POLICE FORM	Vigilante	Public	Private

Table 14.3
A Comparison of Vigilante and Community Policing Strategies

Vigilante Policing	Community Policing
watch and ward	Neighborhood Watch, Block Parents
hue and cry	emergency response systems (i.e., 911 telephone exchanges)
posse	mobile response units
presentments	Crime Stoppers

---

4   Normandeau and Leighton (1990: 43) suggest that contemporary community policing programmes find their roots in the public police practices of the early Industrial Revolution. While there is some truth to this assertion, it is also true that community policing programmes bear a strong resemblance to the vigilante police form used in the late Agricultural Era.

As might be expected with a concept as ambiguous as community policing, evaluation has proved difficult. For example, in their study of Crime Stoppers programmes Carriere and Ericson (1989: 81) concluded that "it is impossible to directly evaluate the effectiveness of Crime Stoppers programmes in apprehending criminal suspects." Similarly, others (Clairmont, 1991: 473) have also noted the difficulty of evaluating community policing programmes.

Given the problems associated with evaluating community policing, it should not come as a surprise to learn that the research results to date have been mixed.[5] For example, in a three-year follow-up study that evaluated the effectiveness[6] of the Victoria community policing programme, Walker et al. (1993) reported that the programme was completely effective only in increasing service delivery to school age children. In all other areas, the programme produced either inconclusive results or was minimally effective or ineffective (ibid.). In their evaluation of the effectiveness[7] of the Edmonton community policing programme, Hornick et al. (1993: 330) reported that the programme "achieved three major programme objectives: reducing repeat calls-for-service, achieving a high degree of user satisfaction with police services, and increasing job satisfaction of the (community policing) constables." In considering the Canadian research evidence to date, Clairmont (1991: 472) noted that:

> The general finding of these studies (evaluations of community policing) has been that the public and the police officers spearheading the CBP development report high levels of satisfaction with the CBP initiative. None of the studies deals in depth with issues of implementation and impact nor do they feature rigorous scientifically-controlled quasi-experiments ...

Research evaluating the effectiveness of American community policing programmes has also produced mixed results. For example, after conducting a national review of Neighborhood Watch programmes, Garofalo and McLeod (1993: 72) concluded that "[t]here is little evidence that Neighborhood Watch, by itself, produces increased neighborhood

---

5   Carrirere and Ericson (1989) notes that it is impossible to directly evaluate the effectiveness of Crime Stoppers programmes in apprehending criminal suspects.

6   The "objectives" of the Victoria programme were: to reduce crime levels; to reduce fear of crime; to increase community involvement in crime prevention; to increase community accessibility to police services; to increase service delivery to the elderly and school age children; to increase the reporting of intelligence information (Walker et al., 1993).

7   The objectives of the Edmonton programme were to reduce the number of repeat calls for service, improve public satisfaction with the police, increase job satisfaction of the participating constables, increase the reporting of information on crime, and solve community problems (Hornick et al., 1993).

attachment or sense of community." Also, in a wide-ranging review of the effectiveness of community crime prevention programmes, Rosenbaum (1993: 84) concluded that "it remains uncertain whether police foot patrols can reduce crime, but they seem to be effective in reducing fear of crime ..." As well, (ibid.) "fear reduction" programmes "focusing on individual residents — such as the distribution of a police community newsletter and recontacting victims of crime to offer sympathy and services — showed virtually no effects, but the more community oriented programmes that encouraged officers to become familiar with local residents and the neighborhood ... were associated with reductions in perceived crime levels and improved citizen evaluations of the police."

One reason community policing programmes in Canada may be producing mixed results is that the police subculture is resisting implementation. For example, repeated attempts to implement community policing in Toronto have met with little or no success.[8] Similarly, as noted in the case study below, when the Chief of Police of Vancouver attempted a "bold strokes" implementation[9] of community policing, he alienated the police rank and file and, eventually, was forced to resigned (Gould, 1995). Also, Hodgson (1993: 258-260) found that the members of the large municipal police service he interviewed were cynical about their experiences with community policing. Finally, Clairmont (1991: 476) reports that at a national community policing conference a "management representative from a large urban department" observed: "the enemy is within; the officers are the problem, especially the middle (sic) management."

Another reason why community policing programmes may not be producing the results predicted for them is because they do not satisfy the security needs of large informational communities. As mentioned above, the effectiveness of a police form is determined by the degree of congruence between it and the social form it reproduces (see Table 14.2). So, for example, vigilante policing effectively reproduced order in agricultural communities; public policing effectively reproduced order in industrial communities; and,

---

8   Police in Toronto have been "implementing" community policing since 1982 when a consultant's report (Coopers and Lybrant, 1982) recommended the implementation of a comprehensive community policing programme in that city. Subsequently, in 1990 the M.T.P.S. released a report entitled "Policing 2000" that committed the M.T.P.S. to the implementation of a comprehensive community policing programme. Despite all these recommendations and implementations, when Toronto hired a new police Chief in 1994, a key selection criteria was the candidate's willingness to implement community policing, thus suggesting that community policing still was not implemented.

9   Clairmont (1991: 474) suggests that there are two basic approaches to implementing community policing: "bold strokes" which is characterized by rapid directed change and "incremental implementation," which is characterized by slow consensual change.

as we will see in the next chapter, private policing effectively reproduces order in informational communities. However, the opposite is not true: vigilante policing does not effectively reproduce order in industrial communities [10] and public policing does not effectively reproduce order in informational communities. [11] It follows that, to the extent that community policing programmes resemble vigilante policing, which is considerable, they will not effectively reproduce the new informational order. In short, while the jury is still out, it appears that community policing is not the panacea public police managers have been seeking.

Case Study

On January 10, 1991, William Marshall became the Chief of Police of the Vancouver City Police Service. Immediately upon assuming office Marshall began a rapid implementation of a community policing programme that included hiring more women and visible minorities and modifying "shiftwork patterns so that officers could serve in communities as steady beat cops." (Gould, 1995: 35). Not long after he began implementing these changes, Marshall became embroiled in a conflict with the Vancouver Police Union (VPU) over contract matters.

In May of 1993 "police sources" informed the media that in 1983 Chief Marshall was the acting duty officer when a constable nearly beat a handcuffed native prisoner to death (ibid., 36). The implication was that Marshall knew about the incident but did not report it. As a result, in March 1994 a commission of inquiry was called to investigate the matter. It was subsequently revealed that the "beating" occurred while the prisoner was forcefully resisting custody and consisted of a single blow from the officer's night-stick that resulted in the prisoner suffering a bruised chest (ibid., 40). It was also revealed at the inquiry that Marshall had reported the incident although there was contradictory evidence as to whether the matter was reported to the Internal Affairs unit as required by police regulations (ibid.). Despite this, the Commissioner found that Marshall had "defaulted in carrying out this responsibility" and, as a result, Marshall was forced to resign by the police board on July 11, 1994.

---

10 Recall, as noted in Chapter 2 (History), this is why Sir Robert Peel created the first public police force — because vigilante policing was no longer effectively reproducing the then new industrial order.

11 Chapter 15 (Future Trends) argues that the dramatic growth of private policing has been driven by the inability of public police to satisfy the security needs of informational communities.

This case demonstrates several important features of community policing programmes. Notwithstanding police managers and politicians may be committed to the principles of community policing, this does not ensure that the police subculture is committed. Also, it is difficult if not impossible to implement a community policing programme without the cooperation and support of the police subculture. Finally, this case suggests that an "incremental implementation" of community policing programmes may be more effective than the "bold strokes" approach attempted here.

Summary

The turmoil caused by the transformation of Canadian society from an industrial order into an informational order has precipitated a "crisis" in policing. Public police have responded to this crisis by developing and deploying community policing programmes that are intended to facilitate a partnership between police and the communities they serve. A few of the "tactics" these programmes use are neighborhood foot patrols, Crime Stoppers, and Neighborhood Watch. Many of these programmes strongly resemble the tactics vigilante police used to reproduce order in traditional farming communities. To the extent that this is true, community policing programmes are relatively ineffective in reproducing the new informational order. This might explain why studies of the effectiveness of community policing programmes have yielded "mixed" results.

15 Future Trends

Introduction

The transformation of Canada from a "modern" industrial society into a "post-modern" informational society is having subtle yet profound consequences for policing. For the past two hundred years public policing has been the average mode of policing in Canada and other parts of the world. During this time, in many minds, public policing has become inextricably linked to the police form, so that now it is recognized as the only form of policing. Despite this dominant position in the public consciousness, public policing no longer is the average mode of policing in Canada — that distinction now belongs to private policing.

This chapter analyses the dramatic growth and development of private policing in the post-modern, Informational Era. In particular, the effects of the privatization of many formerly public spaces and the use of instrumental discipline are considered.

Through the Looking Glass

The social and technological transformation currently underway is, with only a few exceptions,[1] more profound than any other event in human history. Very simply, the old, "modern" industrial order is collapsing and a new, "post-modern" informational order is rising in its place. Rosenau (1992: 62) notes that "(p)ost-modernists have developed a unique counterin-tuitive view of time, geography or space, and history ..." in which time (ibid., 68) is "anarchical, disconnected, and misaligned rather than linear, evolutionary, or intentional" and space (ibid., 69) transcends the individual's ability to locate himself or herself in "hyperspace." As we will see below, this new post-modern reality has profound consequences for policing.

---

1   Arguably, the Agricultural Revolution and Industrial Revolution produced equally profound effects (Lenski et al., 1991).

Marx and Engels [(1989: 50) 1845] were the first to recognize that a transformation of the "means of production" always occurs in association with a transformation of the "means of social organization." This realization helped them to identify the important role played by technology in social development. Similarly, several writers (Schwartz and Miller, 1964; Kelling and Moore, 1988; Tafoya, 1990; Stansfield, 1993) have struggled to demonstrate that the form of policing a community uses to reproduce social order is determined by the level of social and technological development the community has achieved. It follows that as new technologies co-evolve with new forms of social organization, new forms of policing are needed.

A consensus (Toffler, 1981; 1990; Naisbitt, 1984; Laszlo, 1987; Drucker, 1993; 1994) has emerged that a third "wave" of technological development began to sweep over the world in the middle decades of this century. The information(al) society, as it has become known,[2] is characterized first and foremost by the automatic production of data. Whereas agricultural societies were based on the manufacture of food, and industrial societies were based on the manufacture of goods, informational societies are based on the manufacture of data.[3] And, just as agricultural technology transformed hunting and gathering society and industrial technology transformed farming society, informational technology is transforming industrial society. Laszlo (1987: 155) notes:

> The technologies of the second industrial revolution (i.e., the information revolution) are truly revolutionary. Not only are they major advances over previous technologies, but they also require major transformations in the societies that make use of them. A post-industrial society based on abundant and dense energy resources and on information, robotics, and automation reaches new heights in autonomy: it progressively detaches itself from geographic constraints. It generates its own energies and produces its own raw materials with less and less dependence on the endowments of its milieu. This could lead to a brusque rupture of geocultural ties which evolved over centuries ...

---

2   The new social order has been described variously as a "knowledge society" (Drucker, 1992; 1994), "the fourth phase of the Industrial Revolution" (Lenski et al., 1991), an "information society" (Toffler, 1981; 1990; Naisbitt, 1984; Naisbitt and Aburdene, 1992), and "the second industrial revolution" (Laszlo, 1987:155). In this discussion we will adhere to the emerging convention which is to refer to the present technological era as an "information society".

3   Current technology (i.e., computers) does not produce "information", on the contrary, computers produce "data." The difference being that information is data imbued with meaning. Presently, information must be manually synthesized from the data that is generated by computers. A future technological innovation will be needed before it will be possible to automatically produce information.

While it is too early to know the precise details of the informational order, a general outline is beginning to emerge. Preliminary indications are that the Information Revolution, like previous technological revolutions, will dramatically increase the economic surplus (Naisbitt and Aburdene, 1990). In the past this has produced a large increase in the standard of living (Lenski et al., 1991: 271). So, for example, industrialists were more affluent than agriculturalists and agriculturalists were more affluent than hunter-gatherers. If this pattern continues in the present era, informational communities will be the most affluent communities ever.

In the past, the increased economic surplus was used to sustain larger populations; however, it appears that the trend toward lower birthrates that began mid-way through the Industrial Era (Lenski et al., 1991: 264) will continue in the Informational Era (Toffler, 1981: 213; Lenski et al., 1991: 341). For example, the Canadian birthrate at 1.67 children per woman on average is below the replacement rate (McKie, 1991: 270). Also, families are not only having fewer children today, they are also divorcing more often (Lenski et al., 1991: 342) and having and raising children outside of marriage more often (Toffler, 1981: 212; Lenski et al., 1991: 342). Effectively, the nuclear family has become just another lifestyle option for informationalists (Toffler, 1981: 211; Lenski, 1991: 338-339).

Whereas industrial workers were valued by employers for their physical strength and stamina, informational workers are valued by employers for their knowledge and intelligence (Naisbitt and Aburdene, 1990: 308; Drucker, 1993). As well, the emphasis on intelligence and de-emphasis of physical strength in informational work has meant that women can compete with males on equal terms. This may explain why the numbers of women in key informational occupations has increased dramatically (Naisbitt and Aburdene, 1990: 224-225). For example, if the labour force participation rate of Canadian women continues to increase, a woman will soon be the "average worker" (McKie, 1991: 271). Similarly, increasing immigration from predominantly non-western countries is ensuring that Canada's largest information centres — Montreal, Toronto and Vancouver — are becoming racially and ethnically diverse (ibid., 271). The combination of increased participation of women and "minorities" in the Canadian economy and a severe shortage of qualified informational workers suggests that these historically disadvantaged groups and perhaps others, such as the physically and mentally disabled, homosexuals, and the elderly, will have improved opportunities for participating in informational communities — if they are able to obtain the necessary skills.[4]

---

4   Generally, the training needed to be a "information worker" will be advanced studies at the post-secondary level (Drucker, 1993: 210).

An important difference between informational workers and industrial workers is mobility. Industrial workers were tied to their employers place of employment because they needed to be near the means of production (i.e., machines housed in factories) (Naisbitt and Aburdene, 1990: 306; Drucker, 1993). In contrast, when provided with access to the means of production (i.e., computers and telecommunication devices), informational workers are very portable (Toffler, 1981: 196; Drucker, 1993: 66). The rapid development of information technologies such as the World Wide Web and the Internet has made it possible for informational workers to work wherever they reside and reside wherever they choose. Laszlo (1987: 155) notes:

> The new technologies make distinctions between city and countryside almost as irrelevant as geographic location. Space and time constraints are all but eliminated by telecommunications and high speed transportation. There is no further need for urban megacomplexes; high-tech producers and consumers can just as well live in decentralized suburban or rural settings.

Predictably, given their increased options, informational workers choose alternative lifestyles such as living alone (Toffler, 1981: 212), working at home (ibid., 196), living in the country (Naisbitt and Aburdene, 1990: 305), and frequently changing occupations and residences (Naisbitt and Aburdene, 1990: 221; Drucker, 1993). McKie (1991: 272) notes:

> High divorce rates, never-married single mothers, same-sex "families", and persons who live alone throughout their entire adult lives all strain the bounds of traditional notions of "family." These changes in family practice call into question some of the roles traditionally performed in a family context such as nurturance, supervision, and discipline ...

In short, changes in family and work arrangements are revolutionizing informational communities so that they are more racially, sexually, and ethnically heterogeneous than industrial communities (Naisbitt and Aburdene, 1990: 273), just as industrial communities were more heterogeneous than agricultural communities.

An important difference between industrial workers and informational workers is in the ownership of the means and tools of production. Whereas workers in industrial communities owned the means of production (i.e., their labour) and employers owned the tools of production (i.e., machines), workers in informational communities own both the tools of production (i.e., computers) and the means of production (i.e., their knowledge) (Drucker, 1993: 66). [5] As a result, informational workers are the elites in informational societies (Drucker, 1994: 64).

---

5   This has been made possible by the accumulation of vast sums of capital in worker pension plans which have been used to purchase an interest in corporations that may employ the workers (Drucker, 1993: 66).

The dramatic changes in lifestyle and work arrangements in informational communities is producing a radically new form of social organization. For example, Eisler (1988: 198) suggests that, whereas the industrial order was characterized by "dominator" hierarchies that emphasized competition, violence, and male domination of females, the informational order is characterized by "actualization" hierarchies that emphasize co-operation, compromise, and equality between the sexes. Similarly, Drucker (1988; 1993) has argued that, whereas the organizational structure in industrial communities was based on "command and control" hierarchies, the organizational structure in information communities is based on "networks." As a result, informational organizations communicate information more effectively and efficiently than industrial organizations (Naisbitt, 1984; Drucker, 1988).

The networked structure of informational communities is having important consequences for social relationships. For example, informational workers need to be more "self-directed" than industrial workers (Ferguson, 1980: 328; Drucker, 1988: 47) and informational workers need to co-operate and collaborate with colleagues (i.e., form teams) more than industrial workers (Ferguson, 1980: 329; Drucker, 1988: 47; 1993). Also, whereas relationships in industrial communities were organized on the basis of inequality (i.e., superiors and inferiors), relationships in informational communities tend to be between peers. Drucker (1993: 56) notes:

> Because modern organization is an organization of knowledge specialists, it has to be an organization of equals, of "colleagues," of "associates." No one knowledge "ranks" higher than another. The position of each is determined by its contribution to the common task rather than by any inherent superiority or inferiority.

Increasingly informational communities are becoming stratified along the lines of "knowledge" (i.e., information) and "service" workers (Drucker, 1993: 8-9). Individuals who acquire the necessary skills are the first in line for what are well-paying, high-status jobs in the informational sector. Others are destined for employment in what are, at present, low-paying, low-status jobs in the service sector (ibid.). History records that societies that are divided into two unequal groups — one that is small, wealthy, powerful and privileged and the other that is large, poor, powerless, and disadvantaged — are ripe for conflict. To make matters worse, as employment in the manufacturing sector continues to decline, racial minorities in the United States are suffering more than others due to their over-representation in this sector (Drucker, 1993: 70). This situation threatens to perpetuate the current arrangement in American society in which the social order is "white on the top" (i.e., knowledge workers) and "black on the bottom" (i.e., service workers).

Another key trend that has emerged in the Informational Era has been the switch from a national economy to a global economy (Naisbitt, 1984; Naisbitt and Aburdene, 1990). Drucker (1993: 56) notes that the nation state and the mega-state are at a "dead end" and that a new "post-capitalist society" is emerging in their place. In this new, "global" reality, many formerly "national" companies have become "multinational" corporations with property, markets, and "interests" in countries all over the world (Toffler, 1981: 319). As we will see, the transition from a national economy to a global economy has important implications for policing.

Finally, some (Pearson, 1991; Ferguson, 1980; Wilber, 1986; Eisler, 1988) believe that a new awareness is emerging in our species. Very simply, the core of this awareness is that we are more similar (i.e., we all share a common human ancestry) than different (i.e., racial, sexual, religious, cultural, and ethnic differences). Among people who hold this view, violence, in all its forms (but especially against women and children), is unacceptable. As a result, violent conflict resolution is being replaced by non-violent conflict resolution. Also, discrimination, in all its forms, but especially against women, people of colour, gays and lesbians and the physically and mentally disabled (i.e., the historically disadvantaged), is unacceptable. As a result, exclusiveness is being replaced by inclusiveness. As well, dependency, in all its forms but especially on drugs, interpersonal relationships, and government, is unacceptable. Dependency is being replaced by independence. In short, this change in attitudes may have an even more profound impact on society than the technological changes associated with it.

Briefly, the distinguishing characteristics of the "post-modern" informational society are: the automatic production of data, the use of information networks, an increase in social diversity (racial, sexual, religious and other forms) and mobility. These are the conditions in which the most recent evolution of the police form, private policing, is occurring.

Policing in a Post-Modern Community

Given, as noted in Chapter 1, that policing is an activity individuals use to protect themselves and communities use to reproduce order, then a transformation of the social form must produce a transformation of the police form. Just as a new form of policing was needed to reproduce order in industrial society, a new form of policing is needed to reproduce order in the informational society. That new form of policing is private policing.

As mentioned above, there is every reason to believe that the informational order will be as different from the industrial order as the industrial order was from the agricultural order. It follows that private policing will be as different from public policing as public policing was from vigilante policing. To fail to grasp this point is to fail to appreciate the profound changes that are transforming contemporary society.

The emergence of a post-modern, informational order has made the development of a new form of policing inevitable. Many individuals and groups in the new order have realized that public police cannot satisfy all of their "security needs" and, as a result, they are developing alternative forms of policing (Naisbitt, 1984: 171; Stenning, 1989: 181). The precise form these "alternatives" acquire depends on, among other things, the resources available to the individuals and groups that develop them. For example, because they are relatively powerful, elites resort to private policing (i.e., "mercenaries"); whereas, because they are relatively powerless, the poor resort to self-policing (i.e., "vigilantes").

In the previous chapter we discussed how "grass roots" policing initiatives such as "community policing" that have been organized by public police and community groups such as the Guardian Angels are an attempt to revive archaic police practices that were in use during the Agricultural Era. To the extent that these programmes resemble Agricultural Era policing, they are "regressive" police forms. Clearly, an archaic and regressive form of policing will not effectively reproduce the informational order; on the contrary, what is needed is an innovative and progressive form of policing.

The future of policing may be "community policing" but it is not the Industrial Era and Agricultural Era versions of policing currently being proffered by public police authorities and vigilante groups. On the contrary, the future of policing lies with the form of policing that most effectively and efficiently reproduces the networked organizational structure of the new informational order — that is, private policing.

Few people appreciate the massive size of the private policing industry in Canada. Most subscribe to the notion that public police are "real" police and private police are "wannabes." This myth belies the fact that private police already outnumber public police in North America and many other parts of the world (Spitzer and Scull, 1977; Shearing and Stenning, 1987: 9). For example, the number of private police in Canada has been increasing much faster than the number of public police, so that by 1991 private police outnumbered public police by more than two to one (Figure 15.1). Similarly, by the 1980s private police outnumbered public police in the United States by three to one (Naisbitt, 1984: 171). When considering the size and type of private police in Canada, Normandeau and Leighton (1990: 131) noted:

Figure 15.1

Number of Police Personnel, Canada, 1971, 1981 and 1991

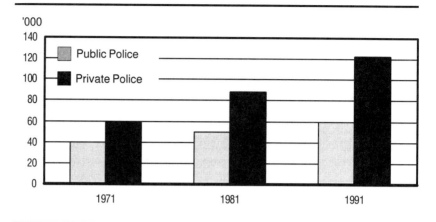

Source: Statistics Canada, Cat. 85-002, Vol. 14 No. 10.

Figure 15.2

Number of Female Police Personnel, Canada, 1971, 1981 and 1991

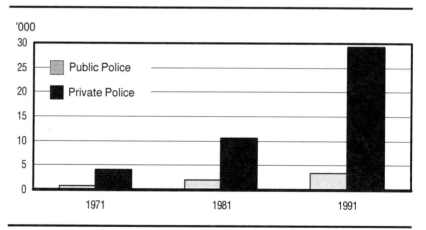

Source: Statistics Canada, Cat. 85-002, Vol. 14 No. 10.

The private security sector has grown to the point where, in terms of manpower, it overwhelms the number of public police officers ... there are about 55,000 full-time public police officers in Canada. The total number of full and part-time private security officers, on the other hand, is estimated to be in the vicinity of 125,000. About 75,000 are employed in private firms which provide services on a contractual basis. Approximately another 50,000 are in-house security personnel working for such concerns as the larger department stores. It is estimated that over three billion dollars a year are spent on private security services in Canada. The scope of private security duties includes assets protection, loss prevention, countermeasures for industrial espionage, drug testing in the work environment, extortion, product tampering, dignitary and facility protection, and communication security.

The dramatic growth of private policing over the past three decades "points to one inescapable conclusion, which is that when Canadians experience policing ... it is more likely to be 'private' policing than 'public' policing" (Stenning, 1989: 172). By most measures one would choose to use, private police accomplish more law enforcement at less cost and with less physical violence than public police (Shearing and Stenning, 1987: 184).

Not only is the number of private police in Canada increasing faster than the number of public police, the feminization of private policing is also proceeding faster than the feminization of public policing. For example, the number of females in private police organizations has been increasing much faster than the number of females in public police organizations, so that by 1991 females comprised almost one-quarter of private police personnel but less than ten percent of public police personnel (Figure 15.2). It appears that the barriers that have been traditionally used to exclude women from public policing are less of a problem in private policing. The rapid growth and feminization of private policing suggests that public police would be well advised to co-operate with their private counterparts.

Public and private police can be expected to co-operate during the transition from an industrial order to an informational order just as public police co-existed and apparently co-operated with vigilante police during the transition from an agricultural order to an industrial order.[6] In some situations both groups stand to gain from a collaborative relationship. For example, in the United States the F.B.I. has collaborated with private police in some large corporate investigations (Marx, 1987). Similarly, in Canada, the Solicitor General has urged public police to co-operate more closely with private police in an effort "to do more with fewer resources" (Normandeau and Leighton, 1990: 138).

---

6   Critchley (1972: 56-57) notes that public police co-existed with agricultural era police in the City of London (i.e., the Bow Street Runners, the Thames River police, and "scattered groups of constables employed in the police offices set up by the Middlesex Justices Act, 1792") for several years before the latter were absorbed into the former. The fact that public police "absorbed" the remnants of the communal police suggests the two groups cooperated for a time.

Public and private police co-operation will continue as long as both sides stand to profit [7] from these arrangements. Eventually, however, their different priorities will force a divorce. For example, whereas public police are committed to keeping the "public" peace, private police are committed to keeping the "corporate" peace; and, whereas public police are pre-occupied with using as much force as necessary to enforce laws that reproduce the economic and social status quo, private police are preoccupied with using as little force as possible to enforce rules (laws) that maximize corporate profits and, ideally, disrupt the economic and social status quo. Add to this the fact that public resources are shrinking as the power and influence of the Canadian state diminishes and the fact that corporate power and influence is increasing as informational technologies create new products and markets, there is no reason to believe that private police will want or need public police cooperation in the future.

As noted above, a key trend in the Informational Era is the expansion of the economic surplus. Much of this new wealth is being used to privatize what were formerly public spaces. Condominiums, stadiums, arenas, shopping malls, and theme parks are private spaces that formerly did not exist or were public. As more and more space is privatized, this will have a profound effect on police jurisdictions and, consequently, on how order is reproduced in the new informational order.

In Canada, private police are authorized by law to exercise special powers on and in relation to their employer's property.[8] The result of linking private police authority to property rights has been to define private police powers in terms of their employer's property holdings. Effectively, private police jurisdiction is coextensive with their employer's property holdings. Consequently, as the employer's property holdings expand, so does private police jurisdiction. If an employer has international property holdings, as many do, private police may also have de facto international jurisdiction.

This arrangement contrasts with public police jurisdiction. For example, typically, public police jurisdiction is defined according to the boundaries of the geo-political unit for which they are appointed. So, for example, in Canada, public police jurisdiction is either municipal (eg., Montreal Urban Community Police), provincial (eg., Sûreté du Québec), or national (eg., Royal Canadian Mounted Police). These "jurisdictions" are based on

---

7   There can be no question that these "arrangements" are driven by the profit motive. Public police profit by being allowed unrestricted access to corporate (i.e., private) property effectively expanding their jurisdiction. Private police profit by gaining access to knowledge and skills that may be difficult or impossible for them to recruit.

8   Reference section 494(1) of the Canadian Criminal Code.

Industrial Era boundaries that were established by using what are now archaic modes of transportation and communication. As a result, public police jurisdictions are becoming obsolete also. The problem is being exacerbated by the privatization of more and more space. The result is that public police jurisdiction is shrinking as private police jurisdiction is expanding. Literally and figuratively, public police have less and less policing to do while private police have more and more policing to do.

The relative "success" of private police vis à vis public police appears to be attributable to the former's use of what Shearing and Stenning (1987: 322) have called "instrumental discipline." They note that instrumental discipline is control that "is embedded, preventative, subtle, co-operative and apparently non-coercive and consensual." [9] Whereas public police have only moral and legal authority to reproduce order, private police also have "instrumental" authority. The practical effect of this situation is that private police can use instrumental authority to reproduce order in many situations where public police are compelled to use legal authority (i.e., force). As a result, private police are less likely than public police to alienate their "customers" and undermine their moral authority.

On those rare occasions when instrumental discipline is insufficient to reproduce order, private police may use physical force — but only as a last resort. Stenning (1989: 182) notes:

> In the course of developing the policing strategies and techniques on which they most commonly rely, (private police) typically give preference to those which will be least likely to engender criticism and complaint from those whom they police. In most cases this has been a conscious priority in their strategic planning and choice of policing philosophy. The way in which the more successful private policing organizations typically insist that their operatives do not use even those coercive powers which the law allows them (especially the use of force) in achieving their policing objectives provides the clearest indication of this approach.

Unlike public police who must routinely use physical force to reproduce order, private police have developed other more refined methods. It is not that public police "like" to use physical force and private police do not; rather, private police frequently have the option of resolving conflict non-violently when public police do not. For example, if a public police officer

---

9   While instrumental discipline may be subtle and co-operative, it definitely is not non-coercive and consensual. Very simply, instrumental discipline is psychologically coercive rather than physically coercive. As a result, while "choices" may be made, because they are made in the context of profound inequality, they are not "free." Shearing and Stenning (1987: 323) implicitly acknowledge this when they compare instrumental discipline to the drug "soma" and note "people are today seduced to conform by the pleasures of consuming the goods that corporate power has to offer."

wants to search a person walking in a public place, the officer must obtain the person's consent, a search warrant or make an arrest. Many people today are reluctant to allow public police to search them without a warrant. In contrast, most people allow private police to search them before they fly on planes, ride on trains or attend entertainment events at theatres and stadiums. They allow private police to search them in circumstances when they refuse public police permission to search because private police control access to the goods and services people want.[10] In short, people will surrender their constitutional rights to private police in exchange for access to the goods and services private police control.

To the extent that private police rely on instrumental discipline to reproduce order and to the extent that this is a new form of social control, private policing is a "progressive" police form. However, the discovery of instrumental discipline has far more profound implications for how order is reproduced than a simple comparison to public policing reveals. As Shearing and Stenning (ibid.) note, the use of instrumental discipline by private police has important implications for how order is reproduced in information communities:

> While this new instrumental discipline is rapidly becoming a dominant force in social control ... it is as different from the Orwellian nightmare as it is from the carceral regime. Surveillance is pervasive but it is the antithesis of the blatant control of the Orwellian State: its source is not government and its vehicle is not Big Brother. The order of instrumental discipline is not the unitary order of a central State but diffuse and separate orders defined by private authorities responsible for the feudal-like domains of Disney World, condominium estates, commercial complexes and the like.

Just as computers have made it possible to replace most people who work in factories with robots, instrumental discipline is making it possible to replace most people who work at reproducing order with new, information-era social control technologies: metal-detectors are replacing frisk searches; closed-circuit cameras are replacing stake-outs; perimeter alarms and electronic locks are replacing guards; condominiums and gated communities are replacing neighbourhoods; and environmental design is replacing architecture.

---

10 Ironically, many people will allow public police to search them at concerts and sports events but not on the streets. Of course, different in contexts makes a difference in attitudes. When public police perform "pay-duties", for most practical purposes, they are private police in the employ of the management.

At the same time private policing is "exploding," public policing is "imploding." Increased sensitivities to the use of force have meant that tried and true public police techniques for reproducing order no longer "work." Whereas once police brutality was an accepted practice, today it invites public complaints and judicial inquiries; whereas once police discretion was accepted, today it is challenged; and whereas once police discrimination was accepted, today it is prohibited by employment equity and affirmative action.

Despite attempts to "reform" public policing to adapt it to the new, "post-modern" informational reality, reality has changed faster than it can be adapted. At the same time as public policing is offering an hierarchical, violent and divisive form of policing, private policing is offering a seamless, instrumental and global form of policing. Clearly, informational communities are demanding the latter not the former. In short, we have seen the future of policing and the future is private not public.

Summary

Two hundred years after the Gordon Riots shook the City of London and foreshadowed the end of vigilante policing and the beginning of public policing, history may record that the street riots in Toronto and Vancouver in the early 1990s marked the transition from public policing to private policing in Canada. Put simply, public policing is in a "crisis" in large urban centres throughout Canada. As these communities reorganize to accommodate the new informational mode of production, the old, "modern" industrial order is collapsing and a new, "post-modern" informational order is rising in its place. And just as "vigilante" policing collapsed under the pressure of industrialization, "public" policing is collapsing under the pressure of informationalization; and, just as public policing became the average mode of policing in the Industrial Era, private policing has become the average mode of policing in the Informational Era. Unquestionably this is difficult to accept, just as it was difficult for people at the time to imagine the scope of the changes wrought by the Industrial Revolution.

Bibliography

Abraham, J., Field, J., Harding, R., and S. Skurka, "Police Use of Lethal Force: A Toronto Perspective," *Osgoode Hall Law Journal* 19: 199, 1981.

Alpert, G., "Police Use of Deadly Force: The Miami Experience," in Dunham, R. and Alpert, R. (eds.), *Critical Issues In Policing: Contemporary Readings,* Prospect Heights, Il.: Waveland, 1989.

Alpert, G., and Dunham, R., "Community Policing," in Dunham, R. and Alpert, G. (eds.), *Critical Issues in Policing: Contemporary Readings* (2 edn.), Prospect Heights, Il.: Waveland, 1993.

Archer, R., "Review of the Minnesota Multiphasic Personality Inventory–2," in Kramer, J., and Conoley, J., (eds.), *The Eleventh Mental Measurements Yearbook,* Lincoln: University of Nebraska Press, 1992.

Asbury, K., "Private Security, Public Police and Mass Residential Space," *Canadian Police College Journal* 14(1): 1–27, 1990.

Axelberd, M., and Valle, J., "Stress Control Progam for Police Officers of the City of Miami Police Department," in Territo, L., and Vetter, H., (eds.), *Stress and Police Personnel,* Toronto: Allyn and Bacon, 1981.

Barker, T., and Roebuck, J., *An Empirical Typology of Police Orruption: A Study in Organizational Deviance,* Springfield, Il.: Thomas Books, 1973.

Bayely, D., *Patterns of Policing: A Comparative International Analysis,* New Jersey: Rutgers, 1985.

Benson, H., *The Relaxation Response,* New York: Avon, 1976.

Bernheim, J., *Police et pouvoir d'homicide,* Montréal: Meridien, 1990.

Bittner, E., "The Functions of the Police in Modern Society," in Manning, P., and Van Maanen, J., (eds.), *Policing: A View From the Street,* New York: Random House, 1978.

Black, D., "The Mobilization of Law," in Manning, P., and Van Maanen, J., (eds.) in *Policing: A View From the Street,* New York: Random House, 1978.

Blackmore, J., "Police Stress," in Terry, W., *Policing Society: An Occupational View,* Englewood Cliffs, New Jersey: Prentice-Hall, 1985.

Blumberg, M., "Issues and Controversies With Respect to the Use of Deadly Force by Police," in Barker, T. and Carter, D. (eds.), *Police Deviance,* Cincinnati: Anderson, 1986.

_____, "Research on Police Use of Deadly Force: The State of the Art," in Blumberg, A., and Niederhoffer, A. (eds.), *The Ambivalent Force: Perspectives on Police,* (3ed.), New York: Holt, Rinehart and Winston, 1985.

_____, "Controlling Police Use of Deadly Force: Assessing Two Decades of Progress," in Dunham R. and Alpert, G. (eds.), *Critical Issues in Policing: Contemporary Issues,* Prospect Heights, Il.: Waveland, 1989.

_____, "Race and Police Shootings: An Analysis in Two Cities," in Fyfe, J., (ed.) *Contemporary Issues in Law Enforcement,* Beverly Hills: Sage, 1981.

Bowsky, W., "The Medieval Commune and Internal Violence: Police Power and Public Safety in Siena, 1287–1355," in Blumberg, A., and Nierderhoffer, A., (eds.), *The Ambivalent Force: Perspectives on Police,* Hinsdale: Dryden Press, 1976.

Campbell, J., *The Hero With A Thousand Faces,* (2 ed.) Princeton University Press: New Jersey, 1968.

Canadian Centre for Health Information, "Firearm Death By Legal Intervention, Canada and the Provinces/ Territories, 1980–1990," Unpublished Report: Ottawa, September, 1992.

_____, "Homicides of Police Officers in Canada," *Juristat* 2(3): 1–6: cat. no. 85–002, 1985.

Canadian Centre for Justice Statistics, "Homicide Project: Police Officers Murdered While on Duty, 1961–1990," Unpublished Report: Ottawa, March, 1992.

Canadian Committee on Corrections, *Toward Unity: Criminal Justice and Corrections,* Ottawa: Queen's Printer, 1969.

Carriere, K., and Ericson, R., *Crime Stoppers: A Study in the Organization of Community Policing,* Toronto: University of Toronto Press, 1989.

Chambliss, W., "Introduction," in Chambliss, W. (ed.) *Sociological Readings in the Conflict Perspective,* Don Mills: Addison-Wesley, 1973.

Chappell, D., and Graham L., *Police Use of Deadly Force: Canadian Perspectives,* Toronto: University of Toronto, 1985.

Chibnall, S. "The Metropolitan Police and the News Media" in Holdaway, S., (ed.) *The British Police,* London: Edward Arnold, 1979.

Clairmont, D., "Community-Based Policing: Implementation and Impact," *Canadian Jounral of Criminology,* July/October 1991: 469–484.

Critchley, T.A. *A History of Police in England and Wales,* (2 ed.) New Jersey: Paterson-Smith, 1972.

Dahrendorf, R., *Life Chances: Approaches to Social and Political Theory*, Chicago: University of Chicago Press, 1979.

Danto, B., "Police Suicide," in Territo, L., and Vetter, H., (eds.), *Stress and Police Personnel*, Toronto: Allyn and Bacon, 1981.

Dash, J., and Reiser, M., "Suicide Among Police In Urban Law Enforcement Agencies." *Journal of Police Science and Administration* 6(1): 18–21, 1978.

Davidson, M., "The coronary-prone Type-A behavior pattern and the policeman: A Cross-cultural Comparison. *Police Stress* 170: 1, 39–41, 1980.

Depue, R., "Turning Inward," in Territo, L., and Vetter, H., (eds.), *Stress and Police Personnel*, Toronto: Allyn and Bacon, 1981.

Drucker, P., "The Coming of the New Organization," *Harvard Business Review,* Jan-Feb. 1988.

⸻, *Post-Capitalist Society*, New York: Harper-Collins, 1993.

⸻, "The Age of Social Transformation," *The Atlantic Monthly* 3: 274, 1994.

Eck, J., and Spelman, W., "Problem Solving: Problem-Oriented Policing in Newport News," in Dunham, R. and Alpert, G. (eds.), *Critical Issues in Policing: Contemporary Readings* (2 edn.), Prospect Heights, Il.: Waveland, 1993.

Economic Council of Canada, *The New Face of Poverty: Income Security Needs of Canadian Families*, Ottawa: Economic Council of Canada, 1992.

Eisler, R., *The Chalice and the Blade: Our History, Our Future*, Harper: San Francisco, 1988.

Engels, F., *The Origin of the Family, Private Property, and the State*, Leacock, E., (ed.) New York: International Publishers, 1972.

Ericson, R., *Making Crime: A Study of Detective Work*, Toronto: Butterworths, 1981.

⸻, *Reproducing Order: A Study of Police Patrol Work*, Toronto: University of Toronto Press, 1982.

⸻, "The State and Criminal Justice Reform," in Ratner, R. and McMullan, J. *State Control: Criminal Justice Politics in Canada*, Vancouver: University of British Columbia Press, 1987.

Ericson, R., and P. Baranek, *The Ordering of Justice: A Study of Accused Persons as Dependents in the Criminal Process*, Toronto: University of Toronto Press, 1982.

Farmer, R., and Monahan, L., "The prevention model for stress reduction: A concept paper." *Journal of Police Science and Administration* 8: 139–144, 1980.

Federal Bureau of Investigation, *Law Enforcement Officers Killed and Assaulted*, Washington, D.C: F.B.I. (1988).

Fell, R., Richard, W., and Wallace, W., "Psychological job stress and the police officer." *Journal of Police Science and Administration* 8: 139–144, 1980.

Ferguson, M., *The Aquarian Conspiracy: Personal and Social Transformation in Our Time,* Los Angeles: Tarcher, 1980.

Forcese, D., *Policing Canadian Society*, Scarborough: Prentice-Hall, 1992.

Foucault, M., *Discipline and Punish: The Birth of the Prison*, New York: Vintage, 1979.

Freidman, P., "Suicide among Police: A Study of Ninety-Three Suicides among New York Policemen 1 934–1940," in Schneidrean, E., (ed.), *Essays in Self-Destruction*, New York: Science House, 1968.

French, J., "A Comparative Look At Stress and Strain in Policemen," in Kores, W., and Hurrell, J. (eds.), *Job Stress and the Police Officer,* Washington: HEW-NIOSH, 1975.

Fyfe, J. *Shots Fired: An Examination of New York City Police Firearms Discharges, 1971–1975*, Albany: State University of New York, 2 volumes, 1978.

⸻, "Geographic Correlates of Police Shooting: A Microanalysis," *Journal of Research in Crime and Delinquency* 17: 101–113, 1980.

⸻, "Race and Extreme Police-Citizen Violence," in McNeeley, R. and Pope, C., (eds.), *Race, Crime and Criminal Justice*, Beverley Hills: Sage, 1981a.

⸻, *Contemporary Issues in Law Enforcement*, Sage: Beverly Hills, 1981b.

⸻, "The Split-Second Syndrome and Other Determinants of Police Violence," in Dunham, R. and Alpert, R. (eds.), *Critical Issues In Policing: Contemporary Readings*, Prospect Heights, Il.: Waveland, 1989.

Gaines, L., "Stress in Police Work," in Dunham, R. and Alpert, G. (eds.), *Critical Issues in Policing: Contemporary Readings* (2 edn.), Prospect Heights, Il.: Waveland, 1993.

Gandhi, M., *Gandhi on Non-violence: A Selection from the Writings of Mahatma Gandhi*, Merton, T., (ed.), New York: New Directions, 1965.

Garofalo, J., and McLeod, M., "Improving the Use and Effectiveness of Neighborhood Watch Programs," in Eskridge, C., *Criminal Justice: Concepts and Issues*, Los Angeles: Roxbury, 1993.

Geller, W. and Karales, K., "Shootings Of and By Chicago Police: Uncommon Crises, Part I," *Journal of Criminal Law and Criminology* 72: 1813–1866, 1981a.

_____, "Shootings Of and By Chicago Police: Uncommon Crises, Part II," *Journal of Criminal Law and Criminology* 73: 331–378, 1981b.

Geller, W. and Scott, M., "Deadly Force: What We Know," in Klockars, C. and Mastrofski, S. (eds.), *Thinking about Police: Contemporary Readings*, New York: McGraw-Hill, 1991.

Getchell, B., and W. Anderson, *Being Fit: A Personal Guide*, Toronto: John Wiley, 1982.

Goldstein, H., "Improving Policing: A Problem Solving Approach," in Klockars, C., and Mastrofski, S., (eds.), *Thinking about Police* (2ed.), Toronto: McGraw-Hill, 1991.

Gould, T., "In the Line of Fire," *Saturday Night,* February, 1995.

Hackler, J., and Janssen, C., "Police Killing in Perspective," *Canadian Journal of Criminology* 27: 227–232, 1985.

Hageman, M., "The Police Suicide," *Journal of Police Science and Administration* 6: 402–412, 1978.

Hamilton, J., and Shilton, B., *The Annotated Police Service Act, 1993*. Scarborough: Carswell, 1992.

Hay, D., Linebaugh, P., Rule, J., Thompson, E., and Winslow C., *Albion's Fatal Tree: Crime and Society in Eighteenth-Century England*, London: Penguin, 1975.

Heiman, M., "The police suicide." *Journal of Police Science and Administration* 3: 267–273, 1975.

_____, "Police Suicides Revisited," *Suicide* 5: 5–20, 1975.

Hislop, G., *Track Two: A History of Toronto's Gay and Lesbian Communities*, Film: Keith, Lemmon, Sutherland Communications Corp., 1982.

Hodgson, J., *Police—Community Relations: Analysis of the Organizational and Structural Barriers Inhibiting Effective Police—Community Exchanges*, Unpublished Ph.D. Dissertation, York University, 1993.

Hornick, J., Burrows, B., Phillips, D., and Leighton, B., "An Impact Evaluation of the Edmonton Neighbourhood Foot Patrol Program," in Chacko, J. and Nancoo, S., (eds.), *Community Policing in Canada*, Toronto: Canadian Scholars Press, 1993.

Illich, I., *Celebration of Awareness: A Call for Institutional Reform*, Garden City, New York: Doubleday, 1970.

Josephson, R., and Reiser, M., "Officer Suicide in the Los Angeles Police Department: A Twelve Year Follow-up." *Journal of Police Science and Administration* 17(3): 227—229, 1990.

Jung, C., *The Archetypes and the Collective Unconscious*, (2 ed.), New Jersey: Princeton University Press, 1968.

Kelling, G., and Moore, M., "The Evolving Strategy of Policing," *Perspectives on Policing*, No. 4. Washington, D.C.: National Institute of Justice and Harvard University, 1988.

Keesling, J., "Review of USES General Aptitude Test Battery," in Mitchell, J., (ed.), *The Ninth Mental Measurements Yearbook*, Lincoln: University of Nebraska Press, 1985.

Kelly, D., (ed.), *Deviant Behaviour, A Text-Reader in the Sociology of Deviance*, (3 ed.) New York: St. Martin's, 1989.

Kimura, D., "Sex Difference in the Brain," *Scientific American*, Sept. 1992, 119–125.

Kirkham, G., "From Professor to Patrolman: A Fresh Perspective on the Police," *Journal of Police Science and Administration*, June 1974, 127–137.

_____, *Signal Zero*, Philadelphia: Lipincott, 1976.

Kline, P., *A Handbook of Test Construction: Introduction to Psychometric Design*, Chatham: Cambridge University Press, 1986.

Klockars, C., "The Rhetoric of Community Policing," in Klockars, C. and Mastrofski, S. (eds.), *Thinking about Police: Contemporary Readings* (2 ed..), New York: McGraw-Hill, 1991.

_____, "Blue Lies and Police Placebos: The Moralities of Police Lying," in Klockars, C. and Mastrofski, S. (eds.), *Thinking about Police: Contemporary Readings* (2 ed.), New York: McGraw-Hill, 1991.

Knowles, M., *Self-Directed Learning: A Guide for Learners and Teachers*, New York: Association Press, 1975.

Kroes, W., *Society's Victim—The Police: An Analysis of Job Stress in Policing*, (2 ed.), Springfield, Il.: Charles C. Thomas, 1985.

_____, *Society's Victim: The Policeman*, New York: Charles C. Thomas, 1976.

Kroes, W., and Gould, S., "Job stress in policemen: An empirical study, *Police Stress* 170: 1, 9–46, 1979.

Kroes, W., Margolis, B., and Hurrell, J., "Job Stress in Policemen," in Territo, L., and Vetter, H., (eds.), *Stress and Police Personnel*, Toronto: Allyn and Bacon, 1981.

Laszlo, E., *Evolution: The Grand Synthesis*, Boston: Shambhala, 1987.

Lavigne, Y., *Hell's Angels: Taking Care of Business*, Toronto: Deneau and Wayne, 1987.

Lee, J., "Some Structural Aspects of Police Deviance in Relations with Minority Groups," in Shearing, C. (ed.), *Organizational Police Deviance: Its Structure and Control*, Toronto: Butterworths, 1981.

Leighton, B., "Visions of Community Policing," *Canadian Journal of Criminology*, July-October 1991: 485–522.

Leitner, L., Posner, I., and Lester, D., "The effects of a stress management training program on police officers. Paper presented to the British Psychological Society (Welsh Branch) at the International Conference of Psychology and Law, July 19–23, 1983.

Lenski, G., *Power and Privilege: A Theory of Social Stratification*, Toronto: McGraw-Hill, 1966.

Lenski, G., Lenski, J., and Nolan, P., *Human Societies: An Introduction to Macrosociology* (6 ed.), McGraw-Hill: Toronto, 1991.

Lester, D., and Mink, S., "Is Stress Higher in Police Officers?: An Exploratory Study," *Psychological Report* 45: 554, 1979.

Lewis, S., *Stephen Lewis Report on Race Relations in Ontario*, Ontario, 1992.

Manitoba, *Report of the Aboriginal Justice Inquiry of Manitoba: The Deaths of Betty Osborne and John Joseph Harper*, (Hamilton, A., and Sinclair, C., Commisioners), Vol. 2, 1991.

_____, *Report of the Aboriginal Justice Inquiry of Manitoba: The Justice System and Aboriginal People*, (Hamilton, A., and Sinclair, C., Commisioners), Vol. 2, 1991.

Manning, P., "Lying, Secrecy and Social Control," in Manning, P. and Van Maanen, J. (eds.), *Policing: A View From the Street*, New York: Random House, 1978.

_____, "Community Policing," *American Journal of Police* 3(2): 205–227, 1984.

_____, "Community-Based Policing," in Dunham, R. and Alpert, G. (eds.), *Critical Issues in Policing: Contemporary Readings* (2 ed.), Prospect Heights, Il.: Waveland, 1993.

Maslow, A., *Toward a Psychology of Being*, New York: Von Nostrand Reinhold, 1968.

_____, *The Farther Reaches of Human Nature*, New York: Viking, 1971.

Marx, G., "The Interleaving of Public and Private Police in Undercover Work," in Shearing, C. and Philip Stenning, P. (eds.), *Private Policing*, Newbury Park: Sage, 1987.

Marx, K. and Engels, F., *The German Ideology*, Arthur, C. (ed.), New York: International, 1989 (1845).

Mastrofski, S., "What Does Community Policing Mean for Daily Police Work," in Eskridge, C., *Criminal Justice: Concepts and Issues*, Los Angeles: Roxbury, 1993.

Matulia, K., *A Balance of Forces: A Study of Justifiable Homicides by the Police*, Gaithersburg, M.D: IACP, 1985.

McKie, C., "Policing and the Demographic Transition," *Canadian Journal of Criminology*, July/October, 269–283, 1991.

Melchers, R., "A Commentary on 'A Vision of the Future of Policing in Canada: Police Challenge 2000,'" *Canadian Journal of Criminology*, January, 49–57, 1993.

Murphy, C., "The Future of Non-Urban Policing in Canada: Modernization, Regionalization, Provincialization," *Canadian Journal of Criminology*, July/October, 333–346, 1991.

Naisbitt, J., *Megratrends: Ten New Directions Transforming Our Lives*, New York: Warner, 1984.

Naisbitt, J., and Aburdene, P., *Megatrends 2000: Ten New Directions for the 1990s*, New York: Morrow, 1990.

National Advisory Commission on Criminal Justice Standards and Goals, *The Police*, Washington, D.C.: U.S. Government Printing Office, 1973.

Nelson, Z., and Smith, W., "The law enforcement profession: An incidence of high suicide," *Omega* 1: 293–299, 1970.

Normandeau, A., and Leighton, B., *A Vision of the Future of Policing in Canada: Police Challenge 2000*, Background document, Solicitor General of Canada: Minister of Supply and Services, 1990.

_____, "Police and Society in Canada," *Canadian Journal of Criminology*, July/October, 251–255, 1991.

Ontario Civilian Commission on Police Services, *Report of an Inquiry into Administration of Internal Investigations by the Metropolitan Toronto Police Force*, August, 1992.

Ontario Ministry of the Solicitor General and Correctional Services, *Police Constable Selection: Community Policing—Selecting Constables for the Future*, Final Report, Phase II—Volume 2, February 1993a.

_____, *Police Constable Selection: Community Recruiting—Selecting Constables for the Future*, Final Report, Phase II—Final Report, March 1993b.

Ontario Police Commission, *Review of Police Tactical Units*, Toronto: Ministry of the Solicitor General, 1989.

Ontario Police College, *1994 Course Calendar*, Toronto: Ministry of the Solicitor General and Correctional Services, 1993.

Peak, K., *Policing America: Methods, Issues, Challenges*, Englewood Cliffs: Regents/Prentice Hall, 1993.

Pearce, F., *Crimes of the Powerful: Marxism, Crime and Deviance*, London: Pluto, 1976.

Pearson, C., *Awakening the Heroes Within: Twelve Archetypes to Help Us Find Ourselves and Transform Our World*, San Francisco: Harper-Collins, 1991.

Piaget, J., *The Moral Judgement of the Child*, Toronto: Penguin, 1977.

Radzinowicz, L., and King, J., *The Growth of Crime*, Basic Books: New York, 1977.

Reiman, J., *The Rich Get Richer and the Poor Get Prison: Ideology, Class, and Criminal Justice* (2 ed.), Wiley: New York, 1984.

Reiser, M., and Dash, J., "Suicide Among Police in Urban Law Enforcement Agencies," *Journal of Police Science and Administration* 6: 18–21, 1978.

Reiss, A., *The Police and the Public*, New Haven: Yale University Press, 1971.

_____, "Police Brutality-Answers to Key Questions," in Niederhoffer, A. and Blumberg, A. (eds.) *The Ambivalent Force: Perspectives on the Police*, (2 ed.) Hinsdale: Dryden Press, Il., 1976.

Report of the Canadian Committee on Corrections, *Toward Unity: Criminal Justice and Corrections*, Ottawa 1969.

Robin, G., "Justifiable Homicide by Police Officers," *Journal of Criminal Law, Criminology, and Police Science* 54: 225–231, 1963.

Robinson, P., "Stress in the police service." *Police Review* 89, 2254–2259, 2308–2313, 2364–2367, 2412–2414, 1981.

Rosenau, P., *Post-Modernism and the Social Sciences*, Princeton: Princeton University Press, 1992.

Rosenbaum, D., "Community Crime Prevention: A Review and Synthesis of the Literature," in Eskridge, C., *Criminal Justice: Concepts and Issues*, Los Angeles: Roxbury, 1993.

Ross, D., Shillington, R., and Lochhead, C., *The Canadian Fact Book on Poverty—1994*, Ottawa: The Canadian Council on Social Development, 1994.

Royal Commission on the Donald Marshall, Jr., Prosecution, *Discrimination Against Blacks in Nova Scotia: A Research Study, 1989,* Vol. 4, Halifax: Province of Nova Scotia, 1989.

Royal Commission on the Police, *Report of the Royal Commission on the Police*, London: Her Majesty's Stationary Office, 1962.

Samuel, T. *Visible Minorities in Canada: A Projection*, Unpublished Report for the Race Relations Advisory Council On Advertising, Toronto, 1992.

Savage, L., and Ault, T., *Police Officer and Public Safety: The Use of Lethal Force By and Against the Police*, Ottawa: Ministry of the Solicitor General of Canada, Research Services, Report No. 1985–13, 1985.

Schwartz, R., and Miller, J., "Legal Evolution and Social Complexity," *American Journal of Sociology*, Sept. 1964, 159-169.

Selye, H., *Stress Without Distress*, New York: New American Library, 1975.

_____, "The Stress of Police Work." *Police Stress* 1: (Fall) 1978.

Sewell, J., *Police: Urban Policing in Canada*, Toronto: James Lorimer, 1985.

Shearing, C. and J. Leon, "Reconsidering the Police Role: A Challenge to a Popular Misconception," *Canadian Journal of Criminology and Corrections* 19: 348, 1976.

Shearing, C. and Stenning, P., "Reframing Policing," in Shearing, C. and Stenning, P. (eds.), *Private Policing*, Newbury Park: Sage, 1987.

_____, "Say 'Cheese!': The Disney Order That Is Not So Mickey Mouse," in Shearing, C. and Stenning, P. (eds.), *Private Policing*, Newbury Park: Sage, 1987.

_____, "Private Security: Implications for Social Control," 5 *Social Problems* 30: 493–506, June 1983.

Sherman, L., "The Subculture of Police Corruption," in Rubington, E. and Weinberg, M. (eds.), *Deviance: The Interactionist Perspective* (4 ed.), New York: Macmillan, 1981.

Shinoda-Bolen, J., *Gods in Everyman: A New Psychology of Men's Lives and Loves*, New York: Harper and Row, 1990.

_____, *Goddesses in Everywoman: A New Psychology of Women*, New York: Harper and Row, 1985.

Silver, A., "The Demand for Order in Civil Society: A Review of Some Themes in the History of Urban Crime, Police and Riot," in Bordua, D., (ed.), *The Police: Six Sociological Essays*, New York: Wiley, 1967.

Solicitor General of Ontario, *Report of the Race Relations and Policing Task Force*, Toronto, 1989.

_____, *Police Constable Selection: Community Policing—Selecting Constables for the Future*, Final Report, Phase 1—Volume 1, June 1992.

_____, *A Police Training System For Ontario: Final Report and Recommendations*, Toronto: Ministry of the Solicitor General, 1992.

_____, *Report of the Race Relations and Policing Task Force*, Toronto, 1992.

Somodevilla, S., Baker, C., Hill, W., and Thomas, N., "Stress Management in the Dallas Police Department," in Territo, L., and Vetter, H., (eds.), *Stress and Police Personnel*, Toronto: Allyn and Bacon, 1981.

South, N., "Law, Profit and 'Private Persons:' Private and Public Policing in English History," in Shearing, C., and Stenning, P., (eds.), *Private Policing*, California: Sage, 1987.

Southgate, P., *New Directions in Police Training*, London: Her Majesty's Stationary Office, 1988.

Spitzer, S., and Scull, A., "Privatization and Capitalist Development: The Case of the Private Police," *Social Problems* 25 (October): 18–29, 1977.

Stansfield, R., *The Evolution of Police Forms and Structure: A Transpersonal Perspective*, Unpublished Ph.D. dissertation, North York: York University, 1993.

_____, *Community-based Policing: Which Police? Which Community?* Proceedings of the 1990 National Police Educator's Conference, Calgary, Alberta, 1990.

Stenning, P., "Private Police and Public Police: Toward a Redefinition of the Police Role," *Future Issues in Policing: Symposium Proceedings*, Ottawa: Minister of Supply and Services of Canada, 1989.

_____, *Police Officer Deaths: Highlights From A Recent Canadian Study*, Proceedings of the Annual Canadian Association of Chiefs of Police Convention in London, Ontario, August, 1991.

Tafoya, W., "The Future of Policing," 1 *F.B.I. Law Enforcement Bulletin* 59, 1990.

Takagi, P., "A Garrison State in 'Democratic' Society." *Crime and Social Justice* 1 (Spring-Summer): 27–33, 1974.

Terry, W., "Police Stress Reconsidered," in Terry, W., *Policing Society: An Occupational View*, Englewood Cliffs N.J.: Prentice Hall, 1985.

Thomas, N., "The use of biofeedback training in the alleviation of stress in the police officer." in Taylor, W. and Braswell, M. (eds.), *Issues in Police and Criminal Psychology*, Washington: University Press, 1978.

Thomas, C. and Hepburn, J., *Crime, Criminal Law, and Criminology*, Dubuque, Iowa: Wm. Brown Publishers, 1983.

Toffler, A., *The Third Wave*, Toronto: Bantam, 1981.

_____, *Power Shift: Knoweldge, Wealth, and Violence at the Edge of the 21st Century*, New York: Bantam, 1990.

Trojanowicz, R., and Bucqueroux, B., *Community Policing: A Contemporary Perspective*, Cincinnati: Anderson, 1990.

Turk, A., *Political Criminality: The Defiance and Defence of Authority*, Beverly Hills: Sage, 1982.

Uchida, C., "The Development of the American Police: An Historical Overview," in Dunham, R. and Alpert, G. (eds.), *Critical Issues in Policing: Contemporary Readings*, 1989.

Valaskakis, K., "Economic Trends and the Future of Policing: What to Expect from the Turbulent Nineties," *Canadian Journal of Criminology*, July/October, 257–268, 1991.

Van Maanen, J., "On Watching the Watchers," in Manning, P. and Van Maanen, J. (eds.), *Policing: A View From the Street*, New York: Random House, 1978.

Vincent, C., *Police Officer,* Ottawa: Carleton University Press, 1990.

Visano, L., *This Idle Trade: The Occupational Patterns of Male Prostitution*, Vitasana: Concord, 1987.

Vitale, F., *Individualized Fitness Programs*, New Jersey: Prentice-Hall, 1973.

Waegel, W., "The Use of Lethal Force by Police: The Effect of Statutory Change." *Crime and Delinquency* 30(1): 121–140, 1984.

Wagner, M., "Action and Reaction: The Establishment of a Counselling Service in the Chicago Police Department," in Territo, L. and Vetter, H. (eds.), *Stress and Police Personnel*, Toronto: Allyn and Bacon, 1981.

Walker, S., Walker, C., and McDavid, J., "Program Impacts: The Victoria Community Police Stations: A Three-Year Evaluation," in Chacko, J. and Nancoo, S., (eds.), *Community Policing in Canada*, Toronto: Canadian Scholars Press, 1993.

Webb, S., and Smith, D., "Police Stress: A conceptual overview." *Journal of Criminal Justice* 8: 251–257, 1980.

Weiner, N., *The Role of Police in Urban Society: Conflicts and Consequences*, Indianapolis: Bobbs-Merrill, 1976.

Westley, W., *Violence and the Police: A Sociological Study of Law, Custom, and Morality*, Cambridge: MIT Press, 1970.

Whittingham, M., "Police/Public Homicide and Fatality Risks in Canada: A Current Assessment—Serving and Being Protected," *Canadian Police Chief* 3(10), 4–8, 1985.

Wilber, K., *Up From Eden: A Transpersonal View of Human Evolution*, Boston: Shambhala, 1986a.

_____, "The Spectrum of Development," in Wilber, K., Engler, J., and D. Brown (eds.), *Transformations of Consciousness*, Boston: Shambhala, 1986b.

_____, *The Atman Project: A Transpersonal View of Human Development*, Wheaton, Il.: Quest, 1985.

Index